ACTIONS and OBJECTS
from HOBBES
to RICHARDSON

ACTIONS and OBJECTS
from HOBBES
to RICHARDSON

JONATHAN KRAMNICK

STANFORD UNIVERSITY PRESS

Stanford, California

Stanford University Press
Stanford, California
©2010 by the Board of Trustees of the
Leland Stanford Junior University

Library of Congress Cataloging-in-Publication Data

Kramnick, Jonathan Brody.
  Actions and objects from Hobbes to Richardson / Jonathan
Kramnick.
      p. cm.
  Includes bibliographical references and index.
  ISBN 978-0-8047-7051-4 (cloth : alk. paper) —
  ISBN 978-0-8047-7052-1 (pbk. : alk. paper)
      1. English literature—18th century—History and criticism.
2. English literature—Early modern, 1500–1700—History and
criticism. 3. Act (Philosophy) in literature. 4. Philosophy of mind
in literature. 5. Causation in literature. 6. Philosophy, English—
17th century. 7. Philosophy, English—18th century. I. Title.
PR448.P5K73   2010
820.9'384—dc22

                                                    2010010565

Printed in the United States of America on acid-free, archival-quality
paper

Typeset at Stanford University Press in 10.75/15 Sabon

Contents

Preface

This book is about the literature and philosophy of action during the last half of the seventeenth and first half of the eighteenth century, the period that begins roughly with Hobbes and Rochester and ends roughly with Hume and Richardson. It features works that examine what happens when someone acts, when someone writes a letter or lifts her feet or kills or kisses, and so on. For many, the difference between actions and other kinds of events turned on the presence of mental states. Someone writes a letter because she *wants* to communicate information and *intends* for her reader to understand her. Her desire for the one or intention for the other causes physical movements of various kinds. And yet how does a mental state like desire or intention cause the body to move? This simple question was of vast significance for all kinds of writers during the period, and opened up literary and philosophical problems for our time as well as theirs, from how a work of writing can represent thought on the page, to how matter can be the locus of consciousness, to whether minds actually cause anything to happen after all.

Writing about the mind during the period took many forms and has been the topic of much important work in literary and intellectual history. The relation between mind and actions, however, remains relatively untapped and points in a number of unusual directions. For example, although this book is above all interested in the language of mental states, it does not make an argument about the growth of inwardness or interiority or the psychological subject during the period. Rather, considering actions leads in a different direction. Minds were understood to do many kinds of things—from represent objects, to work through equations, to grieve—but when they caused someone to act, they were understood to blend in some fashion with the rest of the world. For some, this kind of causal relation meant that minds were at bottom like everything else in nature. When these writers considered actions, they were often led to unexpected or unsettling conclusions: that the will might not be free, that all matter might be sentient or nothing sentient at all, that states of mind extend outside the head. For others, the topic of actions provided an occasion to block just these sorts of conclusions and to distinguish the place of mind and mental causes from other parts of the world.

The late seventeenth and early eighteenth century was indeed a lively time for the consideration of actions, with the combined emergence of empirical philosophies of mind and new literary forms designed to feature experience in often startling ways. Against this expansive backdrop, I follow the problem of actions from the cultures of Restoration-era science to mid-eighteenth-century social theory, from worries about political authority to the consideration of a commercial society. While I place importance on what we might call externalism, I also watch notions of the external shift from physical bits of matter in motion to the elaborate networks of law and exchange. My goal has not been to follow a single perspective as it grows to dominance, however, but rather to examine competing models of mind and action across the period and into ours. I thus examine writers who have been integral for literary studies along with those whose ideas might challenge our expectations on a number of topics: from where seventeenth- and eighteenth-century writers looked to find the sources of actions to what kinds of entities they considered to be conscious.

Actions and Objects has been generously supported throughout by Rutgers University. In the early stages, I received fellowship help from the NEH, the William Andrews Clark Memorial Library, and the Huntington Library. At the end, I was the beneficiary of a wonderful year at the Stanford Humanities Center, which saw the completion of this manuscript and the start of another. As I tried out some of these arguments and readings, a few appeared in print. Early versions of sections of Chapters 3 and 5 appeared in *ELH* and a very different version of a section of Chapter 4 in the *Yale Journal of Criticism*. They have now been completely reconsidered and rewritten, but trace sentences remain.

One pleasure of taking some time to finish is accumulating so many debts of gratitude. I've been extremely fortunate to test some of these arguments among a superlative group of graduate students over the years. I could simply not have written a word without their questions, responses, and quarrels. My period cohort—Lynn Festa, Paula McDowell, and Michael McKeon—has provided invaluable feedback and conversation. Also at Rutgers, I've had the pleasure of working with Billy Galperin, Colin Jager, Meredith McGill, Jonah Siegel, Henry Turner, and Rebecca Walkowitz. The "Mind and Culture" seminar at the Center for Cultural Analysis provided a burst of intellectual energy and renewal just when I needed it most; our many guests and fellows will find their promptings and ideas scattered over these pages.

The same is true for the crew at Stanford, old friends and new: John Bender, Terry Castle, Denise Gigante, Joshua Landy, and Blakey Vermeule. It has come to seem that the broader eighteenth-century world is an expansive set of fascinating interlocutors, including Helen Deutsch, Sarah Ellenzweig, Marcie Frank, Jody Greene, Sandra Macpherson, John Richetti, Helen Thompson, and others who have listened to me talk about actions and minds over the years and who have helped to shape the argument in ways they might not realize. Parts of this book were delivered to audiences at Berkeley, Johns Hopkins, Princeton, Rice, Stanford, UCLA, the University of Chicago, and Yale, where audiences were curious and receptive and challenging in the best ways. James Kierstead, Mike Gavin, and my editor Emily-Jane Cohen all made it possible for this book to come together in the end.

It gives me great pleasure finally to thank those whose continued intellectual presence in my life I consider a tremendous gift: Jared Gardner, Elizabeth Hewitt, Jonathan Goldberg, Adela Pinch, Michael Trask, Michael Warner, and Bliss Kern. Bliss read the entire book and made it better.

ACTIONS and OBJECTS
from HOBBES
to RICHARDSON

Introduction: Nothing from Nothing

Things happen. Often we try to explain them. When Edmond Halley looked back on records of passing comets, he noticed that one seemed to appear every seventy-six years. He then thought hard about orbital velocity and gravity, drawing on what he knew about mathematics and physics. When a fashionable young man cut off a lock of hair belonging to a fashionable young woman, Alexander Pope wrote a poem. He thought hard about human actions, drawing on what he knew about motivation and desire. Halley and Pope both understood that neither comets nor cuttings come into the universe from nothing. Yet for Halley, the comet's return didn't have anything to do with beliefs or decisions. The comet didn't choose to shoot by earth. Rather, its particular mass and distance from the sun put it on an unalterable ellipse. For Pope, the cutting of the lock had little to do with the properties of metal shears or strands of hair. The Baron chose to cut Belinda's hair. Pope would like to know *why* he did so:

> Say what strange Motive, Goddess! cou'd compel
> A well-bred *Lord* t'assault a gentle *Belle*?
> Oh say what stranger Cause, yet unexplor'd,
> Cou'd make a gentle *Belle* reject a *Lord*?[1]

Were we to examine the Baron's motives, Pope says, we might discover why he cut Belinda's hair. Were we to examine hers, we might discover why she rejected his advances. Were we to do either, we would learn how motives serve as *causes*, "am'rous Causes" to be exact. Enclosed in the two couplets therefore is an implicit theory.

Belinda and the Baron are agents. Their actions have causes. Among these causes are states of mind. We may go even further. States of mind distinguish actions like the rape of the lock from events like the appearance of Halley's comet.[2] They do so because they serve a causal role. States of mind make something happen, just like states of physical matter. In other words, Pope plucks minds from other kinds of things only to make us wonder how far the distinction goes.

This book is about minds and actions in Restoration and eighteenth-century Britain. It examines how writers described what precedes and constitutes an agent's doing something, whether writing a letter or fleeing a kingdom. The topic gathered new attention during the period because it opened the possibility for a causal theory of behavior in line with causal theories applied elsewhere in the natural world. If desires, fears, beliefs, and so on were like causes and actions were like effects, some said, then minds were similar to other things in the environment; if minds represent the world in motion, others responded, they were in some special sense distinct from everything else. The discussion animated genres as diverse as the treatise, the lyric, and the novel. Sometimes it concerned matters as ordinary as the lifting of one's feet; other times it engaged topics as broad as what it means to be a person. In each case, the concern was how states of mind might prompt, accompany, or follow the movement of physical bodies. In this introduction, I will set out the conceptual issues involved in the period's consideration of actions. I'll then turn to a chapter-by-chapter summary of my argument. If my sense of this book is right, several of my formulations may be surprising, so I'll present them in some detail.

One might expect a book about minds to validate the long-standing sense that the eighteenth century witnesses a new language of inwardness or subjectivity associated with the joint rise of empirical philosophy and the novel.[3] I complicate this thesis by pointing to the largely unacknowledged role of external factors in the period's conception of mind. In the works I examine, the distinguishing feature of minds is the causal role they do or do not play in physical movement. So while the writers I feature develop techniques to show minds at work, their goal is to describe why certain actions occur and how mental states fit into the rest of the world. The ostensible privacy or interiority of mental states is often not an issue. We may think of this as an important property of actions. *Actions extend mind into the world*. Belinda might conceivably be thinking about all sorts of things in the course of her day, from the taste of tea to troubles with Betty. Pope is interested in why she rejected the Baron, however, and so therefore looks at her reasons for doing so. The same might be said for many of the well-known and incidental actions mulled over in the writing of the period. Why did Evelina accept Orville's invitation to dance? Why did Moll steal that bundle? Any time a writer asks why such an event happened, she pares mental states into those fixed to behavior, the desires or beliefs that form reasons for acting. To the degree to which literary history has focused on inwardness or privacy, therefore, it has missed several important features of mind-talk during the long eighteenth century. This book looks closely at three such features as they take the form of nagging questions: Are actions freely chosen or subject to necessity? How do mental properties cause physical change? How can a physical object be the locus of conscious experience?

Let's start with the first question. The notion that human behavior might be discussed in causal terms brought with it a serious entailment. As soon as we know all the facts about Halley's comet, we understand why it *has* to appear every seventy-six years. The comet doesn't have any say in the matter. An inflexible confluence of causes (mass, gravity, velocity, and so forth) rigidly determines its arrival. The comet is subject to *necessity*. The question thus emerges with some urgency if the same is true for actions. Were we to know all the facts about the Baron's cutting of the lock, or Belinda's refusal of the Baron, would we understand why each had to happen? Pope's language of causes suggests this may be so. Indeed, John Dennis voices precisely this worry in his *Remarks on Mr. Pope's Rape of the Lock* (1728), in which he complains that the word "compel" in line six "is a Botch for the Sake of the Rhyme," because it "supposes the Baron to be a Beast, and not a free Agent."[4] Although he is no friend to Pope, Dennis would still like to save the poet from the charge of determinism. Surely Pope didn't mean to say that the Baron lacked freedom of the will. Pope's emphasis on causation suggests that Dennis was wrong. The poor Baron may have been just as compelled as the comet, unable to do anything other than cut. He too may have been subject to necessity.[5]

Writers like Dennis worry that necessity is a sort of alibi for reprehensible behavior. Don't punish me, the Baron might say; I couldn't have done otherwise. The assumption is that if one isn't free to choose one's actions then one can't really be held responsible for them. The freedom that allows agents to take responsibility for what they do is, on this view, incompatible with the necessity that says they could never have done otherwise. One major contribution of seventeenth- and eighteenth-century theories of action was, however, precisely *not* to pose freedom and responsibility against necessity. It was rather to show how the two could be compatible. Traditionally credited to Hobbes, compatibilism of this kind has had great influence up to the present day.[6] The argument works by a series of redefinitions. First among them is freedom itself. "Liberty or Freedome," Hobbes writes, "signifieth (properly) the absence of Opposition" or "externall Impediments of motion."[7] On this view, freedom does not refer to an ability to choose or will actions. Rather, freedom refers to an ability to perform actions once they are chosen. While "no Liberty can be inferred of the will, desire, or inclination," we can infer a "Liberty of the man; which consisteth in this, that he finds no stop, in doing what he has the will, desire, or inclination to doe" (146). A will may no more be free than a thought may be brittle or a square may be fast. In contrast, an action is free when it may be brought to completion, confined when it is impeded.

This redefinition was useful for Hobbes because it put the freedom of actions together with the safety provided by the state. Absolute power was not a threat to liberty; rather, it provided the protection for agents to act as they would choose.[8] Despite changes in political theory over the course of the period, the idea that freedom could be compatible with necessity had considerable endurance. Hume for example defined liberty as "a power of acting or not acting, according to the determinations of the will" and then argued that this power in no way conflicted with universal causation: "We cannot surely mean, that actions have so little connexion with motives, inclinations, and circumstances, that one does not follow with a certain degree of uniformity from the other, and that one affords no inference by which we can conclude the existence of the other."[9] Surely, he says, we cannot imagine that the will is indifferent to motives or that motives don't serve as causes. Liberty requires only that actions may be completed. For Hobbes, the state performs this role by allowing for common safety and enduring contracts; for Hume a society of commerce and reciprocity draws the behavior of one person to the interests of another. In either case, the will finds its place in a lattice of causes, and actions come under the same fine-grained analysis as the rest of nature.

Although the compatibilist account of agency looms large in the history of philosophy, with canonical British writers like Hobbes, Locke, and Hume at front and center, its importance for questions of literary history has not been much explored. One goal of this book is to do just that. The topic of reasons for acting might be of interest for how we think about such things as the writing of literary character and the placing of actions into narratives.[10] Compatibilism in turn might be of help to refining our sense of how dependent characterization was on notions of internal psychology and how far it extended outward into external objects and events. I mentioned earlier, for example, that talk about actions brought mental causes into the world rather than separating them from it. I would add to this thesis that compatibilism brought the world into the mind. As a matter of definition, no cause ever exists on its own. Causes are paired to effects and, presumably, caused by something else too.

With respect to mental states, this means that reasons for acting extend from experiences or desires or intentions to external objects and back. It is not so hard to see how reasons might be internal. The Baron desires that Belinda's hair be cut. Belinda hopes for the Baron to go away. While the lock and the Baron exist independently of the mind, each is at the same time an object of a propositional statement. They change according to the presiding mental verb (or attitude, as we would now say): the lock is cut in the first case, the Baron ushered away in the second.[11] Mental states are thus able to bear content, like a lock of hair, and mediate behavior, like closing a pair of scissors.[12] It is perhaps not quite so easy to see how these same states might reach beyond the person. No small part of my argument, however, will depend on the period's sense of this possibility. In different ways, Hobbes and Hume both say that every event or object or idea links to another in a long chain of causation. There is no way to view any one precisely on its own, since each has antecedents and effects. With respect to mental states, the result of this intuition is that ideas and intentions ultimately make their way to the social and physical environment. When this relation tightens some, the social or physical hookup actually plays a causal role in this or that action. In our present example, we need only look at the system of external rules and meanings that jointly govern the behavior of the Baron or Belinda. "Am'rous Causes" reach through things like cards and hair and forms like courtship and epic.

I will be interested in accounts of actions that stress the connection between subjective experience and the environment or that show how the meaning of concepts is fixed on the outside or that tie volitional states like desire or intention to physical states like the movement of particles. I will argue in other words for the importance of what I'll call *externalism* in the literature and philosophy of the period.[13] In many of the cases I look at, the emphasis fell on causation as the means by which mental states or properties have at once a real existence and are looped into other things. Even as causation promised to join mind to the world, however, the precise relation between the two became subject to some worry. The question here—the second on my earlier list—was whether mental states instigate physical change. One might be surprised if they didn't.[14] Pope's question about the Baron would only make sense, after all, were his motives able to bring about his cuttings. Yet for all the apparent simplicity of this sort of episode, it became clear to a variety of writers that the process was difficult to pin down. Here are Locke's droll comments on the matter:

> My right Hand writes, whilst my left Hand is still: What causes rest in one, and motion in the other? Nothing but my Will,—a Thought of my Mind; my Thought only changing, the right Hand rests, and the left Hand moves. This is matter of fact, which cannot be denied: Explain this, and make it intelligible, and then the next step will be to understand Creation.[15]

Locke's hand has been writing for some time. It has been forming letters from ink, words from letters, sentences from words, and paragraphs from sentences. The paragraphs read as more than accidents. They make a certain sense and so seem to be the product of an intending agent. Try as he might, however, Locke cannot exactly describe how his will executes the writing. (I can't either. I'm telling myself to type this on the keyboard. So far my fingers are moving as I'd like them to. How and why are beyond me.) Locke does not dismiss the efficacy of mental properties or consign them to a separate kind of substance.[16] Rather, he considers the causal relation between will and writing to be "a matter of fact" and to be an example of a kind of relation that underpins every single act done with deliberate intention. His amused caution has to do with figuring out how the pieces of the causal puzzle fit into each other. Does the relation between will and hand-movement have the same features as the one between, say, heat and the evaporation of water? The evaporation of water from heat happens every time the temperature crosses a certain threshold. The turning of letters into words happens by fits and starts, according to a will described as a distinctively mental property. Locke is therefore sure of two things: that he experiences the decision to move one hand and then the other, and that his experience causes the movement of his hands. There is something that it feels like for him to will hand movement. There is nothing that it feels like for heat to evaporate water. In the face of this sort of relation, however, Locke (as it were) throws up his hands. He knows it exists yet cannot provide an intelligible description of how it happens. Analytic philosophers would call this a problem of mental causation.[17] It is essential to every chapter of the book.

Mental causation is so important because without it there would be no concept of agency and no description of actions, only events. It is important because the scene that Locke provides an expository accounting of here reappears in different guises across the literatures of the period, from the search into the "am'rous Causes" beneath and before the rape of the lock to the prolonged questioning of the motives of a character like Clarissa Harlowe in doing things like writing to Lovelace and leaving her family home. It is important finally because of the very bafflement Locke so limpidly voices. Attempts to resolve the problem of mental causation came in a variety of forms: from the idea that mental states or properties might have no causal role to play—*epiphenomenalism* as it is now called—to the notion that external objects and events do the causing for us; from accounts of the mind's free and independent force on the material world to a recognition that causal relations are best inferred from an outsider's stance. The pleasure in considering this problem over the course of the seventeenth and eighteenth centuries has not, however, been in watching a single answer take shape from the various responses. It has been rather in following the arguments as they take off from their several sources, from Hobbes to Hume, Rochester to Richardson, and in between.

At the heart of the problem of mental causation is the distinction, if there is one, between mind and matter. For most of the writers I consider, the causal relation at issue is not one between two kinds of substance. For some the distinction is between mental and physical description, with the underlying substance question ruled out by metaphysical fiat; for others the problem is fitting the mind into a world that is wholly material; for still others a ghost does in fact haunt the machine. The concerns raised by these responses take me to the last of the three questions I raised earlier. Were we to ask who cut Belinda's hair we would think it odd if someone were to reply the scissors. Why would we think so? On a first pass, we might say because the Baron is a person and the scissors an object. We might then hang a series of further distinctions on this difference. Persons have a kind of value and set of rights, for example, while objects do not. Junk the Baron's scissors and he might be annoyed, but you're unlikely to be arrested. Drown the Baron in the Thames and you might be held accountable for a crime. The concept of person is, as Locke will say, a "forensic category," useful for the assigning of blame or praise, reward or punishment.[18] But to say that persons cause things to happen and objects do not is to take as a premise the difference in roles one is trying to explain. Why then do we say that a person has causal powers while a pair of scissors does not? For many during the period the answer was that persons have conscious experience.[19] There is something that it is like to be the Baron.[20] There is nothing that it is like to be a pair of scissors. Here we can perhaps take matters no further. A person is a kind of thing that is conscious; a pair of scissors is a kind of thing that is not. Full stop.

The premise of this sort of argument is actually twofold. It says that persons have consciousness *and* that consciousness distinguishes one person from another. This claim is made with tremendous influence in chapter 27 of Locke's *Essay Concerning Human Understanding* (1690). For Locke and others, talk of consciousness was hard to have without talk of personal identity, and likewise bringing up personal identity was hard to do without having something to say about consciousness. One linked series of conscious moments wraps the whole into a single entity, making (as the case may be) the young Locke an identical person to the old one. If consciousness and personhood go together, however, they do so with some interesting points of tension. For some writers, including Locke on occasion, consciousness was something that bodies have and do. It was not a separate substance put into them. But how can a physical system be the locus of experience? Matter seems by definition to be without experience, yet put together in certain ways it gives rise to sentience, awareness, pleasure, pain, appetites, and the like. In contemporary work on the mind, the question of how this is possible is known as "the hard problem of consciousness," and it remains decisively unanswered to this day.[21] Following a single thread in the treatment of actions has thus backed me into a large area of concern, one that I try to keep tightly laced to reasons for acting. This topic includes consciousness because it is conscious objects that would seem to have reasons. How precisely that is so, however, does take us into really interesting and difficult issues.

One such issue comes directly out of the seventeenth and eighteenth century's version of today's "hard problem." It went something like this: assuming that material entities are able to have the sort of experiences that lead to actions—conscious reasons for acting, let's say—why are some entities conscious and others not? At bottom, there is little difference between the Baron and the scissors (or the comet). Each is a composite of particles. Yet Baron-particles give rise to consciousness and scissor-particles do not. In the chapters that follow, I will look at a few works that directly ask why that is so. Once again, my interest is not only with period-defining answers but also with some difficulties encountered along the way. I am especially drawn to texts that come at problems of consciousness from an oblique angle or that offer radical or at least off-center responses to the problems at hand. I'll be interested in texts that try to bring consciousness and personhood together, but I will also be interested in those that pry them apart, that present conscious experiences without a person having them or persons without conscious experiences in train. I'll be interested, finally, in texts willing to follow their premises to seemingly unusual conclusions, such as all things having some sort of consciousness or (conversely) nothing having consciousness at all.

Keeping an eye toward the unexpected conclusion has provided one way to narrow a path through a topic as broad as the literature and philosophy of actions. It is also, I think, what happens when you watch writers wrestle with nearly intractable quandaries: An action is the kind of event whose cause includes mental states, but what, after all, does "whose cause includes" really mean? A person is the kind of entity that has consciousness, but how and why is that so? Answer me these and perhaps you will, as Locke says, explain creation. Two guiding principles are at issue here. Questions of agency and consciousness have long concerned literary study in general and the study of Restoration and eighteenth-century literature in particular. I attempt to look closely at the component parts of one critical feature of this concern: how reasons, intentions, and other states of mind do or do not serve as *causes* for acting. This feature then opens up a number of related topics about minds and persons and contexts for acting. The principle is to engage large, period-defining concepts of character or consciousness, such as they are, through incremental examples and debates. The second principle reflects somewhat on the first. I am inclined to tilt the applecart rather than hold it in place. So where the predominant model has favored the growth of inwardness, sympathy, and subjectivity, I tend (again) to favor things external, like the elemental parts of matter or the chains of causes or the forms of contract.

With the exception of the first chapter, this book moves freely between what in retrospect we would call philosophical and literary writing.[22] I take great pleasure in the nonexistence of this distinction in the eighteenth century, a period when David Hume could say his ruling passion was a "love of literary fame" and Samuel Richardson could say that he wrote "*instantaneous* Descriptions and Reflections" of minds and hearts at work. I view this overlap of concerns as permission to stipulate a relation between texts that have grown to seem far-flung. I do track allusion, citation, and debate, but in the main my method has been to follow the appearance and movement of problems, especially those concerning the antecedents to actions and the ontology of persons and objects. These topics obey no boundaries of genre, though they are framed in different ways according to the formal properties and needs of the texts in which they come into view. So, for example, an epistolary novel might choose to distribute its account of causes between writers of letters, while a third-person fiction might try to represent a character's reasons or intentions; a piece of discursive prose might develop a theory in explicit conversation with antagonists while a court satire might make such dialogue internal to its lines. I arrange this movement into a loose chronology: from a new attention to actions amid dynastic anxieties and civil war to a concern with minds and behavior amid polite and commercial exchange. With this backdrop in place, it has been on occasion important to put the texts slightly out of sequence or to put some writers in more than one chapter. I do this to draw out concepts that might otherwise be obscured by a stricter sense of order. I don't think that much is lost in historical presentation by doing so; but the alternative would, I believe, make topics like mental causation and consciousness a little more difficult to track. These topics are of intense interest for Restoration and eighteenth-century writers. At the same time, they have been subject to concentrated attention in contemporary philosophy of mind and cognitive science. While I focus on Restoration and eighteenth-century texts, therefore, I also draw now and again on the persistence of these concerns into our time. Sometimes this is to illuminate older texts with our latest philosophy and science; just as often this is to use the past to shine a light on the present. In either case, I prefer to bore into texts rather than to present a survey. After the first chapter, the rest are case studies, looking at texts that place matters of actions interestingly in the foreground or that have been important for the constitution of the field.

The first chapter presents an overview of the philosophy of action from Hobbes to Hume and features three flash points in a century-long debate over free will. I begin with a quarrel among Civil War exiles, turn to a pamphlet war between Anthony Collins and Samuel

Clarke fifty years later, and end with David Hume's reflections on commercial society. The points of contention among the first two sets of writers concern what the world is made of and whether mental states have a causal function in a person's behavior. Thomas Hobbes and Anthony Collins argue that everything is composed from a single, physical substance and therefore that a chain of cause and effect connects every one event or object to another. On this view, desires and fears have properties like atoms and apples, including the ability to cause agents to act. John Bramhall and Samuel Clarke respond that human agents will their own actions but are themselves not willed. On this view, actions happen outside the laws of causation that apply to physical objects, and human souls bear a spiritual substance different from other kinds of stuff. For his part, Hume pays attention to physical matter only to draw an analogy to actions in the social world. We never know precisely what happens when a physical cause yields a physical effect. Likewise, we never know precisely what happens when a mental cause does the same thing. In either case, we use our habits of inference and correlation to presume a relation between the one and the other. We observe something happen in nature and infer its material cause; likewise, we observe an agent doing something and infer *its* mental cause. The stance with respect to either is from the outside, as the private cause of any given effect recedes from view.

The long debate over free will concerned not only what happens when a person acts but also from what stuff persons are made and from what point of view it is best to describe actions. Over the course of the debate, the meaning of several key terms changed. Hobbes and Hume, for example, share what I call an external outlook on actions. Yet what counts as the external changes from law, reward, and punishment in the mid-seventeenth century to commerce and interpersonal exchange a hundred years later. For Hobbes, one's recognition of legal and political forms provided reasons for acting, while for Hume the elaborate networks of a commercial society were necessary to complete actions and make them intelligible to agents. This difference in perspective might be described, I argue, as one between a first- and third-person view. In the first case, an agent adjusts her desires and intentions to fit into an order of rewards and punishments; in the second, an agent looks at the actions of other people to infer how reasons serve as causes. Likewise, Bramhall and Clarke both defend human autonomy from external determination, yet the former does so in the name of the soul and the latter does so in the name of common sense. Bramhall engages Hobbes in a quarrel at the not yet established borders of philosophy and theology; Clarke engages his readers' sense that they are more than lumps of matter.

The second chapter takes a close look at this relation between persons and physics. The topic is the role of consciousness and mental causation in a universe reducible to particulate matter and structured by physical laws. I say close look because, unlike the first chapter, I slice thinly through a series of late-seventeenth-century texts, looking in particular at Lucretian ideas of matter and agency and a few responses they provoke. I begin with Thomas Creech's 1682 translation of Lucretius' *De rerum natura*, the first complete translation of the poem published in English, and examine how the poem presents the emergence of whole objects from individual parts, thought from thoughtless atoms, and free movement from a universe of causes. I then trace these concerns to two writers subject to extensive treatment in later chapters. I compare Rochester's translation of a few lines of the poem to Creech's and examine their separate views of determinacy. I finish with a look at Locke's long discussion—one equally influential and pained—of consciousness and personal identity in the *Essay*. The question broached by this chapter has two parts: how can insentient matter be the locus of thought and experience, and how can experience play a causal role in the material world? I'm interested in Lucretius because his poem tracked consciousness and mental causation to the movement of particles. The poem proposes that composite entities—people, trees, cows, what have you—take shape from the collision and adhesion of invisible and indivisible atoms. One trouble appears when the poem considers how atoms without thought can give rise to objects that have thought. The solution works through a process of emergence, wherein certain kinds of atoms interlock with others in such a way that consciousness comes out of them. A second area of concern appears when the poem considers what role consciousness has in the physical universe. The answer here is most curious. The poem makes a case for free will by distributing agency to the manifold of particulate matter. Individual atoms are thoughtless, yet they are at the same time possessed of will manifested in their random and unpredictable movement. So where the first response looks at sentience as an *emergent* property, the second looks at will as present in all things, a perspective we would now call *panpsychist*.[23]

Such attention to the small units of matter was of evident interest to Rochester, who translated two bits of Lucretius on his own along with a piece of Seneca about the "lumber" from which all things are made. Both Lucretius and Rochester write past the larger entities in which consciousness and will are incarnated. They are interested in particles, not persons. Locke's treatment of consciousness and personal identity in the *Essay* presents a very different view. In what is arguably the first consistent use of the word "consciousness" in its modern sense as "the perception of what passes in a Man's own mind," Locke argues that consciousness provides a consistent sense of self.[24] Particles come and go but selves persist over time. Accordingly, conscious selves anchor persons who are responsible for their actions and subject to eventual reward and punishment. Having made the topic of consciousness distinct from the topic of matter, however, Locke returns to their relation in the closing books of the *Essay*. There he engages what I describe as an early consideration of today's "hard problem." How is it, he asks, that conscious experience could arise from matter without experience? His answer follows the conundrum to its several ends. Perhaps emergent properties are a brute fact of the world, *or* perhaps all matter bears some sort of experience, *or* perhaps matter is interwoven with spirit after all.

The third chapter picks up on the discussion of Rochester begun in the second and spends considerably more time looking at how his poetry engages questions of consciousness and causation, actions and personhood. I feature Rochester because his poetry engages the physical view he encountered in Lucretius and yet extends the discussion to contexts for acting in the social and political world of the Restoration. *A Satyr against Reason and Mankind*, for example, asks whether mental states are able to cause anything or whether they ride along with physical causes. It toys with the idea that consciousness is only something left behind once physical causes have done all their work, or that mental causes might exist but only without agents to whom they belong. In a similar vein, *Love and Life* presents composite objects that have spatial parts—a hand of a person, a branch of a tree—but no equivalent temporal parts.[25] An object (on this view) neither passes through time nor stretches over time, but exists only in a kind of impossible present. These musings about causation and existence over time combine in the more sexually explicit poetry—like *The Imperfect Enjoyment* and *A Ramble in St. James's Park*—where mental states at turns get in the way of the physical system or provide a language for the system's failure. My purpose in these readings is to show how Rochester attempts physical explanations in terms of the movement of matter. I also examine how he similarly attempts external explanations in terms of the importance of context and environment. The physical and external tend to combine or run in support of each other. Even so, Rochester doesn't so much make neat statements on these topics as range over their many problems and difficulties, often to odd and surprising effect. For example, despite his reputation for having established desire as a basis for action, he mostly locates desire in every place beside the heads, bodies, or persons found in his poems. In keeping with this external view of an ostensibly inner phenomenon, I draw the chapter to a close by exploring the strange fate of a couplet concerning mental causation from *Artemiza to Chloe* that was cited in a variety of works in post-1688 London. My question here is, How does a new context change the meaning of lines committed to the importance of context? The answer takes us from the manuscript coteries of the Restoration to the print public of the 1710s and '20s, and from poetry to the essay and novel.

The Rochester chapter provides one route into the eighteenth century. The fourth chapter on Locke's theory of action provides another. Locke's theory of consciousness had stated that there is something that it is like to have one or another thought, that the background hum of the subjective provides the underpinning of a person's identity over time. What, if anything, do first-person thoughts or feelings have to do with acting? In Locke's first pass at this question, the answer turns out to be "not much." The first edition of the *Essay* says that we may come to full understanding of an action by observing it from the outside. One has reasons to do something and those reasons lead to actions. What it feels like to have some sort of reason has no causal role to play. The entire history of an action may therefore be plotted from an external perspective as a doing of some thing in order to accomplish some good. Locke's frustration with this argument emerges at the outset in a series of letters exchanged with William Molyneux between the first and second edition. Molyneux asks why agents are sometimes led to error or to act against reason. He also poses to Locke his famous thought experiment about a blind man suddenly provided with sight. The point of the thought experiment—the Molyneux Problem, as it will be subsequently known—is to emphasize the importance of first-person experience in understanding the external world. The blind man comes to new knowledge about the cubes and spheres he had previously touched when he sees them for the first time. The analogous suggestion for a theory of actions is that one learns something new about them in light of the feelings with which they were accompanied. The second edition of the *Essay* takes this new argument to heart and presents a thoroughly revised model of actions. In the first edition, the cause of any action was always one's *reason for* doing whatever one did. In the second, it is always one's *wanting to* achieve some desired end. Alongside this new emphasis on desire as a causal faculty, Locke places a new term—"uneasiness"—which describes what it feels like to desire something. Seen from the outside and the third person, desire is the cause of actions. Seen from the inside and the first person, desire is experienced as uneasiness. Without having a sense of this uneasiness, one can't tell exactly what any given agent will do or has done. Consciousness provides additional information to what one gathers from observing the behavior of agents.

This view is in some ways compatible with what we sometimes think we know about early-eighteenth-century literary history. So the chapter ends with a brief treatment of Catharine Trotter, a playwright and novelist who also wrote a treatise in defense of Locke's philosophy. I don't turn to Trotter just to track the controversies surrounding the publication of the *Essay*. (Trotter's was one text among many written against or in defense of Locke at the time.) Rather, I'm interested in Trotter because she provides a concrete example of the explicit and sign-posted theory of actions—the kind of thing that would appear in a treatise—making its way into the implicit staging ground of narrative fiction. Trotter had one foot in each. One of the selling points of the kind of epistolary fiction Trotter wrote was that it provided a first-person perspective on causes of action. Locke had said that desire causes actions and is experienced as uneasiness. Trotter's novel and others like it attempted to color in what that might mean and how it might work. Assertion of this kind has often led to a related claim that novels express the priority of the psychological and of a particular person's private experience, an argument associated with Ian Watt's famous book on the novel, though perhaps one as old as serious consideration of the genre. I don't intend to overturn this argument so much as give it a little bit of trouble. The final two chapters of the book are thus focused on eighteenth-century fiction and attempt to show

how a causal account of actions might or might not make recourse to the interior states of agents.

I've chosen two authors whose works seem to feature problems of agency in interesting and opposed ways, and who are, respectively, a subject of intense, recent interest and a perennial favorite. I look at Eliza Haywood because she sustains the sort of commitment to experience and feelings that Locke and Trotter promote without also committing herself to accompanying notions of the interior point of view or the separateness of personhood from environment. Few writers of the period are more extravagant than Haywood in their language of passionate feeling. So much is intuitively obvious. My argument will be that Haywood stops short of assigning these feelings to discrete persons or objects. The common-sense bonding of experience to a subject of experience begins to loosen across a range of incidents but is especially fraught and intriguing, I argue, with the concept and experience of consent. Consent is a term understood by Locke and others to join private experience to formal contracts like marriage or impersonal structures like the state. In these highly significant venues, it validates external authorities with the imprimatur of the subjective. I wasn't dragged to the altar; I freely consented to marry this toad. The reign of this king or parliament isn't arbitrary; we consent to be governed. And so on. The trouble is how to get from the possession to the expression of consent. How do we know if someone actually consents? How do I know that I have consented? The question poses the real quandary of accessing mental states, phenomena that are difficult, some said impossible, to view directly. The "How can I know if someone has consented?" question is, in this respect, a sharpened version of the "How can I see what another person is thinking or feeling?" question. Locke's answer is that you can't and so you don't. He outlines instead two forms of externalization: the actual "expression" of consent in forms of contractual stipulation, like oaths, charters, and vows, and the tacit enacting of consent in daily life. I'm especially interested in "tacit consent" because it attaches such a consequential entailment to the most quotidian of activities. One person buys an item in a store; another takes a turn in a carriage; both have consented to be governed. Out of the minutest incidents of mental causation rise the grandest edifices of liberal democracy.

Between mental causes and civil societies are a series of finely grained steps: the kind of dailyness of thought and action dwelt upon in works of fiction. Such will be my gambit, at least, in considering Haywood's *Love in Excess* (1719) and *Fantomina* (1725). These will be unsurprising picks for anyone who has been paying attention to the directions of eighteenth-century literary studies for the past decade, and that is partly my point. Our attention has been drawn to these works because, among other things, they are interested in teasing through the kind of problems addressed by the dual nature of consent, as something mental and something external. Locke's problem concerns the enactment of internally held mental states and concepts. Haywood's response is to show that there is no we or I doing the consenting, or, in a slightly different vein, to say that consent is in the doing, not in the expressing. One should, I think, be careful about generalizing across kinds of writing. After all, Haywood does not have the same kind of expository obligations as Locke. Instead, she uses the advantages of formal experimentation, especially in third-person evocations of tremulous feeling, to show how mental states are as much in the world as in the head, as much subject to the needs of plot as something one brings to other people or larger institutions.

Readers might expect an account of Richardson to pursue an opposite line of argument. Arguably no writer of the period is more conventionally associated with first-person experience and the authority of the self in advance of external circumstance. That is not the argument I make, but neither do I simply pursue the contrary line and suggest that our most storied novel of first-person experience really places mental states outside the mind or the person. I end with *Clarissa*, rather, because its multiperspective version of epistolary form is so suited to explore the several models of action available in the eighteenth-century thought world. With this ending in mind, I return to the basic ontological question around actions with which I began, now pitched toward a work of fiction written a century after the discussion of agency took off with Hobbes. The ontological question is, How do we pick actions from the larger class of events? The answer (again) is that actions involve mental states while other events do not. Discussion of the nature of actions thus turned on the status of this involvement. Did mental states cause actions, and if so were they also caused? From what point of view—internal or external, first or third person—should actions be described? *Clarissa* zeros in on these questions by presenting them from more than one vantage, as the few yet weighty events in the novel come under painstaking description from several angles. The novel makes clear, for example, that another way to ask about actions is to count them. We ask about events in general when we ask if anything has happened; we ask about actions in particular when we ask whether anyone has done anything. *Clarissa* is particularly interesting in this regard because so much of the tension comes down to enumeration.

Consider the conflict at Harlowe Place. Clarissa's family treats her refusal of Solmes as an act against them; Clarissa doesn't consider her refusal an action at all. The quarrel isn't just over why she has done one or another thing; it is firstly whether she has actually done anything. So Clarissa finds herself explaining to her family that she hasn't taken any action against them, while they view her as continually acting in ways contrary to their interests. To help make sense of this conflict I make recourse to an updated version of the eighteenth-century philosophy of action, Elizabeth Anscombe's famous account of intentional actions as those "under a description."[26] One point of Anscombe's little volume, *Intention* (1957), was to show how actions come into view when the question "Why?" is asked of them. Events present themselves as a mass of unincorporated detail. Put them under a description and the focus sharpens some. A young woman's legs move up and down. A pair of shoes covers itself with mud. A young woman gets into a carriage with a young man. A young woman runs away with a libertine. A libertine kidnaps a young woman. These are separate accounts of the same thing. The shoes get dirty as her legs move as she gets into the carriage as she runs away *or* is kidnapped. Depending on which description you choose, the event seems very different; indeed, only in the latter two accounts is the event at all recognizable in the terms suggested by the novel. So then the quarrel over enumerating actions revolves around whether and how one apportions intentions in the description one provides. The last two accounts subsume the earlier ones because they provide the intention with which the action is done, and (crucially) the intention belongs to a different agent in each.

Clarissa's way of protecting herself is often to deny a causal role in the actions she appears to take. I did not mean to fly away with a libertine or to harm my family or to lose my honor. I certainly did not *cause* any of these things to happen. She may have intentions but they are rarely intentions with which any actions are done; they are more likely to be intendings to do some future thing. This to say that Clarissa holds on to an internal view of actions and tends to avoid causal accounts of her own behavior. The "direction of fit," as readers of Anscombe would put it, is world to mind.[27] Clarissa attempts to "fit" the world to her intendings. The conflict with Lovelace that preoccupies the middle sections of the novel appears when the "direction of fit" moves in the other way, as Lovelace attempts to shape intendings to a world that precedes them. Richardson writes of Lovelace, in this respect, as one committed to an externalist account of mental states. Nowhere is this more heated than in the consideration of consent. Lovelace arranges appearances and circumstances so that it seems that Clarissa has already consented to lose her virtue and voluntarily live with him out of wedlock. He is frustrated and aghast when her consent does not fit the situation at hand. Both Lovelace and Clarissa are committed to the notion that mental states individuate actions. On his view, mental states emerge out of necessity from the causal order in which they are placed, so the appearance of Clarissa's consent should be the same as the existence of her consent. On her view, one's experience of one's mental states is prior to their place in any outside order of things. *Clarissa* is a nice place to end, in this respect, because the ongoing discussion of actions both shapes and is responded to by some of the features we have come to recognize as integral to the midcentury novel, especially in the Richardsonian mode: from claims to first-person authority, to the contesting friction of overlapping perspectives. In this case, the competition between the several accounts of action takes off *against* the view that would see them as compatible with determination. For his part, Lovelace wants nothing to do with the notion that anyone's behavior is both free and determined. Intentions are supposed to conform to the world in the manner of a belief. For her part, Clarissa insists on her power to act even as it becomes impossible to do so. Intentions outlast the environment they face. The novel is thus among other things a vast tapestry woven around the idea of compatibilism first set forth a hundred years earlier.

I close the book with a consideration of Clarissa's death because it is in the novel's reflecting on whether the death is a suicide that the topic of actions joins to the problems around consciousness and mental causation I feature at the beginning. Clarissa wants to die yet will not kill herself or act in any way that furthers her demise. The avoiding of suicide thus picks out mental properties from the flux of physical causes. Death is one among many physical events. The prohibition against suicide—like that against murder—alights on the mental and, in so doing, fastens on its causal role. The clarity in which this may be stated reveals something interesting, I argue, about the final sections of the novel: mental causation is easier to envisage when it is related to the destruction of the person, precisely the entity imagined to be the locus of such causes. This is not an isolated phenomenon. The long consideration of Clarissa's possible suicide occurs at a historical moment when the materialist questioning of personal identity had reached the topic of ending one's life. First codified in Augustine's ruminations on Lucretia, the prohibition against suicide takes as its premise that a person is distinct from her physical body.[28] On this view, Clarissa is not just a mass of atoms; she is an entity made in imitation of God. Yet on the view of others (including Hume), the prohibition against suicide marks out mental causes only to make them superfluous, rendering the providential design of the causal order something that ought not to be disturbed by states of mind. For some, even, the appropriate response was to say that persons were no different from any other composite entity and mental causes the same as their physical counterparts. On this view, the destruction of the person is merely the return of matter to the cosmos from which all things are made. This is not the view provided by the novel, of course, which endeavors to show how Clarissa is not only more than her parts but also more than a person in the conventional meaning subscribed to by other writers in her midst. The answer the novel provides to the twin problems of consciousness and mental causation thus turns out to be less of a normal or conventional one than one that is, in its own way, just as peculiar as those seen earlier in Rochester and elsewhere.

It is possible to imagine a world in which there are only events and no actions.[29] It is not likely that we, or anything like us, would be in this world. But nevertheless such a world is possible. Subtract every agent and this counterfactual world looms into view: earthquakes happen, comets shoot by, and yet no one does anything. There probably wouldn't be any mental properties in this world, and if there were, they would be causally inert with respect to the pageant of events in their midst. Everything would be caused by physical properties alone. This world has a kind of simplicity and elegance. It is, however, not the world we live in. Were it so, I would not be writing this sentence nor would you be turning these pages. The actual world is one in which some events have mental causes. When we pick these events out, we, as the expression goes, carve nature at its joints.[30] We pare some events into actions, a class defined by their causal history. My argument is that the century roughly between Hobbes and Hume or Rochester and Richardson did just that, and in so doing endeavored to discover the component parts of actions in a way analogous to the discovery of anything else in nature. Once upon a time this sort of argument might have been made with particular reference to the interior life of characters or voice of poems, a life or voice that corresponds to something like the motives and mental causes of human agents. Perhaps for this reason, when Anscombe sought to discount motives in her study of intentions, she said in passing, "I am very glad not to be writing either ethics or literary criticism, to which this question belongs."[31] For Anscombe, motives along with mental causes were inherently obscure, whereas intentions could be read off the surface of one's behavior. An intentional action is not a series of doings plus an inner, private motive. It is rather the kind of action for which one may supply a description of why it was done. Anscombe's attempt to analyze an ostensibly mental-state term while holding at bay categories of the mind is crisp and seductive. Even so, it is perhaps a virtue of writing literary criticism that one sees how even the more mind-centered works of the period do not necessarily imply a language of privacy or inwardness, selfhood or the individual. Some of the works I feature are interested in these categories, but just as many are not. What I will argue in the following chapters is this: the topic of actions involved mental terms (including intentions) as a particular kind of cause. A close look at all kinds of texts shows that these causes move in several directions, sometimes from within but just as often from without. It is (again) possible to imagine a world that has only events, with no actions. It is very difficult to imagine a world that has no causes. Admitting causation into the account of actions left a shudder. The works I look at are a few instances where that shudder is most intriguingly recorded.

1   Actions, Agents, Causes

The period covered by this study witnesses an important debate about actions. For writers like Hobbes and Hume, human behavior really ought to be described in causal terms. When trying to make sense of what a person does, it is always best to examine the reasons that cause and explain her actions. These reasons typically turn out to be the desires and beliefs an agent has about the effects of her actions, attitudes that are in turn caused by events external to the agent herself.[1] The view that actions are caused by attitudes like desire and belief comes under scrutiny, however, from those who think that causal arguments put at risk one's autonomy and freedom, especially when causes are understood to track back to the outside world. While Hobbes and Hume found causal necessity to be compatible with freedom, their opponents saw freedom as incompatible with any sort of external dependence. My goal in this chapter is to show how this debate encloses a range of philosophical, social, and literary concerns. Foremost among them is whether persons are special kinds of agents, endowed with immaterial souls, or whether mental states like desire and belief are made of the same stuff as the rest of the world and thus susceptible to a kind of limitless causation. Within this metaphysical quarrel over personhood, talk about reasons for action—one's motives, say—often entailed further talk about the societies in which actions occur. As a result, debates about agency had considerable bearing on questions of authority in an age that begins with civil wars and ends with a commercial empire. To look at the motives that lie behind actions was for many to examine how states of mind bring about forms of politics or society. Yet states of mind like motive or intention were often impossible to understand apart from the context in which they occurred. And so the moral of this chapter for the larger project of the book is this: if the philosophy of action consistently found itself tugged between an account of agency that secluded the will within the mind and an account that derived it from external causes, so too did the literary forms designed to evoke the reaches of human consciousness and action. In either case, the line between persons and their component parts, persons and society, the mind and the body, one mind and another, all come under meaningful pressure.[2]

Free Will or Necessity, Part 1

Our story begins with Royalist exiles living in Paris during the early years of the Civil War. In 1645 William Cavendish, the Marquess of Newcastle, commissioned Thomas Hobbes and the Anglican theologian John Bramhall to write on the free will problem, a venerable concern of philosophers made relevant again by religious and political upheaval. Bramhall composed a short paper that spring and Hobbes responded quickly; Bramhall rebutted, and the exchange remained for a time within a small group of expatriates. Upon their return to England, however, the debate took a more public face. In 1654 Hobbes's paper was printed and published, without his permission, under the title *Of Libertie and Necessitie*. Bramhall followed the next year by publishing his rejoinder, *A Defence of True Liberty, from Antecedent and Extrinsecall Necessity*. Hobbes replied with a new paper, *The Questions concerning Liberty, Necessity, and Chance*, in 1656. Two years later, Bramhall returned with *Castigations of Mr. Hobbes his Last Animadversions in the Case concerning Liberty, and Universal Necessity*. By this time, the debate had moved from a manuscript coterie to a print public and in the process taken on the formal dimensions of a major controversy, with each writer stating his theses in point-by-point response to the other and anticipating and refuting arguments in advance.[3]

Much of the controversy centered on how one might go about defining what actions are, where they start and where they stop. When Hobbes describes an action, he refers to an event with a causal history. Agent *P* has done action *R* for reason *Q*. It is not enough to say that *P* had *Q* while doing *R*; rather, in order to be part of the description, *Q* must explain the occurrence of *R*. Consider the following set of events: "[W]hen a Travailer meets with a shower, the journey had a cause, and the rain had a cause sufficient to produce it, but because the journey caused not the rain, nor the rain the journey, we say, they were contingent one to another" and not related as cause and effect.[4] The conclusion Hobbes wishes to derive from the example is simple. The rain happened at the same time as the traveler's journey but did not cause him to go, an action that was presumably caused by the desire to get from one place to another. The weather and a person's decisions each have a causal structure that prominently features reasons. This structure bears on the free will problem because it tethers the will to something on its outside. The agent who decides to go on a journey does so for a reason, and, that being the case, her will has locked onto whatever disposition or attitude explains her action. "In this following of ones *hopes* and *fears*," Hobbes writes, "consisteth the nature of *Election*," by which he means that choosing to act refers to a cause (a hope or fear) and does not occur on its own.[5] So when a philosopher leaves London for Paris in the midst of civil war, he does so presumably because he wants to be in Paris and believes that traveling to Dover and getting on a boat is a good way of getting there. He may further believe, given his Royalist sympathies, that being in Paris is a good idea in the hour of Republican victory. Adding further reasons, however, only sews more stitches to the causal net. It's enough to say at this point that he left because he wanted to be in Paris, for by describing events this way we commit to the idea that "all actions have their causes" (*Questions*, 70).

To describe an action that an agent performs, one needs to provide the reason for which it was done. One can do so, Hobbes argues, by looking at the sundry passions of the mind, in particular those organized around "appetite and fear . . . the first unperceived beginnings of our actions."[6] This use of a mental vocabulary is important (for the moment) to satisfy the requirement that the will, like everything else, has a cause. We have on Hobbes's account provided a description of his decision to take a boat to Paris if we say he *feared* the Parliamentary army and *wanted* to be safe among friends. Our description of his actions, however, makes an argument against his will having been free to take them. That is because providing a causal account of actions also supplies the grounds of their necessity, the locking of choice onto the attitude by which it is explained. When, for example, Hobbes argues that the Lord having said to David, "I offer thee three things; choose thee one of them, that I may do it unto thee" (2 Samuel, 24:12), is not evidence for free will, he claims that one cannot show that "such *election* was not *necessitated* by the *hopes*, and *fears*, and considerations of *good* and *bad* to follow" (*Libertie*, 7). God affords to David the opportunity to choose among options, but the act of choosing one thing over another requires there to be a reason for doing so, and this requirement locks the will onto the particular hope or fear that rationalizes the choice. Seen this way, the idea of free will is a category mistake, since it ascribes to an appetite a condition that can belong only to an agent, and since it attempts thereby to shed the causes that explain why one takes the actions one does.

Bramhall holds in contrast that "all the freedom of the agent is from the freedom of the will," a position he articulates in opposition to causal accounts of acting.[7] We have sufficiently described an action, on his view, if we say merely that it was undertaken by the will. No lattice of causes trails behind this singular faculty. And so while agents may be said to have reasons for acting the way they do, those reasons never quite exert the force of a cause into an effect. A reason might "representeth to the will, whether this or that be convenient" but the will always retains the right to choose what to do in response to this information (*Defence*, 10).

When "the will is mooved by the understanding," for example, it is "not as by an efficient, having a causall influence into the effect, but only by proposing and representing the object" (*Defence*, 31). In the gap between the reason that proposes objects and the will that acts upon them lies the vaunted freedom from necessity, for "whatsoever obligation the understanding does put upon the will, is by the consent of the will, and derived from the power of the will, which was not necessitated to moove the understanding to consult" (*Defence*, 30). Where Hobbes tracks motives into actions, therefore, Bramhall reverses course and sets the will apart from any motive one might have, as if the will were a kind of person within the mind. The result is an elaborate allegory of agency, in which "the will is the Lady and Mistris of human actions, the understanding is her trusty counseller, which gives no advice, but when it is required by the will" (*Defence*, 30–1). Lest this seem too close to a cause moving into an effect, Bramhall further observes that "if the first consultation or deliberation be not sufficient, the will may moove a review, and require the understanding to inform it self better" (*Defence*, 31).[8] The effort is at once to sheathe the will from causes and provide for it a kind of psychology of choosing. To be a person, on this view, is to be possessed of a will that can refuse to follow motives or desires. Thus the proper tense in which to describe acts of a free will is the past conditional. Despite the preponderance of causes, free agents "might have suspended or denied [the] concurrence" of past actions or might "have elected otherwise" (*Defence*, 11, 209).[9]

One important corollary of Bramhall's account of actions is that their proper description really ought not to extend beyond the agent. Insofar as the will is always free to do otherwise, the history of an action should make reference to events within the mind only. In pointed contrast, Hobbes argues that the description of actions should be as extensive as possible. This kind of description, as we have seen, begins by making reference to reasons. Hobbes got on a boat because he wanted to get to Paris. Agent *P* did action *R* for reason Q. The more closely one looks at Q, however, the more one sees that it is caused by Q_1, Q_2, and so on. Hobbes wanted to get to Paris because he feared for his safety in London. He feared for his safety in London because he believed his writings had angered the Parliamentary authorities. Once opened up to inspection, the causal horizon is nearly limitless. "That which I say necessitateth and determineth every action," Hobbes writes, "is the sum of all those things, which being now existent, conduce and concurre to the production of that action hereafter, whereof if any one thing now were wanting, the effect could not be produced" (*Questions*, 80).[10] The sum of all things can stretch quite far. At the very least, it can extend beyond the minds of agents to the circumstances and contexts in which agents find themselves. So while it is true that actions depend upon mental states, it is also true that mental states arise from objects, events, and occurrences, from causes external to the head. When Hobbes writes that "nothing taketh beginning from itself" he means to include not only the will but also what we might think of as the efficient cause of the will, the attitude to which the will is locked. Both are brought about by causes not of the agent's "disposing" (*Questions*, 289). While propositional attitudes like *wanting* to get to Paris or *believing* that a boat might do the trick may seem like they begin within us, as mental terms ostensibly should, their proper description, Hobbes argues, ought to reach from the mind to the world. This is because stopping with the mind's internal repertoire of attitudes would fall short of the story in which one comes to have attitudes locked to actions. The route accordingly moves from the outside in: "[E]xternal objects cause *conceptions*, and conceptions *appetite* and *fear*"—and appetite and fear the various acts of the will.[11]

This particular dimension to Hobbes's quarrel with free will is worth a moment's pause. The locking of the will onto attitudes like wanting or fearing, knowing or believing, had seemed to commit Hobbes to a kind of inward account of actions, one that specified their causal history in terms of a mental vocabulary of desires or intentions. But on further inspection it turns out that Hobbes is equally committed to describing the history of actions with respect to their peripheral beginnings, in contexts beyond the person.[12] The long-term result, I will argue over the course of this book, is a balancing of events internal to agents with the external forms by which these events are shaped. Causation casts too wide a net to capture only the propositional attitudes leading up to actions. So it will be important for us to keep an eye on the varieties of external-ism that begin for our purposes with Hobbes and extend into the middle of the eighteenth century with Hume—to look, that is, at accounts of action that track attitudes past agents having them to the worlds from which attitudes spring, to societies and polities, to physical units of matter, or simply to other people.[13] Hobbes's version, as we have seen, places emphasis on the near limitless reach of causation, the "sum of all things" that issue into a particu-lar action. "There is hardly one Action, to the causing of which concurres not whatsoever is *in rerum natura*," Hobbes writes, and then adds as if to explain, that "there cannot be a Motion in one part of the World, but the same must also be communicated to all the rest of the World" (*Questions*, 239). Hobbes thus elaborates a concept of cause that binds atoms to thoughts to persons to kings to God. On this view, actions don't so much begin with agents as fall backward along a continuous web.

The inclusion of any one action within a web of antecedent causes makes an important statement about the nature of persons, as Hobbes's critics were wont to show. If causation doesn't begin with the will, but rather with attitudes and before that with reasons for those attitudes, then the special place of the person in the overall scheme of the cosmos has been taken away. On the most basic sense of things, Hobbes does not consider persons to be differ-ent in substance from other entities in the world. His description of the universe—in which "every *Object* is either a part of the whole World, or an Aggregate of parts"—admits of one substance, reducible in all instances to the atoms that make up minds and bodies alike.[14] I will explore in the next chapter some of the difficulties that come with this sort of physical model of consciousness and mental causation. I would like now to stick to the place of agents in a world where action occurs as a motion across a single chain. Consider Bramhall's writing a response to Hobbes. Bramhall ascribes to this act a "moral" foundation that begins within him. Hobbes retorts, "I doubt not but he had therefore the Will to write this Reply, *because* I had answered his Treatise concerning true Liberty. My answer therefore was (at least in part) the *cause* of his writing, yet that is the cause of the nimble local motion of his fingers. Is not the cause of local motion Physical? His will therefore was Physically and Extrinsecally and Antecedently, and not Morally caused by my writing" (*Questions*, 142–3). The turn to reasons outside the agent flanks an emphasis on physical description. One motion across the surface of things takes us from Hobbes's writing to the movement of Bramhall's fingers to the appearance of another essay, all without much pause for a person having a will that expresses itself in writing. When Hobbes adds to this account that "what it is to determine a thing Morally, no man living understands," he gets rid of the chance that there might be something in agents—a moral center—that stops the motion of cause and leaves space for an authority over one's own will (*Questions*, 142).

Bramhall's feeling that his essay has no cause other than his will to write it, and that having this will is quite close to what it means to be human, misrecognizes on Hobbes's view the nature of causal relations in a physical world. There is no space outside of matter that belongs to the soul or the will or the passions or anything else one might want to use as a platform for autonomy.[15] Hobbes asks Bramhall to give up the intuitive sense that *he* is the cause of his own actions and that any particular action he performed could always have gone otherwise. Bramhall's error, in other words, is to hew too closely to common sense—"that which he sayes, any thing else whatsoever, would think, if it knew it were moved, and did not know what moved it"—rather than to look into the sources of his actions (*Questions*, 41). The feeling one has of free will is intuitive only if one is ignorant of causes, a point that leads Hobbes on a certain rhetorical flourish: "A wooden Top that is lasht by the Boyes, and runs about sometimes to one Wall, sometimes to another, sometimes spinning, sometimes hitting men on the shins, if it were sensible of its own motion, would think it proceeded from its own Will, unless it felt what lasht it" (*Questions*, 41). The notion of human action as a special kind of event is on this metaphorical description vividly reduced, as if to suggest that we are little more than conscious tops, spun by causes beyond our immediate perception. The metaphor makes two related points, first that autonomy is a kind of delusion and second that events internal to the mind follow the same laws of causation as events external to the mind.

Hobbes's inclusion of mental causation under the same laws as physical causation serves an important purpose. If the will is locked to attitudes and attitudes are locked to objects, thoughts, or events, then human action is subject to the same necessity as everything else in the world. At the same time, however, this necessity does not deprive agents of freedom or of responsibility. Here lies one of Hobbes's more notable contributions to models of agency in the early modern and modern periods. Hobbes argues that freedom requires only that a person is able to act according to her wants, not that the will is without a determining set of causes. "A free agent," on this view, is he "that can do if he will, and forbear if he will" and liberty the "absence of external impediments" to action (*Questions*, 304, 46).[16] Freedom turns out to be a particular kind of causal relation, one in which reasons are able to become actions. The condition of freedom is therefore satisfied if the reasons one has proceed uninhibited into the actions one takes. On this account, no amount of determinacy conflicts with freedom, since the having of attitudes is what it means to be an agent and since the translating of attitudes without hindrance into actions is what it means to have liberty. To put the problem in terms of our earlier example, it makes no sense to ask whether Hobbes's will was free to choose going to France but it does to ask whether Hobbes was free to leave or whether the authorities intercepted his boat. "A *Free Agent*" is one "whose motion, or action is not hindered nor stopt. And a *Free Action*, that which is produced by a Free Agent" (*Questions*, 143). The forming of a will to do something, then, is part of the causal history of an action but alone is neither free nor bound; these conditions belong only to the agent and action themselves.

What will later be termed compatibilism is a simple yet important argument: to describe something in terms of its causal history does nothing to put liberty at risk.[17] Rather, it is to take a close look at that thing and examine its component parts. So to say that a person acts for a reason is both to explain why actions occur and to say that a person could not have done otherwise, since doing otherwise would mean only that she had another will, locked to a separate series of events. Freedom therefore does not require that I am set loose from a net of causes; it simply demands that "I can do if I will," a condition met by there being no obstacles to my doing. Hobbes's compatibilism will (again) have a significant influence on seventeenth- and eighteenth-century philosophy, from Locke and Hume, who both embraced it after their own fashions, to Kant, who found it to be a "wretched subterfuge."[18] If one appeal of the argument was its sense that actions become intelligible only once we realize, often against our intuitions, that their sources are extensive, another is the claim that having reasons for acting takes nothing away from the accountability one incurs along the way. The contextual sources of action, on Hobbes's account, bind agents to external structures, a claim he evidently found convenient in a time of political uncertainty. "The *necessity* of an *action* doth not make the *Laws* that prohibit it *unjust*," Hobbes writes in response to Bramhall's worry that a commitment to necessity would mean that "praise, dispraise, reward and punishment are in vain" (*Libertie*, 27). Bramhall believes the doctrine of free will is required for systems of politics and morality to be legitimate, since without it agents would neither be nor feel accountable for their actions; thus even the "perswasion that there is no true liberty is able to overthrow all Societies and Commonwealths in the world" (*Defence*, 91). For his part, Hobbes finds in necessity the very basis of obedience and order. Agents come to have intentions, desires, and beliefs because they witness consequences in the world about them; in this way, "*praise* and *dispraise*, and likewise *Reward* and *Punishment*, do by example make and conform the will to good and evil" (*Libertie*, 34). This exchange repeats their disagreement over the role of causal language in the description of actions, this time with reference to political obligation. Hobbes argues that believing that actions have consequences is reason, in most cases, to conform one's behavior to Scripture and polity, and when it is not, to fear the extrapersonal laws of God and the state. The external antecedents to action turn out to be the very laws one ought to be obeying. From this perspective, Bramhall's claim that the will acts on its own discovers autonomy where there is none and as a result cleaves agents from their sources of compliance.

I will come back in subsequent chapters to the seventeenth-century quarrel over the sources and meanings of actions. Before turning to the next installment, I want to gather some of the threads of the controversy as I have reconstructed it so far. Much centered on the significance of the concept of cause in the description of actions, on whether cause was essential to understanding connections among the diverse phenomena of the mind and world or whether it was a threat to the special nature and place of humans in the cosmos. Under the rubric of cause, Hobbes and Bramhall disagreed about, for example, whether persons are endowed with immaterial souls or whether persons are entirely physical in their composition. As a corollary to that disagreement, they quarreled over the point where actions started and stopped—within the precincts of the will or in attitudes and contexts. Without simplifying too much, then, we might draw the quarrel over cause into one between an immaterialist, dualist, and internalist picture of agency, on the one hand, and a physicalist, monist, and externalist picture on the other. For as much as Hobbes is committed to the second picture, he seems tacitly to concede to Bramhall that our naive intuitions run in favor of the first, that agents tend to think of themselves as having a will under their control and a soul made from spirit. It is, he appears to suggest, the role of philosophy to adjust or correct this naive psychology of action, and so to stand athwart the way in which most people understand their own behavior.

Free Will or Necessity, Part 2

Our story continues with two philosophers engaged in a long-running dispute about actions, agents, and causes: the deist Anthony Collins, heir to the compatibilist materialism of Thomas Hobbes, and the theologian Samuel Clarke, heir to the libertarian dualism of John Bramhall.[19] Moving into the 1710s provides a case of how philosophical ideas do and do not change over time. There is a sense in which the disagreement we've been looking at becomes further entrenched, with Collins arguing that necessity is neither opposed to a proper understanding of freedom nor the basis for lawlessness, and Clarke responding that humans without free will are little more than automata. Yet important transformations occur along the way. For as much as the Hobbes-Bramhall debate became a major controversy in print, one written in the vernacular (as not all philosophy then was) for an audience conceivably as wide as any who might have an interest in questions of agency and motivation, it never completely shed the form of a coterie discussion undertaken within the circumference of the Newcastle circle. Even as they are printed and published, the installments that appeared on both sides after the initial exchange continued to be addressed to Cavendish, with each reproducing the arguments of the other before stating new positions. When we arrive at the moment of Collins and Clarke, the imagined scene of composition is notably different. Freestanding volumes of philosophy, the texts are written at a clear distance from each other, with various levels of circulation standing between one writer and the other. Along with these changes in form, certain key semantic alterations have also occurred. When, for example, Hobbes and Bramhall refer to the world outside the mind, they mean an impersonal structure of rewards and punishments, sovereignty and obedience, a world in considerable turmoil for the duration of their debate. When their positions are returned to in the first half of the eighteenth century, the meanings of terms like "world" and "society" have broadened to include domains of interpersonal and public life not limited to political obligation. For Collins, Clarke, and Hume, that is, the relation we should consider is not only between an agent and the state (or God); it is also between one agent, another, and the society they compose. Within this background sense of what philosophy does, one particular dimension of the debate over actions comes sharply into view. That is the problem of intuitive arguments. If agents feel as though they are in control of their actions, are they in possession of a mistaken view of their own behavior? If they are, what does it mean for philosophers to describe a faulty structure of human intuition? Once opened up for examination, this question of intuitive versus counterintuitive reasoning raises further questions about the way that minds come to have ideas and intentions, especially ideas about their own actions.

When Bramhall argues that his writing an essay has no cause other than his will to write an essay, he claims to have access to the states of his mind that give rise to the actions he performs. And when Hobbes responds that writing an essay has causes that lie before and beyond one's mind, he claims that such access only goes so far. Their disagreement in this respect turns on the relative importance of first-person introspection. The claim that *I* know better than anyone else what causes my own writing rests on the assumption that I have special access to what goes on in my mind. In contrast, the claim that what goes on in my mind takes shape from what goes on in the world assumes that the first-person stance is often mistaken. Hobbes and Collins both allow that the introspective stance with respect to actions tilts strongly to freedom. Given pause to reflect on one's own actions, they concede, most agents tend to think they were free to do them, in the broad sense outlined by Bramhall. That is, looking back on what they've done, most agents tend to believe that they were possessed of a will impervious to cause and were always able to have done otherwise. To the degree to which first-person introspection reveals a will that is free to do otherwise, however, it is for Hobbes and Collins precisely the wrong perspective to have on behavior. "The vulgar, who are bred up to believe *liberty* or *freedom*," Collins writes, "think themselves secure of success, constantly appealing to *experience* for a proof of their *freedom*, and being persuaded that they feel themselves free on a thousand occasions."[20] And yet their appeal to experience looks in the wrong direction or not deeply enough. Agents cannot see their own reasons for acting, in part because they like to believe that they have no reasons, at least none they couldn't resist. "The source of their mistake," Collins continues, is that they "either attend not to, or see not the causes of their actions, especially in matters of little moment, and thence conclude, they are free, or not mov'd by causes, to do what they do" (12). The point is thus not only that first-person introspection is often limited; it is that these limits can only be gotten rid of if one looks closely for the sources of action, including those outside the head. And to look closely at these sources entails that the ordinary or intuitive vocabulary in which actions are conceived—a freedom to choose or forbear from acting—shifts to one that admits of causation. The drift is thus to open mental events to physical description, as if physical language were most suited to describe causal relations and the version of necessity they entail.

The first-person stance is subject to skepticism to the degree to which it reveals a false sense of freedom. The trouble with advocates of freedom is that they have let their unreconstructed feelings get hold of them. They "frequently do actions whereof they repent" and because they regret their past actions, imagine "they might not have done them at the time they did them, and that they were *free* from necessity" at the moment of choice (13). "They likewise see, that they often change their minds; that they can, and do chuse differently every successive moment" and thus picture that every future decision might go one way or another (13). They "frequently deliberate" and are often "at a near ballance, and in a state of indifference with respect to judging about some propositions, and willing or chusing with respect to some objects" and so feel as if nothing influences their actions (13). "Experiencing these things, they mistake them for the exercise of *Freedom,* or *Liberty* from *Necessity,*" when precisely the opposite is the case (13–4). The feeling of freedom, in other words, does not accurately represent the experience by which it is engendered; rather, it arises from a set of conditions it also contradicts. "Ask them, Whether they think themselves *free*? And they will immediately answer *Yes,*" even when—or precisely because—their experience is of necessity (14). When we change our minds or deliberate or regret the past we act from necessity even as we feel that we are free. Each one of these actions elicits a feeling at odds with its causal history. The result is a curious warping among the faculties. Feeling runs one way and cognition another, as the philosopher enjoins his readers to drop their intuitive vocabulary of free will and adopt a more rigorous stance with respect to their actions. The causal history of actions is not so much sealed from introspective access, therefore, as made available through a dramatic change of perspective.

Agents can have access to the states that give rise to actions in part by coming to the view that these states are not only mental but admit of a description in a physical language of cause and effect as well as a psychological language of freedom and choice. The effort then is to push the description of mental states downward, as it were, so they may be expressed in physical terms. "Whatever has a beginning must have a cause," and this includes the "opinions, prejudices, temper, habit and circumstances" we are likely to consider most defining of who we are and what we do (57, 47). On a first pass, opinions, prejudices, tempers, and the like don't fit into the kind of lawlike regularity that defines relations in the physical realm. And that is precisely why our initial first-person sense of agency tends toward error. Mental-state words like "temper" seem to resist description in terms of causes, while physical-state words like "sense" do not. The result is a mistaken feeling that one's mental states exist on their own, without dependence on external or antecedent sources. So the point for Collins is to shade the idiom of the first with that of the second, to emphasize the causal interaction between experiences that might seem peculiar to the mind—opinions, perceptions, beliefs, and the like—and objects and events that exist independent of the mind. Seen this way, received notions of first-person access start to unravel some. What is it we retrieve when we reflect on experience? The answer, Collins proposes without much surprise, is the ideas in our head. Sit down and think about your thoughts and it will turn out you think about your thoughts. Yet the content of minds has two properties important for Collins's larger point. First, "idea's both of sensation and reflection, offer themselves to us whether we will or no, And we cannot reject 'em" (32). Ideas come for free. So the mere having of them does not make a case for free will. The second property follows from this first. Ideas have to begin somewhere, and since the mind has no innate content, their origins must lie in the world. Admitting this condition then opens the door for a broad thesis about actions: "[As] we necessarily receive Idea's, so each Idea is necessarily what it is in our mind; for it is not possible to make anything different from itself. This first necessary Action, the Reader will see to be the foundation and cause of all other Intelligent actions of Man, and to make them also necessary" (32). Minds come by their ideas by copying and representing some sort of object or event, one prior to and outside of them. Were this not so, minds would have no content at all. So the laws that cover the physical domain should also cover what happens in the head, or else the proximity between the original and its copy would be broken.

These two properties lay the basis for how Collins thinks one might describe first-person access in such a way that is consistent with necessity. Because causes lead to effects in objects outside the mind, so must they also in the mental representations derived from these objects. The idea and its original share the same substance, with the same laws of cause and effect; therefore, to say that the one follows laws and the other does not would be to propose that a thing could differ from itself. Seen this way, it is impossible to say that mental states resist description in physical terms, or that the will is free in a way that matter is not. We come to understand our own mental states as soon as we place them under the same formal rule as the physical states to which they ultimately reduce: "[We] may know that the least circumstance in the extensive chain of causes, that precede every effect, is sufficient to produce an effect; and also know, that there must be causes of our choice (thô we do not or cannot discern those causes) by knowing, *that every thing that has a beginning must have a cause*" (49). With respect to actions, in other words, the first-person stance is not wrong to conceive of antecedents in a language of mental states. It is only wrong to conceive of mental states as separate from laws. So when we turn to reflect on our own agency, what should be revealed to us is that "our *passions, appetites, sensations*, and *reason*, do determine us in our several choices" (69). To say that passions, tempers, reason, and other attitudes admit of a physical description in terms of cause and effect, however, is also to say that first-person access only makes sense once we change what we mean by the person who is gaining access and the states she discovers. The knowledge of necessity in this respect runs against what Collins takes to be common notions or feelings about each.

The sustained tension between Collins's point of view and what he represents as a "vulgar" type of introspection turns on several related dimensions of what it means to be an agent. Once we grant the idea that every part of an agent—ideas, attitudes, soul, will, arms, and legs—falls under a causal description, we are in place to understand what is wrong with the intuitive feeling of free will.

And once we are in such a place, we begin to lose our feeling that humans have a special exemption from a world otherwise structured by causes. Like nonhuman animals and children (but unlike rocks and turnips), "man" is an "intelligent necessary agent" (70). All act according to reasons, and each is free to the degree to which his or her actions are unimpeded. The only difference between intelligent agents like men and sheep and nonintelligent entities like rocks and turnips is that the former include mental states in their causal histories while the latter do not. The process of introspection Collins enjoins on his reader is in this respect something of an austere one, as it asks that readers come to the view that their sense of freedom is built on such a mistaken view of personhood.

It is in turn the very austerity of this view that provokes and becomes the target of Clarke's response. There is on his account nothing naive or ill-conceived about the feeling that we choose our actions freely, since there is no logical way to distinguish between how this feeling might present itself to us in truth or in error. "All our Actions do now in experience *Seem* to us to be *Free*, exactly in the *Same Manner* as they *would* do upon *supposition* of our being really *Free* Agents."[21] Clarke asks us to suppose that we are possessed of free will in the way that we tend to think we are, and then to suppose that we are not free but only think that we are; in either case, the subjective sense of our actions remains unchanged. The point is that from the perspective in which we are situated we can never see into the condition of necessity Collins alleges, at least not with respect to our own mental states and our own actions. Since this is the case, the putative fact of necessity has no priority over the intuitive sense of freedom; it is rather one belief asserted against another. Collins has thus asked us to entertain a paradox, "a contradiction in Terms," in which we believe that we are free and unfree at the same time (9). The logical impropriety of this position, on Clarke's view, lies in the reduction of "*Reasons, Motives* and *Arguments*, which are mere *abstract Notions*," to "*physical, necessary*, and *efficient Cause* of *Action*" (10). Collins has placed mental-state terms under the same set of laws as things like "a *Clock* or a *Watch*" and so defined the properties of the mind in such a way that gets rid of the mind entirely (27).[22]

Clarke's response is not entirely what one might expect. Across the long arc from Bramhall, certain features of the defense of free will have been preserved and others altered. The resistance to external sources of action once more couples a sense that their description ought to begin within the mind. And this accent on internal or endogenous description again links up with a claim that agents could always have done otherwise. What is different in Clarke's account is the reluctance to claim that mental states like "reasons, motives or arguments" compose an entity separate from the body in which they are housed. The dualist edges, rather, are softened considerably.[23] "'Tis the *Man*, that freely *determines himself* to act. *Reasons* or *Perceptions of the Understanding*, can no more (properly and strictly speaking) determine an Action, than an *abstract Notion* can be a *Substance* or *Agent*, can strike or *move a piece of Matter*" (11). Clarke's aim is to turn Collins's physicalism against itself and show that reasons are by definition too abstract to produce material effects. It is men who act, not their attitudes. But this does not mean that some ghostly dimension of their minds stretches onto a physical frame. In fact, Clarke's point is close to the opposite. Reasons or intentions are abstractions with no power independent of agents having them; they are merely another way of describing the very freedom that agents possess. Seen this way, Collins either has no account of the mind, or if he has one, no account of mental causation: for "[if] the *Reasons* or *Motives* upon which a Man acts, be the *immediate* and *efficient Cause of the Action*: then either *abstract Notions*, such as all *Reasons* and *Motives* are, have a *real Subsistence*, that is, are themselves *Substances*; or else *That which has it self no real Subsistence*, can *put* a Body into *Motion*: Either of which, is manifestly absurd" (43). Either reasons are as physical as rocks and so are not mental properties or they are mental and so outside of causal explanation. On Clarke's view, both lines of argument would separate agents from their mental states and place them in some sort of net. The argument for necessity thus reduces to one of two impossibilities: states of mind that aren't really states of mind, or states of mind that have no plausible role to play in the world. This being the case, it is best to conceive of the agent as an entire being, possessed with a freedom to initiate actions in the way she sees fit.

Clarke's alternative is thus to argue, on behalf of common sense, that one ought to describe actions with reference to the agents who initiate them. The first-person stance is precisely the right view to have, since there is no closer perspective on the sources of behavior. Or to put it another way, agents do not typically separate themselves from their attitudes or join these attitudes to external events. Softened as the dualism may be, the emphasis on *internal* description has not gone away. "To be an *Agent*," Clarke writes, "signifies, to have a *Power of beginning Motion*" (6). And having such a power of motion means that one is free to act or not act at will: "If he has within himself a *Principle or Power of Self-Motion*; then (which is the Essence of *Liberty*,) That *active Substance*, in which the Principle of Self-Motion inheres, is it self the only proper, Physical, and immediate *CAUSE* of the Motion or Action" (26).[24] Nothing "*extrinsick* to the Agent" ought to be included in the roster of causes (26). This being the case, introspection reveals at once a complete history of any given action and a proper sense that one could always have done otherwise.

Clarke's metaphysical point about where actions begin is in this way recruited to an ethical point about how we come to behave in ways that are moral and civil. "Every *Action*, every Motion arising from the *Self-moving Principle*, is *essentially free*," and for that reason is essentially "joined with a Sense or consciousness of *moral good* and *evil*, and . . . therefore *eminently* called *Liberty*" (27). According to this model, one brings a set of moral principles to relations with other agents, and the result is a society of reciprocity and exchange. For Collins, in contrast, principles of reciprocity and exchange are by definition antecedent and external to the agents they shape. Agents are guided less by principle than by pleasure and pain, the causes of which lie in structures that precede them: "[R]ewards will be of use to all those who conceive those rewards to be pleasure, and punishments will be of use to all those who conceive them to be pain; and rewards and punishments will frame those Mens wills to observe, and not transgress the Laws" (Collins, 87–8). So while pleasure and pain provide a disposition to act in one or another way, their sources come from the already existing order in which actions occur. The difference between Collins and Clarke in this final respect comes down to a disagreement about where to look for the sources of moral actions. Clarke looks inside agents for the "Sense or consciousness" of right and wrong; Collins looks to the "foundations of morality and laws, and of rewards and punishments in society" (Collins, iv). The quarrel between internal or external description turns into one over whether agents constitute social forms or such forms "frame" agents.[25]

This fundamental conflict will reappear in later chapters, between writers like Locke and Haywood, and within single works like *Clarissa*. The idea is that agents either bring principles to relations with other agents, and so constitute a larger civil order, or this order pre-exists and structures encounters between agents, and so provides a sort of template in which intentions and desires become intelligible to whoever is having them.[26] In the episode we've been examining, Clarke embodies the former, Collins the latter position. One interesting feature of their debate, however, is that both make recourse to the view that agents allegedly have of their own intentions and their own actions. For Clarke, this first-person stance is the naive or automatic account that one typically gives about why one did or did not do something. Actions are for him the result of a kind of internal deliberation that includes a feeling of being responsible for one's choices. Elaborated into a philosophical language, this feeling goes by the name of free will. Collins attempts in contrast to undo a great deal of what it means to be a person taking a view of such things. The commitment to physical description means that a human is really no different from any other agent responsive to pain and pleasure, such as a sheep, fox, or turtle.[27] The commitment to externalism means that states of mind like intention, desire, and belief leak into and take their cue from the contexts in which actions occur. These twin commitments allow agents to see the sources of their actions, perhaps, but from Clarke's perspective only at the price of losing an important sense of what agency might mean, the price of relinquishing a sense that thoughts and actions are things one can own, or own up to, or bring to the world.

Free Will or Necessity, Part 3

For a philosopher sympathetic to the kind of commitments that Collins holds, the attempt to sustain a first-person perspective might seem like a losing wager. What use is it to bully readers out of their prized sense of self? When Hume turns to the problem of free will in *A Treatise of Human Nature* (1739–40) and again in *An Enquiry Concerning Human Understanding* (1748), it is this feature that is fundamentally altered. The change is in certain respects quite simple: in order to understand the nature of the will, Hume argues, agents should not look to their own actions; they should, rather, look to the actions of other people. Hume thus responds to the quarrel over first-person access—its specific nature and relative authority—by turning to the third-person, objective perspective from which one views any item of concern. As Collins had pointed out, one's own motives can often be misperceived as disinterest or freedom from cause. Hume's response is neither to suggest that we should take a more rigorous stance with respect to minds nor to say we should accept at face value the intuitive sense of freedom. His response instead is to say that we should trust our feelings about material objects and then about other people (if not, at first glance, about ourselves). Agency is in this sense something that ought to be situated within the particular circumstances and occasions of social life.[28] The intuitive sense of freedom may be held in check or corrected by the recognition of necessity elsewhere in the natural and social environment.

Among the philosophers looked at in this chapter, Hume boasts the most extensive treatment in contemporary criticism, usually in consideration of the literatures of sympathy and sensibility.[29] My reading here will hew quite closely to his treatment of actions and thus arrive at these more familiar concerns from what is for Hume the structuring problem of causation. I thus look exclusively at the two chapters on "liberty and necessity" and their environs in the *Treatise* and the chapter on the same in the *Enquiry*. For as much as Hume wants to argue on behalf of necessity in these chapters, he does not want to claim, like Collins, that intuitive feelings are misleading or wrong. His philosophy is nothing if not an attempt to generalize and describe the set of customs, habits, and beliefs commonly used to explain human behavior and physical events alike.[30] "Vulgar" feeling is for him the inescapable ground and object of philosophy.[31] The "long disputed question concerning *liberty and necessity*" is on this account particularly tricky because it concerns the instinctive sense that agents seem to have of their own freedom to do as they please, feelings that seem at first blush different from what Hume wants to say they are.[32] His response is to say that this difference is in fact just a seeming, that, in words of Saul Kripke, the language of free will is a "philosophical misconstrual" of the way that agents ordinarily conceive of actions.[33] "Rather than repudiating common sense," Hume "asserts that the conflict comes from a philosophical misunderstanding of common language."[34] What Kripke describes as Hume's "professed determination never to deny or doubt our common beliefs" thus persists across the description of actions (64). How can this be so? Hume begins with a turn from internal impressions to the external world, from psychology to physical matter. We can easily agree that "every object is determin'd by an absolute fate to a certain degree and direction of its motion, and can no more depart from that precise line, in which it moves, than it can convert itself into an angel, or spirit" (400). "The actions, therefore, of matter," we may further agree, "are to be regarded as instances of necessary actions; and whatever is in this respect on the same footing with matter, must be acknowledg'd to be necessary" (400). The trick is to see how human actions are on this same footing and so not in conflict with our common sense and ordinary beliefs. "In judging the actions of men," he asserts, "we must proceed upon the same maxims, as when we reason concerning external objects" (403).

When Hume says this, however, he adjusts the meaning of reasoning upon external objects considerably. The account of how the actions of men resemble the contours of matter repeats the skeptical model of causation provided by book one of the *Treatise*, which he cites, in summary form, in the discussion of the will in book two. Each depends upon an act of habitual or customary inference on the part of whoever is noticing a causal relation between one thing and another, whether a rock colliding with a tree or a person deliberating on an action.[35] In both situations, we perceive a relation between a cause and an effect, yet "in no single instance the ultimate connexion of any objects is discoverable, either by our senses or reason" (400). That is because "we can never penetrate so far into the essence and construction of bodies as to perceive the principle, on which their mutual influence depends" (400). The opacity of the cause holds whether we are talking about the physical structure of rocks or the cognitive structure of minds. In either case, the constant conjunction of one thing and another leads us, through custom and habit, to believe that there really is a connection between the two, so much so that the appearance of cause X will escort us, unawares, to the immediate appearance of effect Y, or the appearance of effect Y will lead us to assume the preexistence of cause X, without our ever knowing the precise reason why this is so. "All those objects, of which we call the one *cause* and other *effect*," Hume reminds his reader (having dealt with the issue exhaustively in the first book), "are as distinct and separate from each other, as any two things in nature, nor can we ever, by the most accurate survey of them, infer the existence of the one from the other" (405). The connection exists solely in the mind that infers a relation between two objects "from experience and the observation of their constant union," and even then "the inference is nothing but the effects of custom on the imagination" (405).

When Hume says that human actions are on the same footing with matter he means to include both under an argument about causal relations. The discovery of inductive patterns requires particular events to belong to common types. Every type X we've observed in the past has led to a type Y, so therefore every X event we might discover in the course of daily life may reliably be expected to produce Y events. The relation between one event and another lies entirely in the constancy of this connection, our ability to sense that any present X is an example of a type X we've already encountered, and that this type X has reliably produced a type Y whose present example we also see in front of us. On this view, the correlation one makes by habit and custom makes no claim upon the actual constituency and makeup of individual Xs and Ys, only their falling under patterns. Hume thus declines to prioritize the particular individual (object, mind, what have you) when establishing the relation between an action and its cause. As Kripke puts it, "Only inasmuch as these events are thought of as instances of event types related by a regularity can they be thought of as causally connected. If two particular events were somehow so *sui generis* that it was logically excluded that they be placed under any (plausibly natural) event types, causal notions would not be applicable to them."[36] Kripke names this line of reasoning alternatively the "impossibility of private causation" or the "argument against private causation" because it suggests that no single event considered on its own ever yields its causal connection to another.[37] Only when two events are considered as examples of a regular pattern does causation become intelligible. Therefore it is wrong to look inside of a cause, whether the atomic structure of rocks or the internal motives of humans, and expect to find the properties that lead to its subsequent effects. The ordinary stance with respect to actions is to remain on their outside, so one may view a cause and its effect at once and then abstract from both into some regularity.[38]

In this way, the actions of men are indeed a lot like the falling of rocks, the purling of rivers, and the ticking of watches—not because they are mechanical in the way that Collins would understand the term, something that can be entirely predicted because it is so thoroughly known. Try as we might, we will never peel back the husk of a private cause to reveal its inner workings. "We must not here be content in saying," Hume avers, "that the idea of cause and effect arises from objects constantly united; but must affirm, that 'tis the very same with the idea of these objects" (405). Ideas of causation don't "arise from" objects because that would require a complementary "located within" that is always beyond our grasp. So the causal relation of one object to another is the "very same" with the concepts we have of them. The "*necessary connexion*," Hume continues, "is not discover'd by a conclusion of the understanding, but is merely a perception of the mind" using its habits of inference (405–6). Looking at the world we see that "motion in one body" is always "follow'd upon impulse by motion in another" (406). On the basis of this regular occurrence alone we come by our belief in their necessary connection. "'Tis impossible for the mind to penetrate further. From this constant union, it *forms* the idea of cause and effect, and by its influence *feels* the necessity" (406). Mind and matter thus remain on the same footing, yet their ground shifts considerably. Hume does not, like Collins, identify shared laws between ideas and their objects. Rather, he argues that we use the same form of induction in relation to each. If Collins makes ideas seem like the objects to which they refer, Hume makes objects seem like the ideas by which they are grasped.[39] He thus turns from the inner workings of minds that cause actions to happen to the perception of actions reliably inferred to have causes.

Although Hume here commits to a language of mental states,

in other words, he also argues that the mind at issue belongs to the person who observes the world in action, not to whoever may be acting in a given situation. "The necessity of any action, whether of matter or of the mind, is not properly a quality in the agent, but in any thinking or intelligent being, who may consider the action" (408). To remain on equal footing between mind and matter, therefore, we have to grant that while we suspect that rocks do not have feelings, we wouldn't know if they did, and that while we suspect that agents act out of reasons, we never know precisely what those are. We can never exactly penetrate into the essence of objects and discover what happens when cause turns into effect. The feeling of necessity that accompanies all actions, human or natural, is located outside the agent performing them, where it has the propositional status of a belief. I see a rock fall into a river and I believe it will cause a splash. I watch a man fall into a river and I believe he will later change his clothes. What the rock or the man thinks, at least in this instance, is not really at issue.

Does a rock believe that it is free as it tumbles through the air? For Hume, the question is beside the point because the belief under consideration does not belong to the rock but rather to whoever views the rock on its downward curve and pictures the splash before it happens.[40] Collins's quarrel with feelings will always miss its mark because it is so focused on the agent herself. If we widen our view enough to take in the perception as well as the performance of an action, we will discover that there is no reason to attack the feeling of freedom, because that feeling cannot properly be said to exist. The "intuitive proof of human liberty" said to lie in our account of our own actions, according to Hume, is a peculiar mistake of philosophers, who misconstrue the "certain looseness which we feel in passing or not passing from the idea of one [object] to that of the other" into a "false sensation" that "our actions are subject to our will on most occasions and . . . the will itself is subject to nothing" (408). Philosophers come to this false sense of freedom when they retrace past actions with a mind to discovering how their wills might have settled elsewhere. "This image or faint motion, we perswade ourselves, cou'd have been compleated into the thing itself" (408). The error is to be corrected, however, by a moment's reflection on customary belief, one undertaken as a shift from the first to the third person: "We may imagine we feel a liberty within ourselves; but a spectator can commonly infer our actions from our motives and character; and even where he cannot, concludes in general, that he might, were he perfectly acquainted with every circumstance of our situation and temper, and the most secret springs of our complexion and disposition. Now this is the very essence of necessity" (408–9). Other minds are steadily committed to the proposition that actions follow from motives and motives from reasons and reasons from causes.

Hume's account of actions might appear to become, at the conclusion of the second chapter on necessity, committed to the sort of depth and intricacy some associate with a rise of inwardness during the period.[41] Yet if this is so, it is at most inwardness at a considerable distance. In keeping with his model, mental causes can never be conceived in private terms. What Hume calls "motives" become intelligible only when reliably inferred from the outside.[42] Hume gives some indication that inferring motives loops backward, that agents come to know their own intentions by recognizing that they have the same properties of motive and necessity as those whose actions they observe.[43] In an influential study of the *Treatise*, Annette Baier makes something like this argument in paraphrasing Hume to be saying that "I must be to mine whatever I take you to be to what is yours, and what you take me to be to what is mine."[44] To Baier's description, I would add only that such back and forth inference occurs as part of ordinary social exchange; the "kind of reasoning" that goes into reading the "motives, temper and situation" of other people "mixes itself so entirely in human life, that 'tis impossible to act or subsist a moment without having recourse to it" (404, 405). When Hume observes in the midst of his discussion that "nothing more nearly interests us than our own actions and those of others," and for that reason "the greatest part of our reasonings is employ'd in judgments concerning them," he means to suggest therefore that coming to will something is built on a kind of external scaffold (405). Agents consider the motives of others in the same way that they would consider any other cause and at the same time discover their own motives by locating themselves in a reliably patterned network.

The final point of this argument moves from the recognition of necessity in others to the coming (necessarily) to intentions on one's own, a claim Hume develops with considerable finesse in the next chapter, entitled "The Influencing Motives of the Will" (413). It is this chapter that contains his oft-quoted aphorism, "Reason is, and ought only to be the slave of the passions, and can never pretend to any other office than to serve and obey them," a statement conceived in tight relation to the immediately preceding discussion on necessity (415). Since he has shown "that all actions of the will have particular causes," he may "proceed to explain what these causes are, and how they operate" (412). The argument begins with a claim for tremendous originality:

> Nothing is more usual in philosophy, and even in common life, than to talk of the combat of passion and reason, to give the preference to reason, and to assert that men are only so far virtuous as they conform themselves to its dictates. . . . In order to show the fallacy of all this philosophy, I shall endeavour to prove *first*, that reason alone can never be a motive to any action of the will; and *secondly*, that it can never oppose passion in the direction of the will. (413)

What is particularly novel about this formulation is not so much the assignment of actions to passions as (again) the joining of passions to a kind of external perspective.[45] Reason can never alone be a motive because "it's proper province is the world of ideas" (413).[46] Passions are better equipped to direct the will because they respond to the "prospect of pain or pleasure" presented by events one encounters (414). A passion is not a reflection or representation of an event, moreover, but rather part of the world itself, "an original existence" that "contains not any representative quality" (415). To say that passions have an existence is therefore to say that they act as causes and to say that they act as causes is to say that they may be inferred only from the outside. Our relation to the passions of mind, on this view, is similar to our relation to anything else in nature. We observe other people's behavior and infer the existence of underlying passions.

Hume takes this structure of inference as the basis for supposing that one's own actions have a cause similar to what one infers about others. I suppose the existence of a motive for someone else's actions and then do the same for myself. The account he provides of this sort of self-attribution, however, widens the scope of the argument by turning to the constitution of a social order out of discrete agents. The argument here moves swiftly. Coming to understand one's own motives by considering those belonging to others implies also that one often acts on behalf of others, as the process of inferring seems to slide the motive from someone else to oneself. To infer a cause is to assume a connection between events, a falling under types. To take on another's motive is to assume an interest *of* someone else or some other group. The instrument of this sort of inference is one or the other of the so-called calm passions— "benevolence and resentment, the love of life, and kindness to children . . . the general appetite to good, and aversion to evil"— on whose lead agents adopt the reasons, interests, or intentions of others (417).[47] Such calm passions operate "without producing any sensible emotion," and therefore we often take on the interests of others without ever quite realizing we are doing so, as simply part of ordinary social exchange (417). Once again, the argument abjures any sort of private causation. It is impossible to come to an action alone, without the side-by-side presence of others whose interests, motives, or reasons fill in one's own. To act in solitude, by contrast, would be something like having a singular cause, taken out of the larger framework that provides motives and meaning for what one does.[48]

Hume's subordinating of reason to passion in other words turns to a kind of social externalism, according to which one's intentions commence with and are completed by someone else or some other group. Nearly ten years later, Hume would clarify and expand the point in the *Enquiry*, in the section entitled "Of Liberty and Necessity." Revisiting the argument from the *Treatise*, Hume explains that the influencing motives of the will extend to the limits of the societies in which agents are located. The argument begins with the simple proposition that the "experimental inference and reasoning concerning the actions of others enters so much into human life, that no man, while awake, is ever a moment without employing it."[49] Agents are as comfortable in everyday social calculations as they are in everyday physics. I drop a cup and assume it will fall to the ground; I pay the cashier money and assume I will receive change. We use the same powers of abstraction and correlation with respect to human actions as we do with lifeless matter. "The same motives always produce the same actions: The same events follow from the same causes" (64). In human affairs, we come by the association of a type of motive with a type of action by observing their repeated connection, not in oneself but in others, who in this respect are like billiard balls—external objects whose "constant *conjunction*" leads to a "consequent *inference* of the one to the other" (64, 65).

Society both educates us in the way of actions and serves as their medium. The experience "acquired by long life and a variety of business and company" works "to instruct us in the principles of human nature," one important dimension of which is that actions never happen in a vacuum (65). One's actions take into account the response of other agents, who are themselves calculating their actions in regard to others. This constant and reciprocal inferring of motives—those belonging to others and one's own, those of others who are contemplating one's own, those who are not—stretches across the networks of society and commerce. Hume's description of how this is so weaves the metaphysical argument of the *Treatise* through the very structure of the social order. "The mutual dependence of men is so great, in all societies, that scarce any human action is entirely compleat in itself, or is performed without some reference to the actions of others, which are requisite to make it answer fully the intention of the agent" (68). On their own, actions can never be complete because they require social coordination and the activity of others. To make this point, Hume asks his reader to consider how locked into the causal patterns of social organization are even the most solitary individuals: "The poorest artificer, who labours alone, expects at least the protection of the magistrate, to ensure him the enjoyment of the fruits of his labour. He also expects, that, when he carries his goods to market, and offers them at a reasonable price, he shall find purchasers; and shall be able, by the money he acquires, to engage others to supply him with those commodities, which are requisite for his subsistence" (68). At every moment, the artificer presumes that other agents will respond as they have before, an expectation that in turn supplies the reason for the work he does. As with commerce, so with metaphysics. The private cause no more yields its effect than the lonely artificer spins his web; each requires a scaffold to bring work to fruition. One cannot complete an action without its belonging in some sense to another person, nor can one have one's intentions answered until they are brought to an end by someone else. Without an aggregate of others, the idea of agency makes no sense because society realizes intentions and makes actions intelligible: no intention is felt until it is recognized in someone else; no action is performed until it is finished (or registered) by someone else. To find one's place in this network of commerce and causation one must, so to speak, remain calm.

To put things this way is to show how much ideas about the external sources of actions change from Hobbes to Hume. I will summarize these changes now with a view toward the particular texts I examine in the chapters that follow. I maintain over the course of this book that the meaning of philosophical works should not be limited to

a background or context for the poems and novels that circulate
in their midst, that the lines of affiliation and influence among the
works I consider are extraordinarily porous. Even so, the writers I've
featured so far stand in a line, for two related reasons: first, because
they engage each other's ideas—explicitly or sotto voce—and second
because they formulate their arguments with a kind of abstraction
useful for picking out and signposting the topics that will concern
me from chapter to chapter. The first point carries over into the
second. Hobbes, Bramhall, Collins, Clarke, and Hume wrote with a
self-consciousness and formality that brought the terms of art to the
surface. Looking at their texts, we don't have to clear much away
to track the definitions of action, cause, and agency. The middle
term, for example, takes on tremendous importance. "Cause is the
cement of the universe," wrote Donald Davidson, in words that
apply equally to the British philosophers of the seventeenth and
eighteenth centuries; "the concept of cause is what holds together
our picture of the universe, a picture that would otherwise disinte-
grate into a diptych of the mental and the physical."[50] For Hobbes,
the concept of cause could be extended from the objective study of
matter to the subjective states of mind. Causes link thoughts forward
to actions and backward to reasons, weaving a web that stretches to
the limits of the political and physical world. For Hume, our habits
of induction and association apply equally to humanity and nature.
We infer the causal structure of each by observing the customary
appearance of one thing after another. As contemporaries took note,
the introduction of causal language into the description of actions
made a case against a certain understanding of free will. The use of a
causal language meant that choosing, deliberating, and deciding all
now had antecedents. As a result, freedom belonged only to actions
and not to the will, and so was compatible with external determination so long as agents could act without restraint. For Hobbes,
actions took their cue from and were understood in relation to
one or another law. Persons were agents to the degree to which
their actions could be rewarded or punished. For Hume, actions

were compatible with an external order at once closer to home and more comprehensive: not only the law but also the transactions of market and social exchange. Persons were agents to the degree to which they understood their own actions in terms of other people who were in turn doing the same. One concern was what composed persons and thoughts in the first place. I turn to that problem in the next chapter, where I look at the vexing question of how matter can think and act in the world.

2   Consciousness and Mental Causation: Lucretius, Rochester, Locke

The previous chapter looked at some philosophers with a view to their treatment of actions. I focused on several moments in an unfolding debate on free will and highlighted several new and controversial models of external determination. I'll now slow the discussion down to a case study of the treatment of Lucretius' *De rerum natura* during the closing decades of the seventeenth century. Like others, I am interested in the Lucretius revival because his poem provided a way to think about actions and objects in a world composed only of matter.[1] My particular concern is with the description of how physical particles compose conscious entities and how the actions of humans and other animals could be modeled on the unpredictable motion of the atom. These are specific versions of the two guiding threads of this book: the interrelated problems of consciousness and mental causation, how thinking happens and what thinking does. I'll begin by looking at some passages from Thomas Creech's celebrated and widely read translation, *The Nature of Things* (1682), the first complete version of the poem published in English.[2] I'll then turn to the treatment of Lucretius by John Wilmot, the second Earl of Rochester, a poet preoccupied throughout his work with the reduction of mind and behavior to matter in motion. I close the chapter with a consideration of the problem of consciousness and personal identity in Locke's *Essay Concerning Human Understanding*. Like Lucretius and Rochester, Locke was concerned with the relation between states of mind and the movement of matter. Unlike them, he attempts to keep ideas of the person and conscious experience at a remove from ideas of material objects.

Lucretius and Conscious Matter

When writers became interested in Lucretius during the seventeenth century, they confronted a novel thesis: the entire world and everything in it could be reduced to atoms and void.[3] There was no separate realm for the soul, just simple bits of matter moving about in the emptiness of space; and there was no afterlife of reward or punishment, just the death that awaits all living things. In this respect, the Lucretius revival sharpened the ongoing debate between the dualism of official Christianity and the monism of Hobbes and other materialists.[4] And as it made the case for materialism and monism in verse, the poem confronted several concerns of pointed interest for this study: How do small bits of matter add up to larger entities? How do nonthinking atoms create thought and experience? And how do thoughts and experiences cause events to happen? I'll consider these problems one at a time, beginning with the creation of large-scale objects from simple particles. I will show how the same laws of nature that cause small things to rise to great have difficulty explaining how things are capable of being conscious, although (strangely) not so hard a time explaining how states of mind play a causal role with respect to the matter from which they emerge.

On the face of it, the idea that the world is composed only of atoms and void is somewhat puzzling, even for the materialist. When we open our eyes, we see all sorts of different entities: from persons to pumpkins to mountains to chickens. According to *The Nature of Things*, however, these sorts of entities are not the basic furniture of the universe. Mountains are really piles of atoms in the shape of mountains, and persons are really piles of atoms in the shape of persons.[5] When Lucretius asks his reader to see "How Things are made," therefore, he enjoins her to look past large objects to their smallest parts.[6] The idea that everything in the world is composed of small bits of matter lies at the heart of the poem's most basic law of nature, *ex nihilo, nihil fit*:

But Because Things on certain Seeds depend
For their Beginning, Continuance, and End.
Therefore unfruitful *Nothing*, nothing breeds
Since all things owe their life to proper Seeds. (i.8 [1.205–7])[7]

The rule that everything must be made from something leads to an argument about composition. Since nothing comes from nothing, we can examine things and reduce them to their component parts. Large-scale objects of the kind that can be seen or walked upon or manipulated accordingly break down to individual atoms (or "seeds," on Creech's translation): small, invisible bits of matter that have no parts.

The opposite seems to hold true as well. Just as observable objects and entities break down to smaller, constituent atoms, so too individual atoms add up to make larger-scale things. And yet here the story begins to get a bit thorny. The rule that everything must come from something entails that objects reduce to the atoms from which they are made. There is nothing in this rule that entails that atoms must add up to large things. The trick is to find the principles according to which "small things rise to great" (i.38 [2.123–4]).[8] Here is such composition at work:

Now those small Seeds, that are more closely joyn'd,
And tremble in a little space confin'd,
Stopt by their mutual twinings, Stones compose,
Iron and Steel, or others like to those.
But those that swim in a wide Void alone,
Or make their quick and large rebounds, or run
Thro a large space, compose the Air, and Sun. (i.38 [2.100–8])

The universe on this first view is quite like we imagine it to be. Open your eyes, and stones and suns will be presented to you. These stones actually exist. How they come into existence from the movement of individual atoms is a question of *mereology*, or the relation between small parts and the larger wholes they compose, like grains and a pile of sand or bricks and a building.[9] Why are there large things and not just a myriad of small things? Why do some atoms take the shape of people and others stones or suns? The existence of atoms does not itself ensure that atoms will compose anything. So in order to have "small things rise to great," Lucretius invokes one more law of nature: the intrinsic nature of atoms to swerve or *clinamen* (i.38). Atoms don't move on straight lines. They fall on a kind of random and unpredictable curve, which leads them to pile together into larger shapes.

> Now *Seeds* in downward motion must *decline*,
> Tho *very little* from th' exactest line;
> For did they still move *strait*, they needs must fall
> Like drops of Rain dissolv'd and scatter'd all,
> For ever tumbling thro the mighty space,
> And never *joyn* to make one single mass. (ii.41 [2.216–24])

The universe is filled with more than just atoms because atoms tend to collide, stick together, and make things: whence people, rocks, oceans, worms, stars, and so on. Described in this fashion, the physical structure of the world is consistent with the emergence of whole objects from constituent parts. Were there no atoms, the universe would be simply empty space. Were there no swerve, there would be nothing larger than an atom. One doesn't have to add anything else to the picture to get composite objects—objects with parts—out of the universe.[10] With the laws of nature being what they are, composites like persons and rocks come into existence on their own.[11]

This model of composition solved the problem of why things exist and yet introduced other difficulties for the writers with which I'm concerned. It left ambiguous how material entities could have the kinds of properties (desires, intentions, and the like) that lead to discernible actions. It also left unstated who or what is having these desires or intentions in the first place. Both problems stem from the commitment to there being nothing outside of the physical world. Everything in the world is composed of atoms. Some entities seem to bear conscious experiences, to think or feel pain or desire or grieve. How is this possible? Creech notes on the side of a long passage from book three of the poem that Lucretius means to show how "the Mind is Material" because it is "composed of Seeds small and round" (iii.74). On the face of it, this is hardly surprising. Lucretius has already committed himself to the notion that all things that exist must trace their origins to other things that exist, not to the void where there is nothing. Since the mind is clearly something, it must be made from the atoms or seeds that create all things. How is it then that "*sensibles*" could "rise from *seeds* void of *sense*" (ii.61 [2.930])?[12] In their very nature, "sensibles" seem to be immaterial. Try to hold onto a thought and it will run through your fingers. Throw a ball against an idea and it will sail through the air. Yet clearly thoughts or experiences are something. How are they created by the swerve and collision of atoms?

The trouble is that the seeds are void of sense. In the poem's account of every other kind of creation, the thing made adds nothing to the world but size. Here the world acquires a new property seemingly from nowhere, and we know from the first law of nature that nowhere and nothing cannot create anything. Since the poem cannot make recourse to the idea that consciousness is the property of a soul distinct from matter, it has to come up with some account of how consciousness could rise from the elemental material of the universe. This is nothing less than "the hard problem of consciousness" as it has come to be known in contemporary cognitive science and philosophy of mind.[13] The hard problem, in the words of David Chalmers, is "how could a physical system give rise to conscious experience."[14] The point isn't to cast doubt on there being just one substance to the world or to open a space for immaterial things. Rather, it is to wonder how matter could have the property of being conscious in the first place. "It is widely agreed that experience arises from a physical basis," Chalmers writes; the problem is that "we have no good explanation of why and how it so arises. Why should physical processing give rise to a rich inner life at all? It seems objectively unreasonable that it should, and yet it does."[15] The universe contains a variety of objects, but only some have the further feature of being conscious. Only some have what we would now call "qualia"—that is, states of mind that are experienced, like emotions or pains or occurrent thoughts.[16] For Lucretius as for Chalmers, qualia are puzzling. Were we to look closely at all the particles in the universe and all the things they make, we would not have any reason to include consciousness in the picture, and we would have no idea, in Thomas Nagel's famous phrase, "what it is like" to be one or another entity.[17] The organization of particular atoms in certain ways entails that these atoms gather into shapes; it does not entail that these atoms are conscious. Consciousness is a further fact above the distribution and collection of atoms.[18] How then does consciousness come from atoms and void, sense from the absence of sense?

Several possible solutions to the hard problem circulated in Creech's time. One was to deny that there was a problem at all. For Cartesians as well as Christians (like Creech), our brains have a physical substance and our souls an immaterial substance. The soul can think because that is what it does.[19] Atoms compose tangible objects and obey laws of nature, like swerve and collision. Souls have thoughts and don't perish. Body is extended and subject to division. Soul is unextended and indivisible.[20] Creech claims this view as his own in the notes, where he distances himself from the poem he is in the process of translating: "Another fancy of [Lucretius'] is this," Creech complains: "*Animals*, those things of *sense*, can spring from *senseless* Seeds, and there is no need of any *Superiour Principle* to Matter, but a fit Combination of *Atoms* can *Think*, *Will*, or *Remember*."[21] By drawing mental properties out of particles in motion, Creech continues, Lucretius "imploys all his Forces against the *Immortality* of the Soul" (22).[22] The sort of dualism proposed by Creech runs contrary to the poem he translates, therefore, because it supposes that there is something other than atoms and void in the universe—a third category of immaterial substance that does all the thinking for us, in fact is "us" in the subjective sense of the term.

Without recourse to a separate, conscious substance, materialists following in the tradition of Lucretius tended to move in one of two other directions: either consciousness is intrinsic to matter, or consciousness emerges from matter. According to the first view, individual atoms are really not "void of sense" after all; rather, they bear some sort of consciousness on their own. According to the second view, consciousness is a higher-order property that somehow emerges out of the activity of lower-order, senseless atoms. In deference to contemporary philosophy of mind, we may call the first option the argument for *panpsychism* and the second the argument for *emergence*. Opting for the first view, for example, Margaret Cavendish claimed in *Observations on Experimental Philosophy* (1668) that matter was "rational and sensitive" down to its "smallest particles."[23] The ultimate material of the world, she argued, has a kind of consciousness out of which the consciousness of larger entities is made. The advantage of this view is that it would grant the existence of consciousness without having to violate the principle that nothing should come from nothing. If "things commence / *Sensibles*, from *seeds* endow'd with sense," as Creech has Lucretius put it, then consciousness would be part of the elemental and simple structure of the universe (ii.60 [2.902–4]). The prohibition against acquiring something from nothing would be met. As we will see, the poem adopts something close to this perspective with respect to the will. With respect to consciousness, however, the distribution of mind to the smallest particles of matter would solve some problems but introduce others.

> If all the Seeds have *sense*, that *sense* must be
> Or of one *single* member, or of *all*,
> And so be like a *perfect Animal*.
> But now the parts, in a divided state,
> Enjoy no sense; the *hand*, if separate,
> Can feel no more, nor any member live
> Divided from the *body*, nor perceive. (ii.60 [2.907–13])

Creech's compressed couplets mask a simple point. Were consciousness a property of every single atom, sense would belong to parts and the whole they compose. There would be two orders of sense at once. Each seed would be like a perfect animal, having its own thoughts and perceptions and emotions.[24] At the same time, these micro-experiences would somehow add up to the macro-experience belonging to the whole. The lines express some unease with this possibility by concluding with individual parts that are once again insentient. What is more, if it is difficult to conceive how many particle-level experiences add up to a single animal-level experience, it is no easier to see how any one particle could itself be the locus of experience. The difficulty is not only in imagining what a microscopic variety of consciousness might be like, but also in explaining how such a particle got to be conscious in the first place. Were the parts that together make instances of consciousness themselves conscious, something would need to make *them* so, ad infinitum:

> It follows, that the *seeds* are things unfit,
> Or to be toucht with *pain*, or with *delight*;
> Because they are not made of other Seed,
> Whose *change* of Motion or of Site may breed
> Vexing pain, pleasure, or delight; and hence
> It follows too, that they are void of *sense*. (ii.62 [2.967–71])

The effort to resist finding mind in each unit of matter gives some indication of the eventual solution to the problem of consciousness the poem will offer. Qualia like pain or delight depend on "change of Motion or of Site" at a lower level. Seeds are "unfit" to have experiences because they *are* this level. Seeds are by definition indivisible and for that reason are unable to have anything within them that would move or give rise to experience.

The poem thus finds it no easier to distribute mind to every particle than to divide mind from particles entirely. The only plausible solution to the problem of consciousness lies in the second option, the argument for *emergence*.[25] When put together in specific ways, certain seeds without sense give rise to (*gigno*) sentience. Or as Lucretius puts it, "[T]hose *Composures* that *perceive*, / Enabled all

with various *sense*, derive / Their Beings from *Insensibles*, and live"
(ii.59 [2.865–7]). Individual atoms are insensible, yet composures of
atoms have sentience. The idea is that mental properties can emerge
from clumps of atoms that have no such properties, as something yet
unknown happens in the journey from part to whole that puts sentience to the mix: "*discursive* things can rise / From *seeds*, that neither *reason*, nor are *wise*," for example (ii.63 [2.986–8]). On a larger
scale, emergence is responsible for all experience-bearing entities.

> Whence *Animals*, those things of *sense*, she frames
> As out of *wood* she raiseth *fire* and *flames*.
> From hence, as we discours'd before, you find
> It matters much with what, first *seeds* are joyn'd. (ii.59 [2.880–4])

Just as fire emerges from wood, things of sense emerge from particles of matter. The ostensibly simple analogy, however, raises some
further questions. For one, there appear to be two things that emerge
out of the movement of insentient particles: the animal composed
from atomic swerve and the consciousness that the animal is having. How is this possible? For another, what is the relation between
things like wood or atoms and things like fire or sense such that we
can say that the second emerges from the first? It would seem that
the second comes out of the first as a higher-order phenomenon.
Atoms are a more basic part of the world than sense; wood is more
basic than fire.[26] Only in certain arrangements do some atoms give
rise to sentience or pieces of wood burn. It "matters much" how the
elementary particles are joined because some configurations bring
sense and others do not, but why and for what reason?

The bringing of sense out of particles that have no sense has a
structure similar to the emergence of anything else in nature while at
the same time raising the difficult problem of how a new and salient
feature could appear where previously there was none. Consciousness would seem to obey a relatively unique kind of emergence,
with some important consequences. The laws of the universe bring
wholes out of parts. Composite objects are not properties of their
parts; they are just larger. Were we to know the direction a certain

set of particles might swerve, we would have no difficulty deducing the larger object they would make. Atoms bouncing in close proximity make stones; atoms gliding at a distance make the air and sun. The shape and swerve of the atoms yields the object. We are not in a similar position with respect to consciousness. Individual particles are insentient. Were we to know the direction a set of particles might swerve we would know they would create something without having any idea that the thing would be conscious. While the laws of swerve and void entail the emergence of composite objects, therefore, they are consistent with the absence of consciousness, with there being no sense or belief or hope or fear.

Consciousness is not a separate feature of the world, drawn from its own substance, but neither may it be deduced from the laws of matter and motion. Consciousness would seem to be an accident, and yet, as the poem happily acknowledges, some things in nature are conscious. The intuition seems to be that there is something about certain kinds of insentient atoms that gives rise to sentience when put in collision, and therefore that we should direct attention to the particular features of matter from which conscious things are made: "[T]hose Seeds, whence *sensibles* arise / Must all have a *convenient shape*, and *size*, / Position, motion, order*" (ii.60 [2.894–6]). Certain kinds of atoms have the property of being conscious when they come together in special kinds of ways:

> For things which do enjoy the faculties,
> And powers of *perfect Animals*, must rise
> From other Seeds, and those must be begun
> From others, and so to *infinitum* on.
> For thus I'le urge: Whatever can perceive,
> Discourse, laugh, reason, flatter, weep or grieve,
> Must be *compounded*, and must owe their frame
> To proper Seeds, which can perform the same. (ii.63 [2.980–4])

All powers of animals rise from the seeds out of which they are composed. So we are urged to consider these seeds when we attribute mental states and actions to composite objects. Should we care to know why atoms composed in the shape of dogs or persons are conscious while atoms composed in the shape of trees or berries are not, we need to look at the composure itself. One important consequence of this attention to the way that atoms give rise to conscious experience therefore is the literal scaling down of the subjects whose experience is at issue. Were immortal souls the source of sentience then we could say that the important question was whether any given entity was the kind of thing that had a soul. The description of emergence in the lines above points instead to the coming together of parts that give rise to this or that conscious experience. It does not point to the subject having that experience. Atoms that take the shape of persons may well be linked in such a way that gives rise to consciousness, while atoms that take the shape of trees are not, but consciousness comes from the kind of atom and the kind of collision, not from the separate status of the person.

I will return at several points in this study to this unexpected separation of consciousness and personhood, just as I will also look at moments when they come together. My point is to reveal various strands of mind-talk in play during the long period and highlight moments that take a form different from what we have come to expect. What do I mean by this? Critics as various and talented as Ian Watt, Marshall Brown, and Deidre Lynch have presented the seventeenth and eighteenth centuries as a heyday for the importance of consciousness, and doubtless it was, but perhaps not entirely as a move toward subjectivity or the individual person.[27] One legacy of Lucretius was to distinguish consciousness from personal psychology so it could be seen as an emergent property of the stuff from which all things are made. The following chapters will explore the persistence of views like this, along with others of a quite different variety. Before doing so, however, I will need to put in place another piece of the Lucretian puzzle: the relation between minds and actions.

Lucretius and Mental Causation

The solution to the problem of consciousness provided by *The Nature of Things* lies in emergence. Every single thing is made of particulate matter. Individual pieces of matter are insentient, while some combinations of matter have sentience. So consciousness *rises from* atoms. Having located the origin of consciousness in certain "composures" of particles, the poem moves in its middle sections to ask whether consciousness plays any role in the causal structure of the universe. Answering the question How do things think? thus does only half the job; the other problem turns out to be, How does thinking redound on things? Moreover, this concern with mental causation comes from the very answer to the problem of consciousness the poem had given. The poem had proposed that physical particles give rise to conscious thoughts and experience. It had also proposed that these particles cause things to happen. The trouble arrives when it further proposes that emergent properties like beliefs and desires cause things to happen too. At issue is a two-way causal circuit: physical particles cause beliefs and desires; these beliefs and desires cause physical events (hand movement in the event of writing a poem, say, or swatting a fly). So the question arises how states like beliefs and desires could exert a causal role independent of the matter from which they emerge.

The question may be examined in reverse from the vantage of a completed action. Physical particles cause the movement of one's hand; so too does the desire to write a poem and the belief that putting pen to paper will do the trick. Where does the one start and the other end? How is any completed action the result of a mental state independent of the matter that gives rise to this state? Consider the N atoms that compose Y conscious entity. Fit together in a certain way, these atoms have the property of being conscious. At the same time, these atoms enter into causal relations of various kinds. The problem of mental causation concerns whether there is anything special about consciousness that initiates or alters these relations, or whether these relations would remain the same in the absence of consciousness.[28] By the time of the publication of Creech's translation, the problem had already rattled Cartesian dualism, whose account of radically distinct substances of mind and matter left little room for interaction between the two.[29] While the materialism proposed by *The Nature of Things* does not have to worry about interaction, a completely physical universe does not by itself describe how mind fits into the picture either. When, for example, the cow misses her slaughtered calf, she tries her best to locate her. "Mad for her young, she every field doth trace / With *Passionate* eyes she visits every place" (ii.45 [2.355–8]). The cow's madness and passions are properties of some atoms arranged in the shape of a cow. These atoms should, however, be sufficient to bring out effects on their own. Were we to write the causal history of the tracing and the visiting we would have to look no further than atomic motion. But, while physical particles cause the movement of the cow's legs, so too does the madness to find her calf and the belief that by looking she might do so. The trick is to show how this is possible.

The recourse to emergence that worked for consciousness does not make this concern go away. The logical form of thoughts rising from seeds void of thought stitches the causal relation from the physical to the mental. Mental causation would require the sequence to run in the opposite direction, from the mental to the physical. The account of consciousness emerging from atomic motion is thus logically compatible with consciousness having no causal power at all. (In the extreme, this position is referred to now as epiphenomenalism: the idea that consciousness exists yet has no causal role.)[30] The problem for the poem turns out to be how to throw "rise from" in reverse and endow states like desire or belief or memory with the capacity to act on states empty of such attitudes. This is the problem Lucretius confronts when he moves to explain "why men can *move*, can *run* / *When er'e they please*, what force the members on" (iv.128 [4.877–8]). The lines pose a nearly perfect instance of mental to physical causation, since it is after all the pleasing that initiates the running and not the other way around. What is it then that allows an event described in a mental vocabulary to push downward as it were on an event described in a physical vocabulary? Once more, the capacity to have one's pleasings cause one's runnings is not entailed by the capacity for "sensibles" to "rise from seeds void of sense." For thoughts to cause actions, they must turn their course and "force" something on seeds void of sense—that is, a certain set of beliefs or desires must be able to bring about a corollary set of motions or acts. My wanting to type a sentence of this chapter must be able to cause my fingers to move across the keyboard. Only if this is so may we then conclude that the mind has a real set of causal powers and is not an epiphenomenon or shadow of an atomic substrate. In the case Lucretius has provided, the set of mental terms that fall under the attitude of pleasing (wanting, desiring, intending, and the like) yields a standard set of responses (feet on the ground, pushed forward, lifted up, on the ground again) that fulfill the physical event of running. The fulfillment in turn is backed by a lawlike regularity of connection between the two. One can never want to run and end up singing.

The poem's solution to the problem of mental causation is to insist on the closeness of this connection, so much so that the mental event begins to seem indistinguishable from the physical event it causes. If pleasing is able to cause running, then it is no less part of the world and, as will become of tremendous importance, may be explained by the very same laws. In this respect, the discussion of actions presents a very different kind of model from the discussion of consciousness. The nature of atoms and swerve do not entail that anything is conscious; they do entail, however, that the mind has causal powers. This seeming paradox only works by a steady reduction of the mind to individual particles in motion.

> First then, the *subtile Forms*, extreamly thin,
> Pass thro the Limbs, and *strike* the *Mind within*:
> That makes the *Will*, for none pretends to doe,
> None strives to act but what the *Mind* doth know.

Now what the *Mind* perceives, it only *sees*
By *thin*, and very *subtle Images*:
So when the *active Mind* designs to move
From place to place, it gives the *Soul* a shove:
The *soul* spreads o're the *limbs*, ('tis quickly done,
For *soul* and *mind* are joyn'd, and make up *one*,)
That strikes the *limbs*: so *all* is carried on. (iv.128 [4.881–91])

The important thing to notice about these lines is the thin distinction between "subtle forms" and "active Mind."[31] One flies from external objects and the other initiates behavior, but both are physical entities. And in this case, the identity means that the same laws of causation inhere for each. Just as atoms cause things to happen in virtue of their motion through space, so thoughts cause things to happen in virtue of their "shoving" and "spreading" over the body. The puzzle is ostensibly solved. Mental to physical causation occurs in this world because, strictly speaking, mental events are identical to physical events.

On this radical form of externalism, the content of any one mental state is potentially indistinct from the world in which it is situated. As we saw in the last chapter, the commitment to external sources of action seemed to many to court necessity. Once the mental is made identical to the physical it is hard to know where one cause starts and another ends, or (and this was the rub) when a person is responsible for her actions and when actions happen for reasons outside a person's control. Creech makes this point with considerable unease in the notes. "The *Liberty* of the Will," he argues, "is a power to choose, or refuse any thing after the Understanding hath consider'd it, and propos'd it as good or bad" (19). On this basis rests not only our sense of self and individuality but also all institutions of state and society. That "such a power belongs to every Man is evident from the general consent of Mankind, for every man finds such a *power* in himself and thence proceeds that agreement; tis the foundation of all *Laws*, of all *rewards*, and *punishments*" (19). There has to be a real difference between thought and the world that lies external to thought or else we have no way of choosing our actions in such a way that would leave us accountable for them. Materialism in Creech's view violates our intuitive sense of agency—that I am responsible for what I say and do—and all systems of human morality alike. His response is not so much to defend the poem he has translated as to make it clear that he, for one, does not believe a word of its philosophy: "[T]hose who imagine the Soul material" tend to conclude "all her actions *necessary*" because "matter once moved will still keep the same motion, and the same *determination* which it receiv'd, which must needs destroy all *Liberty* and evidently proves the *Epicurean Hypothesis* to be inconsistent with it" (20). For humans to have free will, thoughts must originate inside of us, not in some external or physical source. Lucretius' "Epicurian principles," Creech concludes, "are pernicious to society" (43).

The worry about determinism, however, reads against the grain of the poem Creech translates, or rather, selects one form of freedom against another. It turns out to be a good thing that mind and matter follow the same laws of causation, since the aleatory swerve atoms take on their declining path means there is no predictable direction to their movement.[32] The tight connection between the physical and the mental being what it is, the crooked path of the one is the freedom of the other. While it is true that all mental events are caused, in other words, there is no way to extrapolate an effect from its cause when all motion is capricious:

> . . . did all things move in a *direct* line,
> And still one motion to another joyn
> In certain order, and no *seeds* decline,
> And make a motion fit to dissipate,
> The well wrought Chain of Causes, and *strong* fate;
> Whence comes that *freedom* living creatures find?
> Whence comes the *Will* so free, so unconfin'd,
> Above the power of *Fate*, by which we go
> When e're we please, and what we will we do[?]   (ii.42 [2.251–60])

The version of free will on offer in these lines is quite distinct from what Creech reminds his reader of in the notes. For the will to be free, according to Creech, agents and their choices must be prior to and separate from their actions. Agents come to have desires and beliefs before they act, or else the results of their actions cannot be pinned on them. The freedom of the will we see above does not require this sort of temporal bracketing, or indeed any sort of separation of agents from the actions they take. The question is, Whence comes the will so free? There is no sense that the will must belong to anyone. The will acts *like* the happy atom, swerving from whatever course might have been expected were we to extrapolate from its past motion, and is *identical* to the aggregate of such atoms and so free from the "well-wrought chain of causes." The "little *Declination*" breaks through "strong *necessity*" and overcomes "fates rigid laws" (ii.43 [2.889–93]). That's all.

Wills have causes, but none of them are internal to agents, since the very model of agency—the atom—has no insides. Willing may be explained only by the course of free motion, in the same manner in which one would trace any physical cause to its accidental effect. The overall pattern of free agency thus comes to seem like a ripple on the surface of a lake. The example is, suitably, a horse.

> For sure the *Will* first moves, and thence,
> The motions spread to the Circumference,
> And vigorous action thro the *Limbs* dispense.
> For look, and see, when first the *Barrier's* down,
> The *Horse* tho eager, cannot start so soon
> As his own *Mind* requires, because the force,
> And subtle matter that maintain the Course,
> Must be stir'd thro the Limbs, then fitly joyn'd,
> Obey the eager motions of his *Mind*;
> Which proves these *Motions* rise within the *Heart*
> Made by the *Will*, thence run thro every part. (ii.42 [2.261–71])

The pause before the horse's actions is not deliberation or forethought. It is rather the amount of time it takes for the atoms of the mind to move to the limbs. This movement is free because the entire course—from the beginning of the thought to its terminus—is subject to the arbitrary swerve of the atom, as are all things made of matter. Since the mind is merely a different arrangement of the same kind of stuff as the limbs (and, inter alia, blueberries and doorknobs), the causal sequence at issue is one single motion covered by the way in which particles swerve, collide, and swerve again. Freedom in this respect is not so much a condition of the agent as a quality inherent in the universe. Were there no void, atoms would not be able to move and nothing would be capable of action.[33] Were there no swerve, no forms of life would emerge out of collisions.[34] Since there is swerve, we know that the will is free. Once again, the freedom of the will does not mean that any one person is free. It does not mean that there are persons at all.

I mean this in a literal sense. The will is a property of atoms, a way of accounting for their motion. Bramhall and Creech would make freedom an integral part of what it means to be a human, an ability to choose actions for which one may be held accountable. Lucretius makes freedom a quality of the particles from which humans and other objects are made. So in this respect the story the poem tells about the will is in an interesting tension with the story the poem tells about sense and other features of consciousness. Consciousness emerges only from certain kinds of atoms configured in special kinds of ways. Will, however, is present in every particle of the universe. David Skrbina has called this a "limited form of panpsychism," since it attributes "the psychic quality of will to all atoms and hence to all matter."[35] Even if the poem makes consciousness an emergent property, and so deprives atoms of sentience, in other words, it at the same time leaves to atoms the entire scope of freedom and action. By this limited form of panpsychism, in Skrbina's words, "we are given no evidence that there is something ontologically unique about human beings."[36] The reduction of will to a property of all bits of matter in this respect completes the disentangling of consciousness from psychology I pointed to earlier.

The will to do something does not track back to the thoughts of an individual person. Rather, the will is to be found in the stuff from which persons and other objects are made. This is the final importance I would draw from the Lucretius revival. The immense popularity of *The Nature of Things* at the end of the century allowed some writers to conceive of mind without concomitant notions of subjectivity and to think about actions without pinning them to inwardness. The rest of this chapter will follow this development in two separate directions: first, with Rochester, toward matter and away from mind, and then, with Locke, toward mind and away (slightly) from matter.

Rochester's Atomism

I've drawn from Creech's translation two related concerns around mind and action. The poem celebrates the idea that the universe is made entirely of particles in motion and then asks how particles in motion might be the locus of conscious experience. The poem also celebrates the will of the swerving atom as a model of how minds might fit in the causal order of things. In this section, I'll move from Creech to Rochester, one of the more unusual and controversial readers of Lucretius in Restoration England. I'll take a look at one of Rochester's translations from *De rerum natura* and at some related lines he adapted from Seneca. Rochester is especially interesting in these respects because he appears to trouble the recourse to emergence without opting for the ubiquity of the will. The trick of emergence was to show how a property like sense could emerge out of atoms that were insentient without violating the maxim that nothing should come from nothing. I've argued that this was the Restoration's version of today's hard problem. Rochester's response to the hard problem was to say that emergence may be impossible and emergent properties may not exist, either because all matter has some kind of mindlike quality or because the mind itself is a kind of illusion and all there is is insentient matter.

I'll look at this response now because it is articulated in such a close relation to Lucretius. I'll develop my reading of Rochester at greater length in the next chapter. "Lucretius was Rochester's favorite ancient," according to Sarah Ellenzweig.[37] This is to phrase the matter in somewhat poignant terms, but we do know that he translated two groups of lines from the poem. The first is an address to Venus that is one of the few pieces of verse to survive in his holograph. The second is a section on the indifference of the gods to human affairs that is of immediate importance to the topic of actions. According to the passage Rochester translates, the gods do not judge human behavior, but rather live without anxiety or desire for things they cannot have. This unconcern of the gods presumably serves two purposes: an alleviation of any fear that our souls await divine judgment, and an elaboration of an ethos suitable to mortals. The gods shouldn't be a source of dread; they should instead provide a model for how to enjoy the time we are given in this, the only world there is. Yet Rochester's translation is revealingly different from Creech's on the location of mind and the meaning of actions. Here is Creech's version:

> For every Deity must live in peace,
> In undisturb'd and everlasting ease,
> Not care for us, from fears and dangers free,
> Sufficient to His own felicity,
> Nought here below, nought in our power He needs,
> Nere smiles at good, nere frowns at wicked deeds. (ii.53 [2.646–51])

Here is Rochester's:

> The *Gods*, by right of Nature, must possess
> An Everlasting Age, of Perfect Peace:
> Far off remov'd from us, and our Affairs:
> Neither approach'd by *Dangers*, or by *Cares*:
> Rich in themselves, to whom we cannot add:
> Not Pleased by *Good* Deeds; nor provok'd by *Bad*.[38]

The first thing one might notice about the two versions is that Rochester's attempts to turn emotions from a possession of the

Gods to a property of time and space. For Creech, Deities live in peace and ease, whereas for Rochester, Ages have perfect peace. In the first case, serene states of mind latch onto the Gods as an object of a prepositional phrase; in the second, a singular emotional state modifies an impersonal and endless stretch of time. As much as they can, Rochester's lines endeavor to pare down the emotional language and separate it from agents. Compare the third line to Creech's version; the mental state of "not caring" has been replaced by the spatial relation of being "far off remov'd." The fourth line in Creech has the Gods experiencing felicity, whereas the same line for Rochester has dangers and cares lurking on their own. Rochester's version is almost as peppered with language of the mind as Creech's, but the various thoughts and feelings belong to no one in particular.

I will consider in the next chapter how Rochesterian erotics stage what might happen if we no longer consider desire as something that originates within agents and begin to consider it as something that emerges from matter with no insides at all. My interest in this chapter is with more basic questions of consciousness and mental causation. As we have seen, Lucretius discovered in atomic motion both an account of consciousness and an argument for free will. Rochester adopts the atomist commitment to physical explanation yet moves the argument outside of agents who are conscious. These commitments may be clarified some by turning to another of his translations from classical materialism. This is not from Lucretius but from the chorus of Seneca's tragedy *The Troades*. The translation takes up the question of soul and afterlife, and presents an account of matter both similar to and distinct from what we see in Lucretius. In this poem, Rochester's dispersion of mind to all of matter switches to a subtraction of mindedness from the world. Unlike his Lucretius, that is, Rochester's Seneca watches mental states fall apart to matter that is without mind at all.

Creech's Lucretius turns to matter to find a principle of creativity and freedom. Rochester's translation of Seneca moves in a different direction and finds in matter a kind of insentience, as if emergence and panpsychism were equally impossible and lifeless particles all there is:

> After Death nothing is, and nothing Death,
> The utmost limit of a Gasp of Breath.
> Let the ambitious Zealot lay aside
> His hopes of Heaven; whose Faith is but his Pride.
> Let slavish Souls lay by their Fear,
> Nor be concern'd which way, nor where,
> After this Life they shall be hurl'd;
> Dead, we become the Lumber of the World:
> And to that Mass of Matter shall be swept,
> Where things destroy'd, with things unborn are kept.
> Devouring Time swallows us whole;
> Impartial Death confounds Body and Soul.
> For Hell and the foul Fiend that rules
> God's everlasting fiery Jayls,
> (Devis'd by Rogues, dreaded by Fools)
> With his grim grisly Dog that keeps the Door,
> Are senseless Stories, idle Tales,
> Dreams, Whimsies, and no more. (1–18)

Like Lucretius, Rochester looks at the inevitable turning of life into death and death into life, and again the point is to rid us of any faith we might have in the persistence of the soul in an afterlife. The only eternity promised by the poem is the matter from which life emerges and to which death turns. It is of real interest then that nothing like "Dead we become the Lumber of the world: / And to that Mass of Matter shall be swept / Where things destroy'd, with things unborn are kept" is in the original.[39] Added by Rochester, the lines at once insist upon the materiality of all life-forms and emphasize the near proximity and always tilting of life to the death that "swallows us whole." In this respect, the lines unwind the path of emergence from consciousness to the inert matter from which it springs. Matter is not so much the potential for sentience, should it happen to cohere in the forms that give rise to consciousness; it is instead the always-present specter of insentience, the lumber of the world from which all future things are made. The poem comes to indivisible, lifeless matter, moreover, by a sort of logic of emotive subtraction. We are to stop feeling one or the other passion generated by a belief in an afterlife. Hope, faith, pride, concern, and fear drain out until all that is left is a lumber defined by a want of thought. In keeping with Lucretius, Rochester follows the trail of matter past the person to smaller particles. Yet his model of emergence seems insistent on watching emergent properties decompose to their constituent parts, this time without the swerve and free will. One begins to sense that all complex entities are ready at all times to return to their smaller and insentient units.

In a letter sent just before Rochester's death, the deist and free-thinker Charles Blount wrote the poet at once to celebrate the achievement of the Seneca translation and argue against its materialism:

> I had the Honour Yesterday to receive from the Hands of an Humble Servant of Lordship's, your most incomparable Version of that Passage of *Seneca*'s, where he begins with,—— *Post mortem nihil est, ipsaque mors nihil*, &c. —— and must confess, with your Lordship's Pardon, that I cannot but esteem the Translation to be, in some measure, a confutation of the Original; since what less than a divine and immortal Mind could have produced what you have there written? Indeed, the Hand that wrote it may become *Lumber*, but sure, the Spirit that dictated it, can never be so: No, my Lord, your mighty Genius is a most sufficient Argument of its own Immortality; and more prevalent with me, than all the Harangues of the Parsons or Sophistry of the School-men.[40]

Blount is well aware of physical accounts of soul and person. The letter to Rochester goes on to survey various theories of life and death from the ancients to the Christians. Later that same year, he would publish *Anima Mundi, or the Opinions of the Ancients concerning Man's Soul after this Life, according to unenlightened nature*. Later still, his deist miscellany *Oracles of Reason* (1693) would include a letter from Charles Gildon arguing that the soul is a "Congregation of Atoms, or other invisible particles of *Matter* solid or subtle."[41] So it is of some interest that Blount clearly divides "the hand that wrote" the poem from "the spirit that dictated it." Rochester adds the lines about the lumber and thus fills in an atomist ontology to Seneca's argument that nothing follows death. Blount would have Rochester confute the original in an entirely different sense by insisting on a strict dualism. The spirit is distinct from the hand because without it the hand wouldn't move. Rochester's genius is an argument for immortality because it executes the writing of the poem. Were everything made of matter, Blount argues, there would be no reason for anyone to do anything, just a "hum drum Deity chewing his own Nature" (126–7).

Blount turns the translation to an argument against materialism because he believes that a completely physical universe with no afterlife supplies little incentive for actions. He avoids the problem of how an immaterial substance could have a causal relation with a material substance—Descartes's interaction problem—by asserting that a *belief* in spirit and the afterlife, irrespective of their truth, prompts agents to do things like write poems.[42] The best argument for the immateriality and immortality of the soul is "the absolute necessity and convenience that it should be so" (126). Blount's turn to belief nervously moves from what the world is made of to what it ought to be like. Rochester's Seneca had reduced states of mind like hope, fear, and belief to matter in order, it would seem, to dispense with them entirely. The effect was not to show how bodies and minds arise from lumber; rather, it was to sweep the two back to that great mass. For Blount, we need to believe in the soul because otherwise we would have no reason to do anything. The ultimate nature of things on this view is less of a concern than what we think about this nature. Blount shies away from metaphysics because it alienates us from our understanding of soul, mind, and bodies. In contrast, Rochester's twin translations present a simple austerity, robbed of comfort in anything other than the matter of the world.

Locke on Consciousness and Personal Identity

I've looked at Rochester's translations because they pose such an extreme reduction of mental states to matter. We might think of this reduction as a two-part elimination: in the first poem an elimination of the person as the locus of states of mind and in the second an elimination of mental states altogether. I'll close the chapter with a turn to Locke because Locke presents a very different treatment of these same concerns. Locke does not so much eliminate persons or states of mind as attempt to coordinate their relation to each other. This attempt at coordination turns out to be extraordinarily influential. The modern philosophical meaning of the word "consciousness" arguably dates to the *Essay Concerning Human Understanding*, where Locke's definition is quite close to the "what it is like" meaning found in writings on the hard problem from Nagel to Chalmers.[43] Moreover, the discussion of consciousness occurs chiefly in a chapter on personal identity, the first philosophical treatment of a topic that persists through Derek Parfit, Sharon Cameron, and beyond.[44] While I will devote a separate chapter to Locke's serially revised and tortured account of actions, I want first to show how his discussion of these topics engages Lucretian questions of emergence and particulate matter.

This account will differ a little from what criticism has often had to say about Locke's relation to the specifically literary culture of the period. Critics have long associated Locke and empiricism with the rise of the novel and new ideas of the self and person. They are right to do so, if for reasons I will argue are (again) slightly different from what we have often assumed. Locke has tended to stand for a commitment to the individual experience "punctually" recorded, as Charles Taylor has put it, in the literary works of the period.[45] In her influential discussion of literary character, for example, Deidre Lynch has argued that Locke provides "the eighteenth century's most important description of the production of personality" because he gives an account of "human consciousness as a documentary genre, founded not just on observation . . . but also on transcription," the "imprinting of a surface and the acquisition of characters" that produce, on Lynch's view, " 'character,' or personality, where before there was a blank."[46] On this account, Locke's model is important because it ties a theory of knowledge to an idea of the inner life. The mind takes in ideas and makes of them the persons who are subjects of fiction and history. In the more recent formulation of Nancy Armstrong, Locke's commitment to the person stands as the model of "self-enclosure" because his "account of how the mind exercises reason allowed him to explain how men ideally developed into individuals capable of self-government and therefore capable of governing others."[47] The enclosed individual is here the stuff at once of fiction and philosophy, as "the mind in Locke's theory" makes its way to "the fiction of Daniel Defoe and other eighteenth-century novelists."[48]

My point is not to dispute the importance of Locke's theory of personal identity to the literary forms of character writing during the period. Rather, it is to situate this theory within the philosophical context of matter and consciousness in which it occurs. Locke does make a great deal about experience and self in the all-important chapter on personal identity, but the discussion is not centrally about either enclosure or the accurate representing of objects. If criticism since Watt has looked to Locke to see how such epistemological concerns make their way into literary fictions, it has not paused long over the metaphysical corners of the *Essay*. Yet Locke's worries in the chapter on personal identity, consciousness, and self are pervasively ontological: What kind of thing is a man? What kind of thing is a person? Are they the same? How should we sort the world into its basic categories? His answers to these questions are engaged in the ongoing attempt to locate consciousness in a physical world.[49] While Locke does not try to reduce consciousness to matter, he does engage in a painstaking series of distinctions. He associates the physical system of atoms in motion with *life* and *man* and conscious experience with *self* and *person*. Man is a kind of object supported by life, whereas person is a kind of self, supported by consciousness. Much depends on keeping the two orders apart, which Locke is not always able to do.

Locke's remarks on consciousness appear very early on in the *Essay Concerning Human Understanding* (1690), spread into the controversial chapter "Of Identity and Diversity" added to the second edition in 1694, and culminate with a long discussion of thinking matter near the end.[50] The term first appears in chapter 1 of the second book, in the beginning of his anti-Cartesian argument that the soul does not always think. Were we to think while asleep, our thoughts would happen without our awareness of them, and that is impossible since "thinking consists in being conscious that one thinks."[51] At this moment, the quarrel with Descartes admits of a distinction between the functional processing of the mind and the experience with which this processing is accompanied. Thinking is one thing and consciousness another. Thinking consists in copying simple ideas from the outside world or manipulating the complex ideas drawn from them. Consciousness consists in the experience that accompanies these processes. Were I to think about Lucretius' sad cow, I would put together an idea of an emotion with an idea of animal, both of which I acquired at some point during my waking life. Joined to this would be my conscious experience of sad cow thoughts, which, were you to ask, I could relate to you in some manner of expression. The cow has brown spots, a lowered head, a mournful sigh. "Consciousness is the perception of what passes in a Man's own mind," Locke writes; "Can another Man perceive, that I am conscious of any thing when I perceive it not myself? No Man's Knowledge here can go beyond his experience" (115). So while thinking refers to the assembling and running together of ideas, consciousness refers, in Nagel's phrase, to "what it is like" to have such ideas and how they are experienced. Anyone might be able to say what the thought "sad cow" consists in (the complex idea of sadness and cow combined as one), but no one except the person having the thought could describe the experience with which it is accompanied.

At this early point in the *Essay*, the distinction between thinking and consciousness is between a third- and first-person account of mind: the acquisition and association of ideas on the one hand, and the experience with which they are accompanied on the other. The word "consciousness" does not appear again until considerably later, when Locke drifts from these concerns to more metaphysical topics in the added chapter on "the very Being of things . . . at any determin'd time and place" (328). What, Locke asks, is an object? According to the materialist line we've been tracing, an object is the sum of its parts. That sad cow is a mass of atoms arranged in the shape of a cow. Locke disputes this view, at least so far as it applies to living entities: "[T]heir Identity depends not on a Mass of the same Particles; but on something else" (330). Were we to subtract or add any one particle the mass would change yet the entity would not. "An Oak, growing from a Plant to a great Tree, and then lopp'd, is still the same Oak: And a Colt grown up to a Horse, sometimes fat, sometimes lean, is all the while the same Horse: though, in both these Cases, there may be a manifest change of the parts" (330). The oak and the horse lose some parts and gain others, yet remain in some real sense the same thing over the course of their lives. Therefore the identity of a living thing cannot be reduced to the parts from which a thing is composed. The oak tree, for example, "continues to be the same Plant, as long as it partakes of the same Life, though that Life be communicated to new Particles of Matter vitally united to the living Plant, in a like continued Organization, conformable to that sort of Plants" (331). During the time when any one part contributes to the life of a plant (or a horse or a man), the part shares in the "organization" of the life. As soon as the part no longer has that role, it ceases to contribute to the life. Lop that branch off the tree and it is merely a branch, not part of a tree. Cut off my finger and it is only a bleeding digit. Its role in the supporting of my life has gone away, and this supporting relation is what it means for any one unit (finger, atom, cell) to be a part of me.[52] While parts and particles come and go, therefore, a single life has a continuous existence across them and may be distinguished on that basis from other lives. The branch is part of this oak and not another because it supports the life of *this* oak not the other.

Were we to ask what sorts of entities are out there in the world, Locke says, we would have to grant that there are lives as well as objects, and that each may be counted separately.[53] As Peter van Inwagen has put it, a life, for Locke, "is at any given moment spatially conterminous with an object that is numerically distinct from it."[54] Were we to inquire into the identity of an organism, therefore, we would have to give precedence to the life over the object in which it is momentarily housed. "If the activity of xs at t_1 constitutes a life, and the activity of the ys at t_2 constitutes a life," van Inwagen continues, then, according to Locke, "the organism that the xs compose at t_1 is the organism that the ys compose at t_2 if and only if the life constituted by the activity of the xs at t_1 is the life constituted by the activity of the ys at t_2."[55] Van Inwagen's neat formalization of Locke's ontology illustrates the relative distance it places between physical objects and discrete lives. This distance only grows once Locke moves to place persons alongside lives and objects. A man is not the same as the mass of matter from which he is a made; likewise, a person is not the same as the man with which it is typically aligned. On August 29, 1632, a living man named John Locke was born into the world. The identity of that man remained the same until his death on October 28, 1704. The infant and the grown man look entirely different. Not a single particle of the first is present in the second. Yet they are the same being because a single life has stretched from the one to the other, has taken some parts and lost others yet remained continuous throughout. "The identity of the same *Man* consists," Locke writes, "in nothing but a participation of the same continued Life, by constantly fleeting Particles of Matter, in a succession vitally united to the same organized Body" (331–2). The "*Idea* in our Minds, of which the Sound *Man* in our Mouths is the Sign, is nothing else but an Animal" (333). The idea of a person, however, is something else. To "find wherein *personal Identity* consists, we must consider what *Person* stands for; which, I think, is a thinking intelligent Being, that has reason and reflection, and can consider it self as it self, the same thinking thing in different times and places" (335). Whereas man refers to a life stretched continuously over time, person refers to continuous states of mental activity. Were we to ask Locke why he is the same man over time, he would respond because he has been alive all the while. Enough of his body passes from one moment to the next for the whole to be continuous even if Locke the senior citizen has none of the same parts as Locke the child. (He is in this way like the Ship of Theseus, whose planks are gradually replaced, but never wholly scrapped, and so is always the same ship.)[56] Were we to ask Locke why he is the same person, his answer would be different. His answer would be because he can consider himself as a self now as in the past, here as well as there.[57]

Like men and oak trees, persons may also be counted, but in order to do so one must look elsewhere than at the living organisms. One must look at the number of selves. But what does that mean? To answer this question, Locke returns to a concept he had introduced many pages earlier. An intelligent being considers itself as a self "only by that consciousness, which is inseparable from thinking" (335). The earlier difference between thinking as a functional process and consciousness as a mode of experience returns to some effect. I described earlier John Locke's "sad cow" thought; if I am right, you now are in possession of his thought. But what is it like for Locke to have the thought of a sad cow? Were we able to answer that question we would be in possession of Locke's consciousness and thus *be* the person named John Locke. Thought and consciousness accompany each other, but the one tracks the experience, the other the logical form of the same mental state. "Consciousness always accompanies thinking, and 'tis that, that makes every one to be, what he calls *self*; and thereby distinguishes himself from all other thinking things, in this alone consists *personal Identity*, *i.e.* the sameness of a rational Being" (335). While it may be hard to extract this language of self from the penumbra of associations later applied to the term, for Locke the point is rather simple: the conscious dimension to a thought creates a self insofar as it distinguishes one person from another just as a life distinguishes one man or oak from another.

To illustrate his case Locke asks us to consider a prince and a cobbler. Were the cobbler somehow possessed of the prince's past experiences and the prince likewise possessed of the cobbler's, the two persons would switch yet the men would remain the same. The cobbler's living body would be unchanged and thus "he would be the same Cobler to every one besides himself" (340). To himself, he would remain the prince. Suppose, however, that this prince had been guilty of some crime. Would it be just to punish the man who looks like the prince or the one who looks like the cobbler? Intuition runs in favor of the latter. Whoever "has the consciousness of present and past Actions, is the same Person to whom they both belong" and who is "justly accountable" for them (340, 341). The point of Locke's thought experiment in this respect is for the reader to draw the conclusion that person goes with consciousness and not with the living body. He supposes we feel instinctively that the prince is still the prince when he is in the cobbler's body and that he ought to be responsible for the prince's actions, not the cobbler.

Locke includes misdeeds in his stories because he wants to show that intuitions place personal identity with the having of experiences not with bodies. Were there no misdeeds, the question of where such identity lies might not matter so much. Talk of persons confers a kind of honor, a membership in a community above that of mere particles or animal life, but it is useful primarily in matters of assigning responsibility. Person is "a Forensick Term appropriating Actions and their Merit; and so belongs only to intelligent Agents capable of a Law, and Happiness and Misery" (346). Are you the man who broke the china vase? Yes, but I was only three at the time and cannot remember having done so. I am the man but not the person, so please don't punish me now. Seventeen witnesses all say you stole that loaf of bread, but since you were so drunk at the time perhaps you are a different person, though (again) the exact man we have in custody. "If it be possible for the same Man to have distinct incommunicable consciousness at different times, it is past doubt the same Man would at different times make different Persons; which, we see, is the Sense of Mankind in the solemnest Declaration of their Opinions, Humane Laws not punishing the *Mad Man* for the *Sober Man*'s Actions, nor the *Sober Man* for what the *Mad Man* did, thereby making them two persons" (342). Statements like this place a category of experience together with a system of rules in a somewhat delicate balance. It is unclear how forms like the law are able to peek inside experience in such a way that could discern whose consciousness belongs with which body. The idea of a person picks out conscious entities, and a system of laws picks out persons. So by a sort of transitive movement the law should be able to gain access to consciousness, but of course it cannot. We have the concept of person therefore because we need to have some "forensic" language for placing blame, assigning value, or rewarding conduct. In the end, the law recruits persons by erring on the side of consistency. Even "though punishment be annexed to personality, and personality to consciousness, and the Drunkard perhaps be not conscious of what he did," often he will be punished anyway and not without justice, since the "want of consciousness cannot be proved for him" (344). Only God can prove whether he was conscious as himself, so final justice will have to be reserved for the afterlife, "wherein the Secrets of all Hearts shall be laid open" (344).

On Locke's account, the law may be sensitive to signs of discontinuous personhood, but assumes that one person tends to be the same over time. As do we: I can remember myself in a past, and so in all likelihood will continue to exist in the future. To this feat of memory and imagination, Locke adds an important corollary. "Every intelligent Being, sensible of Happiness or Misery, must grant, that there is something that is *himself*," because there is something "he is concerned for, and would have happy" (345). Personal identity on this view is special not only because its elemental property, consciousness, is available only to the person whose identity is at issue, but also because its apperception is not simply a question of knowledge. I know what it is like to be me in a way that others do not; at the same time (Locke thinks) I *care* about myself in a way that others do not, and so I monitor my actions to ensure I remain happy. It is on the last point that the internal and external criteria of personhood begin to match. "By this consciousness, he finds himself to be the *same self* which did such or such an Action some Years since, by which he comes to be happy or miserable now" (345–6). I eat well today because I would like to be healthy tomorrow. Likewise, I refrain from stealing that loaf of bread now because I would prefer not to be punished later. Both cases require that persons are able to project themselves into the future and also care about the happiness of that future person.

This imagining of future states of the same person and care for the person's happiness would seem to stitch ideas of the self to some sort of physical system.[58] While Locke attempts to remain agnostic on the physical nature of consciousness, his recourse to care as a defining feature of what it means to be a person takes the argument back to the hard problem it had bracketed with the distinction between self and life. The mere fact of self-persistence does not require physical persistence, as he maintains at several points. Here is one near the end of the chapter: "I that write this am the same *my self* now whilst I write (whether I consist of all the same Substance, material or immaterial, or no) that I was Yesterday" (341). At the same time, the transience of particles does not mean that consciousness and self are immaterial either, since, as Locke grants, one could imagine that different particles give rise to the same consciousness. Locke's solution at this point in the *Essay* is to say that the question is not at issue. "*Self* is that conscious thinking thing," he writes, and then immediately adds in parentheses, "whatever Substance made up of whether Spiritual, or Material, Simple, or Compounded, it matters not" (341). Once we have answered all the questions about persistence over time, consciousness versus thinking, and care of the self, we have done all we need do to explain personhood. Probing into what gives rise to consciousness would supply no further facts or deeper truths, at least about persons.

Or at least so much is true at this point in the argument. Later on in the *Essay*, he observes that while "[we] have the *Ideas* of *Matter* and *Thinking*," we might "never be able to know, whether any mere material Being thinks, or no" (540). This careful sidestepping leads to a sentence that would prompt swift response from religious orthodoxy.[59] It is "not much more remote from our Comprehension to conceive, that GOD can, if he pleases, superadd to Matter a Faculty of Thinking, than that he should superadd to it another Substance, with a Faculty of Thinking" (541). God might have seen fit to endow matter with the capacity to be conscious on its own or might have seen fit to house in matter a conscious, immaterial substance. Either consciousness is material or matter sits alongside a conscious soul. The answer lies beyond our knowing. It is "impossible for us, by the contemplation of our own *Ideas*, without revelation, to discover, whether Omnipotency has not given to some Systems of Matter fitly disposed, a power to perceive and think, or else joined and fixed to Matter so disposed, a thinking immaterial Substance" (540–1). These sentences were written at an earlier date than the chapter on persons, but there is an important sense in which they fit the discussion of consciousness in chapter 27.[60] In that chapter, Locke had assumed that a person was made of consecutive states of conscious awareness. The source of this consciousness was in large part not an issue, though at crucial moments a caring for the future state of one's body meant that a relation between consciousness and matter had to be at least briefly entertained. The final sections of the *Essay* then take a longer and considerably troubled look at this relation.

In this respect, the hard problem remains as much a concern for Locke as it was for Lucretius, Creech, and Rochester. Suppose, Locke says near the end of the *Essay*, consciousness is a property of matter after all.[61] How might this be so? The options are similar to what is available to *The Nature of Things*. For a material object to be conscious qua material object, matter would have to be the locus of thought and sentience. Since matter is at bottom particulate, and all composite objects are made from smaller parts, consciousness would either have to "rise from" particles without consciousness or every single particle would have to itself be conscious. Either emergence is true or panpsychism is true. Let us imagine, Locke says, that a wholly material entity is conscious. Are we then prepared to imagine "that all Matter, *every particle of Matter, thinks?*" (626). Were we to accept the premise that matter might be the locus of consciousness we would have to consider at least the possibility that "there would be as many eternal thinking Beings, as there are Particles of Matter, and so an infinity of Gods" (626). We would have to consider this possibility because it would get us out of the conundrum of emergence, which Locke tartly explains as follows: "[If] they will not allow Matter as Matter, that is, every Particle of Matter to be as well cogitative, as extended, they will have as hard a task to make out to their own Reasons, a cogitative Being out of incogitative Particles, as an extended Being out of unextended Parts" (626). Suppose there is no emergence, Locke continues; suppose that nothing without thought yields something with thought, just as nothing without extension yields something that is extended. Were matter all there is in the universe, the panpsychist conclusion would follow as a matter of course: everything is made of matter and there is no way of assembling material that isn't conscious to produce material that is; then either the material that everything is made of must itself be conscious or nothing is conscious at all. (Galen Strawson has recently made this sort of argument and urged along the way that "if this seems a little colourful then it's time to read Locke on substance again.")[62] Perhaps there really are "as many thinking beings as there are particles of matter . . . an infinity of Gods."

The alternative (emergence) may sound more attractive, Locke argues, but it is impossible to work into metaphysical sense. The premise of emergence is that individual particles are insentient yet give rise to sentience in humans and other animals. Arranged in a certain way, incogitative particles produce cogitation. For Locke this is a kind of dodge. One can no more get sentient wholes out of insentient parts than extended objects out of unextended points of light. In order for one thing to emerge out of another, there must be something about the first that gives rise to the second. Were that not so, we might expect any one thing to come out of another: frogs from turnips or will from mist. Citing Lucretius, Locke writes that emergence of this sort would violate the "great Maxim, *Ex nihilo nil fit*" (626). For emergence to work, there must be something about the base property that gives rise to the emergent property, and, contrary to Lucretius, Locke does not think there is anything about insentient particles that could intelligibly be said to give rise to sentience. "For unthinking Particles of Matter, however put together, can have nothing thereby added to them, but a new relation of Position, which 'tis impossible should give thought and knowledge to them" (627). In other words, if particles aren't conscious, there is no way that consciousness can emerge out of them. This does not necessarily entail that panpsychism is true. After all, consciousness might be a property of a soul-like, nonmaterial substance. What is more, panpsychism solves the emergence problem but introduces some familiar concerns. Consciousness on Locke's view individuates persons as subjects of experience. If panpsychism is true then the individual particle would be a self (of some sort), and these smaller selves would somehow add up to the larger selves that are me, you, and everyone else, though not that table over there or the apple I'm eating. This "infinity of Gods" is, Locke thinks, as much a concern as the failure of emergence to get something from nothing. His conclusion lies neither with substance dualism nor emergence nor panpsychism. Rather, the point seems to be to illustrate how little we know about the substance of the universe and how intractable the problem of consciousness really is.[63]

What then is the lesson of looking at the problems of consciousness in Locke? We are (again) in no shortage of accounts that emphasize Locke's influence on the literature of the period. Yet this influence has been insistently posed in terms of how agents come to know things about the world in which they are situated. One way of framing the concerns I've put forward in this chapter is that epistemology tells only part of the story, that it leaves some important questions about the period unasked. The question for eighteenth-century writers was not just how do agents know things, but rather what are agents and agency in the first place. Whereas the story about epistemology tends to look at the first two books of the *Essay*, and to emphasize on that basis a model of self-enclosure and inwardness—a mind like a camera obscura transcribing objects and events on its interior spaces—the story I would tell about consciousness and persons looks also at the later parts of the *Essay* and has a more ontological bent. How does consciousness arise from matter, and where are we to locate the sources and limits of actions?

The hardness of the hard problem of consciousness returned in full force to the philosophical scene some three hundred years after the publication of Locke's *Essay*. "Consciousness is all the rage just now," as Jerry Fodor put it in the Spring 2007 issue of the *London Review of Books*.[64] While the present-day interest in consciousness crosses over established disciplines of neuroscience, philosophy of mind, and psychology, Creech's period had no firm disciplines to bring together. Even so, the reason for an interest in consciousness and the form that the hard problem took were similar then to what they are now. The more one knows about the physical composition of the universe, the more the causal relation between matter and experience becomes important to pin down and yet still elusive. Conceived in this fashion, the problems of consciousness and mental causation might still seem a bit abstract. I've tried therefore to show in this chapter how the problems involve specific issues around agency that will concern this book to the end: what kinds of entities have conscious reasons for acting? Is it necessary that such reasons are distinct from the mere movement and flux of matter? The alternative stories of emergence and panpsychism attempt to answer the first question; the finding or not of a causal role for the mental attempts to answer the second. Where one stood on the two, finally, had considerable impact on some important concepts, like soul, life, and person. Rochester and Lucretius alike describe soul, life, and person in terms of elementary particles, and Rochester especially wonders whether anything larger than a particle really exists. With different ends in view, Locke pushes up from these particles to the entities they create and endow. This puts him in the unenviable position of standing behind an idea of consciousness seemingly dependent on, yet with no clear relation to, the physical world. We may never know whether and how matter gives rise to consciousness, Locke says, but we do know that consciousness makes the person and that persons are the fundamental units of law and society. From the attention to matter, therefore, came different accounts of the basic furniture of the world. The next two chapters retrace this movement and look again at Rochester and then Locke, with closer attention to the problems of mental causation. These chapters also provide separate routes from the Restoration into the eighteenth-century novel, where this study will conclude.

3   Rochester's Mind

The last chapter turned to Rochester because his translations locate the origin and meaning of actions in the impersonal motion of atoms. This chapter considers a broader range of his writing, including the obscene poems for which he would become notorious. The animating problem in all these poems concerns acting on desire, a process whose difficulties Rochester examines in the period's vexed language of mind, consciousness, and physical matter, and with reference to varied locations in court and town. Rochester has long struck readers as oddly indirect or "imperfect" in these regards. In Carole Fabricant's influential formulation, the poetry "is characterized not by an exaltation of sexuality as commonly assumed, but by an unequivocal demonstration of the latter's transience and futility."[1] For Fabricant, sexuality is Rochester's "comprehensive metaphor of man's failure to realize his desires in the mortal world" (348). In what follows, I will argue something close to the opposite. While we might expect desire to begin with the person and then move outward to others, Rochester tends to go in reverse, from external forms like parks and poems back to bodies and desires. I will begin by looking at poems that consider the physical reduction Rochester encountered in his reading of Lucretius. I'll then turn to poems that examine consciousness and mental causation in particularly sexual terms or that copy their model of action from what is provided for them by the court and town. My attention in the latter part of this chapter will be as much with the outside as the inside of poems; I'll attempt to show how the manner in which Rochester's poems circulated—published in manuscript, copied out in miscellanies, transmitted among reading communities—instantiated their version of desire. I test this hypothesis at the end by tracing a single passage concerning erotic agency from its origin in a Rochester poem to its varied citation in subsequent decades, from the moment of court and manuscript exchange to the moment of civil society and print publication.

Reasons and Persons

I have argued so far that problems of action in Rochester's period often concern the mind's place in a physical world. If mental states were physical, how were they different from other kinds of physical things? If they weren't, how could they interact with things that were? These kinds of questions placed actions in the heart of the new science and philosophy. I will begin this chapter therefore with two of Rochester's more philosophical poems before turning to poems more embodied or political and social in their concerns. The first, *A Satyr against Reason and Mankind*, outlines a version of epiphenomenalism in which states of mind either lag behind or are indistinguishable from the machinelike workings of the body. The second, *Love and Life*, pays close attention to the structure of time in order to consider how actions might happen without agents that precede them. Both take up the mereological concerns found in Lucretius, and ask whether parts add up to wholes or act on their own.

Consider the hapless "scholiast" who comes along midway through *A Satyr against Reason and Mankind* as a sort of straight man to the materialist antirationalism and antihumanism of the speaker.[2] Hearing that the speaker has taken on the vaunted faculty of reason, the scholiast comes to defend "Reason, by whose aspiring Influence / We take a flight beyond Material sense."[3] The couplet establishes a spatial relation between cognitive faculties and matter. But what does it mean to say that reason flies beyond material sense? The question is tricky because the statement is made by someone the speaker introduces in order to dismiss. Turn the couplet over and read it from its opposite meaning and we arrive at a certain physicalism.[4] One way to see this is to take seriously the adjectival nature of matter. The scholiast not only says that reason transcends the senses; he also says that the senses are physically composed. He places reason outside the physical world and claims that rational thoughts and brute matter are distinct and separate substances. From the monist perspective of the speaker, this flight beyond matter is literally impossible. So the departure turns to a series of doomed attempts to climb out of or beyond the physical world (or nature, instinct, and the like). Here are some well-known lines at the beginning of the poem illustrating the failure. The perspective is the monist's taking stock of the scholiast's dilemma:

> The Senses are too gross, and hee'll contrive
> A sixth to contradict the other five:
> And before certain Instinct will preferre
> Reason, an Ignis fatuus of the Mind,
> Which leaving Light of Nature, sense, behind;
> Pathless and dangerous wandring wayes it takes,
> Through Errours fenny boggs and thorny brakes:
> Whilst the misguided follower climbs with pain
> Mountains of whimseys heapt in his own brain;
> Stumbling from thought to thought, falls headlong down
> Into doubts boundless Sea, where like to drown,
> Books bear him up a while, and make him try
> To swim with bladders of Philosophy. (8–21)

The lines begin with the scholiast's unmarked voice—"the senses are too gross"—layered on top of the voice of the speaker, who thus begins his account of mind by mimicking the misguided follower of reason's distaste for the coarse material of the five senses. The speaker's point is not simply that sensory perception provides better access to nature and the physical world. It is rather that the five senses are part of the physical world, unlike the spurious sixth sense, which has no existence anywhere. The relation of flying over is sustained by the placement of a kind of sham faculty on top of the actual movement of matter. In the all-important ignis fatuus metaphor, for example, reason turns to a "will-o'-the-wisp" or mist that hangs over a bog and retreats when approached.[5] Reason seems to lie on top of matter and yet disappears when looked at closely.

Readers of the poem have tended to see the importance of the metaphor as a false light within the mind, and so an attack on forms of knowledge ("errour") or types of religion.[6] The metaphor is equally concerned, however, to ask whether a causal role may be assigned to mental states once they are mistakenly considered as their own substance. The reason beloved of theologians and philosophers is something thrown off or given rise to, a steam or froth that is both misleading and inefficacious. The image is a precursor to the canonical description of epiphenomenalism provided by Thomas Huxley almost exactly two hundred years later. "Consciousness," Huxley writes, "would appear to be related to the mechanism of [the] body simply as a collateral product of its working, and to be as completely without any power of modifying that working as the steam-whistle which accompanies the work of a locomotive engine is without influence upon its machinery."[7] On this view, consciousness plays no role in a creature's behavior. It is merely the aftereffect or steam or bell playing that accompanies the hard work of the physical system. Huxley's metaphor identifies consciousness as something that comes off of the physical system without causing any actions on its own. Is the same the case for Rochester's metaphor? The sliding inside of the scholiast's perspective managed at the start of the lines makes it unclear if "whimseys" exist yet have nothing to do, or if the scholiast is wrong even to believe in them. In either case, the ignis fatuus metaphor would classify as epiphenomenal all thinking that cannot be identified with matter. Reason is not so much a procedure or faculty, therefore, as the movement of "thought to thought" as such. In its place, the speaker prefers a "right reason" that "distinguishes by Sense" (99, 100). As opposed to epiphenomenal mental states, right reason is fully within the causal flux of particles or things made from them.[8] (Sense, after all, is "material.") With this constraint in place, the speaker is able to find a place for mental causes: "Thoughts are given for Actions government / Where action ceases, Thought's impertinent" (94–5).[9] Mental causes have a role in the production of action and reach no further. This is because actions are physical movements, extensions of bodies in space, as in, for example, eating when hungry (107). Having established the borders of thought at the beginning and end of actions, the speaker solves a problem of mental causation by making the mental identical to matter in motion: thoughts govern actions because they aren't really thoughtlike.

Either mental states tack along with actions without actually doing anything, or they have the same sort of causal role as any other piece of matter. By making recourse to right reason, that is, the speaker allows himself to talk about mental states without evaporating them into a mist. The same cannot be said for the second item on the list of targets:

> Thus I think Reason righted, but for Man,
> I'le ne're recant, defend him if you can.
> For all his Pride, and his Philosophy,
> Tis evident Beasts are in their degree,
> As wise at least, and better farr than he. (112–6)

As elsewhere in the poem, beasts stand in for systems of input and output relatively unburdened with the sixth sense or will-o'-the-wisp of false reason. The refusal to let go of the attack on Man thus follows from the finding of a place for mental causes. Thoughts cause actions. Men do not. Were men to cause actions *and* thoughts to cause actions, then one action would have two equal causes. And were one action to have two equal causes it would be difficult to say which one did the actual work. There is no reason to assume, however, that a thought must belong to anyone for it to bring about its effects. In fact the very assumption is a prideful redundancy.

Anything a man could be said to cause must also be caused by his individual thoughts. So all this consideration of "those strange prodigious Creatures, Man" is a strange kind of talk (2). In contrast, beasts do not causally reduplicate their effects. They are nothing over and above their actions and so acquire "by surest means, the ends at which they aime" (118).

The poem extracts from its treatment of mental causes a claim about the men who are or are not their agents. For the speaker, accounting for the causal role of this or that mental state ought to be sufficient to describe a given action. Once we have explained the role played by desire or right reason, for example, no further question remains. We do not need to know whom, if anyone, desire or right reason belong to, or whether desires or right reasons are organized in any coherent manner. Rochester seems to say that false reason and mankind may be subtracted from a causal story of a creature's behavior without any loss. He seems even to advocate the subtraction of the two. The *Satyr* is given over largely to the negative case of establishing the irrelevance, danger, or fictiveness of mental states or entities that cannot be reduced to their causal roles. In paired contrast, the short lyric *Love and Life* takes on the positive case of establishing what a view from subtraction and reduction might look like. No longer tied to reason or mankind, actions only happen, and so are events that belong either to no one or to someone else.

> All my past Life is mine no more,
>   The flyeing houres are gone
> Like Transitory dreams given o're
> Whose Images are kept in store
>   By memory alone.
>
> What ever is to come is not:
>   How can it then be mine?
> The present moment's all my Lott
> And that as fast as it is gott
>   *Phillis* is wholly thine.

Then talk not of Inconstancy,
  False hearts and broken vows:
If I by miracle can be
This livelong Minute true to Thee
  'Tis all that Heaven allowes. (1–15)

We might begin our consideration of this poem with Howard Erskine-Hill's observation that it "questions the continuity of the self,
thus relegating on new grounds the notion of fidelity in love."[10]
On this view, the self disappears and resurfaces along the warp of
vanishing time: a past that fades into memory, a future that has no
substance, a present slipping into yesterday. Discontinuity is thus
taken to be a fortunate ploy for whoever lurks behind these punctuated selves. That wasn't me who made you a promise yesterday, nor
can I say for sure what I will be tomorrow. So speak not of broken
vows, please, and let me get on with my business. To maintain this
reading, however, we would have to put in place an unspoken first-
person perspective across the first two stanzas that manages to gain
its voice in the third. Read in this way, the "I" that declares its transitory fidelity at the end would come out once it is sure it will not be
made responsible to some other moment or version of itself.

The first thing I would say about this approach to *Love and Life*
is that it does not really address the poem's interrelated concerns
about time and personal identity.[11] The reading would present the
poem's understanding of time as a ruse and its account of identity as disingenuous. It would do so by framing the concerns of the
poem in terms of psychology, so that personal identity turns on the
continuity of experiences or feelings. The reading I will pursue is
less interested in a psychological account of personal identity than
a physical one. The persistence of persons across time, on this view,
is the same as the persistence of any spatially extended object. The
poem says that persons may have a certain three-dimensional coherence, as objects with parts, but that parts do not stick together as
persons for more than an instant. I'll begin by following the poem's
train of philosophical allusion, which stretches from Augustine

through Hobbes, and then turn to its peculiar model of identity. Rochester takes from these works a certain problem about continuity over time that he then uses to consider instances with another person. Seen this way, continuity is not about the self in the abstract but about whether persons stretch into a past and a future in the same way that they fill out a region of space.

Love and Life wonders how any moment passes from the past into the future, how, in Derek Parfit's words, it can be true "that certain things are happening *now*, and then be true that other things are happening *now*, and then be true that other things are happening *now*."[12] The question in this preliminary sense is whether time can be said to have a structure across which objects move. The poem's way of framing the question makes reference to a passage from late in the *Confessions*, where Augustine asks, "What is time then?"[13] Admitting the real difficulty of the question, Augustine's response separates the three-part time of earthly living from the timelessness of eternity:

> If nobody asks me, I can tell: but if I were desirous to explayne it to one that should aske me, plainely I cannot tell him. Boldly for all this dare I affirme my selfe to know thus much; that if nothing were already *passed*, there should bee no *past* time: and if there were nothing *to come*, there should bee no time *to come:* and if there were nothing in *present* being, there should now bee no *present* time. Those two times therfore, *passed* and *to come,* in what sort are they, seeing the *passed* is now no longer, and that to *come,* is not yet? As for the *present,* should it alwayes bee present and neuer passe into time *past*; verily it should not bee *Time,* but *Eternity.* (755–6)

Augustine's bewilderment leads to an important end. Time passes because, were it to stop, were the present moment ever to pause, then experience in this world would be like experience in the next. The passing of time is nothing to bemoan, therefore, because it draws our attention to heaven, where "nothing is flitting" (749). Time has a structure independent of our subjective perception and occurs in intervals, whether or not one ever senses one is in a present moment or has any idea of what the future holds. Without punctual time, there would be no contrasting dimension of the timeless.

Viewed simply in terms of temporal structure, Rochester turns the Augustinian meditation to secular erotics, where concerns over one moment turning into another are no longer answered by an otherworldly sense of the eternal but rather by the presence of another person. While the first two stanzas follow the beginning of Augustine's question and contemplate the difficulty of finding a place in time, the last sets out a place where no time passes. A language of the sacred transposes onto the profane, as if by a miracle one might discover "all that Heaven allows" in a "livelong minute" on earth. Rochester works through the transposition on two levels. Within the scene set by the poem, the address to Phillis says that time with her—*time at P*, let's say—is miraculously taken out of time. The view of ceaseless flux turns to a fantasy of stasis, as *time at P* never turns into *time at P +1* or *time at Q*. Alternatively, and considered from the outside, the stasis occurs at a distance from the addressee and is formalized by lines of poetry that occupy and fill out "this livelong minute." The miracle from this perspective is the lyric itself, which considers time but has none of its own, which has spatial extension with no temporal change. In either case, timelessness requires an external support that contrasts to the internal experience of time passing; it can be gotten to only by a certain divestiture, a making of a moment "wholly thine," in which the perspective of the first person is given over to a punctual unit occupied by someone else or to the form of the poem itself.

This requirement of external support means for Augustine that one should consider a heaven that comes after a life marked by intervals, while for Rochester the role of the external will always be played by some form or entity that exists in this world, the only one there is. Phillis and *Love and Life* both augur a fantasy of timelessness, but neither subsists beyond or outside the atoms that compose all matter. (It may seem less strange to say this about persons than about poems, but Rochester's monist ontology includes both. On his account, a person is a physical thing in the sense that she is composed out of particles in motion, while a poem is a physical thing in the sense that it is made by thinking matter and, if written, is in ink and on the page or, if spoken, is in particles of sound.)[14] If the trick is to sustain the stopping of time without conceding the existence of anything beyond the physical, it is quite important that the minute is phrased as a deictic, as "*This* livelong minute." For were the poem not able to point to *this* minute and so locate it in the present tense, livelongedness would just be another version of the immaterial and, in the terms set by the translation of Seneca we looked at in the last chapter, would follow the path to the "nothing" that is "after death." Syntax happily constrains the speaker to pick *this* livelong minute from the mass of matter in his vicinity.

The moment loses none of its palpability and immediacy, its liveness, even as it is made long.[15] (That this feat is equally impossible for poems and persons hardly matters and may be precisely the point.) In keeping with the immediacy of external forms, the poem reworks the second layer of the allusion, to a passage from Hobbes's *Leviathan*. Hobbes frames Augustine's problem as such: "The *Present* onely has a being in Nature; things *Past* have a being in the Memory onely; but things *to come* have no being at all; the *Future* being but a fiction of the mind, applying the sequels of actions Past, to the actions that are Present" (22). Like Lucretius, Hobbes provided for Rochester a source to view all reality as physically constituted. Moreover, Hobbes's version of Augustine is absent of any appeal to the afterlife.[16] Possible events in the future always come to mind in the present and bring with them concerns about security. We gain some calm by using experience to guide behavior, a habit that Hobbes calls "prudence," or "a *Praesumtion* of the future, contracted from the *Experience* of time *Past*," but only once safety is guaranteed by an impersonal system of rules (23). In the state of nature, a state without common rules, the tendency of the future to follow the same pattern as the past brings no comfort. The prospect of violence makes everything uncertain and the future something to fear. This is "the notion of *Time*" that "is to be considered in the nature of Warre" (88). It "consisteth not in actuall fighting; but in the known disposition thereto, during all the time there is no assurance to the contrary" (88–9). The role of the external in Hobbes is accordingly to supply assurance and keep the peace, and so it has a kind of remoteness and formality—"Lawes and publicke Officers, armed, to revenge all injuries" (89)—adjusted by Rochester to things closer at hand. Rochester takes one version of external support and turns it to another: the state to the person, legal to poetic form.

So far we have looked at *Love and Life*'s question of whether time has a structure through which persons and other objects pass. We haven't yet looked at the embedded question of whether objects have a persistent identity over time. This question requires the first, because were time not to have a structure then the issue of whether and in what ways identity is relative to time would have no meaning. Yet the question of identity animates the poem as much as the problem of structure, and it is identity on which criticism has regularly fixed. According to James Gill, for example, the speaker "not only communicates the fragmentary, discontinuous quality of his conflict-ridden existence . . . but also is somehow able to sum it up with a modicum of coherence as well as great suggestiveness."[17] This reading shares with Erskine-Hill and most others a sense that there is someone doing the summing up, one who has a mind to convince Phillis not to worry. On this view, the poem assumes that objects exhibit both fragmentation and endurance.[18] They fragment because the present version of an object turns to the past; they endure because this present version is only part of what the object is. I don't think this is what the poem wants us to imagine, though it will be useful to sketch out the argument so the somewhat more elusive and counterintuitive alternative is easier to see. The idea that objects both endure and fragment over time assumes a part-whole relation between an object at a certain time and the identity of an object over time. The perspective is four-dimensional insofar as it holds that, in the words of the philosopher Theodore Sider, "Persistence through time is like extension though space."[19] Considered from four dimensions, temporal parts are as real as spatial parts, each a distinct way of understanding the composition of objects: "When applied to space, the idea that things have arbitrary parts means, roughly, that for any way of dividing the region of space occupied by a given object, there is a corresponding way to divide that object into parts that exactly occupy those regions of space. Applied to time, the idea is that for any way of dividing up the lifetime of an object into separate intervals of time, there is a corresponding way of dividing the object into temporal parts that are confined to those intervals of time."[20] So it is from a four-dimensional perspective that the speaker of the poem seems disingenuous in his argument to Phillis. If the speaker may be divided into parts and then put back into a whole in spatial terms, so may he be in temporal terms. Just as the tongue and the toe are parts of a whole that is him, so too are *time at P* and *time at Q*. The past and future tense of the speaker form pieces of an identity that has no tense.

The distinctiveness of the poem lies on my view in its *not* representing the identity of objects in four dimensions.[21] Objects don't have temporal parts. Rather, the past and future versions of things are disjoined from a common identity and thus only the present tense of them is real. While this may sound deeply counterintuitive as metaphysics, it is I think rather intuitive as an account of the poem. For one, it is closer to what the speaker seems to be saying. The argument of the poem, if we want to call it that, consists in the steady cutting of time slices from the block of experience. No one slice of time should be taken as a part of a whole. Rather, each splinters into a point of nonexistence. A moment is "mine" if part of me, "thine" if part of you. Since the past of me is no longer "mine" it doesn't exist, and since the future cannot be "mine" it too doesn't exist. The present is all my "lott," but it exists only because it is owned by Phillis. Objects don't pass through time or exist over time. Their being given to Phillis/taking form in a poem is therefore a kind of miracle, though one achieved by the forfeiting of any claim to be an object or person oneself.

This argument is supported by the poem's form in the simplicity of its grammar and the barrenness of its spatial arrangement. The poem is structured almost entirely through the use of present tense verbs. With the exception of the embedded "given o're," the first stanza is entirely in the simple present tense ("is mine," "are gone," "are kept"). The second sustains the present tense syntax, though slips an infinitive within a present ("is to come") and adds an interrogative ("How can it then be mine?"). The third sustains the present again, from the imperative at its beginning all the way through the long conditional at the end. The effect of the minimal subject-verb grammar of the poem's sentences is to put a set of constraints on the speaker, especially since the verb is in most cases some form of *to be*. By phrasing things the way he does, the speaker cannot be understood to say that a tensed version of himself expresses or refers to a reality that has no tense. Or to put this another way, were he to use the past and future tense ("was mine" or "will be gone," for example), the predicates would link to a subject who exists out of time. So the austere force of grammar leads to the conclusion that slices of time are not parts of being, or, as the poem puts it, that the present is all the lot. This grammar leads also to a locale similarly bereft of parts. Across the fifteen lines, the poem includes not a single familiar object. The noun closest to something one could see or hold or use is the "store" of line five, a container for the mass of memories sliced from the speaker's time. Other than this store, the nouns are almost entirely abstract (hearts, vows, dreams, miracles). They provide no information about the occasion and make curiosity about setting or persons seem out of place. The result is to inhibit a comparison between spatial and temporal parts. For objects to persist over time, moments of their existence should seem like pieces of their structure. Yet the indistinctness of the spatial parts makes this analogy difficult to sustain. Hearts, vows, and miracles do not read like parts of a person in the way that elements of a blazon do, though they do read as parts of the poem. The simplicity and sparseness of the grammar has the final effect then of maintaining the present tense in reference only to the poem itself. In this way, the external form of things (three points in time, three stanzas of the poem, one point taken by someone else) endures while the objects underneath do not.

Both poems in this respect explore a consequence of material reduction. The *Satyr* gets rid of extraneous states of mind or watches them follow along with the movement of sense. *Love and Life* makes a strong and strange case for conceiving of persons as present-tense things. If it is a misreading of the poem to say that it advocates the infidelity of the speaker, that is because the poem is finally interested in physical rather than psychological states. What might it mean for only a present tense of something to be real? Do objects exist outside of tense? The poem doesn't so much answer these questions as shift to the perspective of someone else, from whose "livelong" view there might be agents, but only in the flash point that never ends, when all the physical parts line up as a whole.

The Forms of Sexuality

The previous section pursued a two-pronged reading of Rochester's philosophical verse, looking first at mental states and then at the objects in which they might be realized. The poems toy with the notion that states of mind might have little to do with acting or that acting might not trace back to agents. This section situates these questions within the embodied dynamic of sexuality, long an integral concern for Rochester criticism. Perhaps the most frequently discussed of all of Rochester's poems, *The Imperfect Enjoyment* is a good place to begin because it explicitly frames its concerns—impotence and priapism—in terms of mental causation and temporal parts and wholes. The poem begins in a flurry, as bodies prepare and tumble through a course of action:

Naked she lay clasp'd in my longing Armes,
I fill'd with Love and she all over Charmes,
Both equally inspired with eager fire,
Melting through kindness, flameing in desire.
With Armes, Leggs, Lipps, close clinging to embrase,
She clipps me to her Breast and sucks me to her face.
Her nimble tongue (loves lesser lightning) plaied
Within my Mouth; and to my thoughts conveyd
Swift Orders, that I should prepare to throw
The all dissolving Thunderbolt beloe. (1–10)

This portrait of action seems designed to present the mental as an interruption along an otherwise smoothly running chain. Until the strange interlude of line eight, all terms of the mind are laced tightly to their physical supports. In Rochester's belated and ironic Petrarchan vocabulary, it is the arms that are longing at the same time that it is desire that is flaming. The effect is a certain crossing of mind-body properties that sets the relevance of inspiration, desire, longing, and eagerness in terms of the actions into which they feed. Placed against this fervid blending, the clunky language of "thoughts" in line eight is quite jarring, as if the mind comes into the story only to gum up the machinery of the physical system.[22] The "orders" make a curious roundabout to the conscious preparation of a mock-heroic. Compared to the nimbleness of the woman's tongue, consciousness seems once more inelegant and inefficacious (or epiphenomenal).

And it will turn out of course that consciousness is spectacularly inelegant and inefficacious. In one of literary history's most celebrated evocations of impotence, the mind proves altogether unable to provoke the body. This problem has an intellectual history stretching back again to Augustine, for whom the inability to control erection was a consequence of the fall.[23] (The literary antecedents stretch further still.)[24] In what follows, I'll attempt to show that it is not only the specter of dualism and feeble minds that haunt the poem, but also the unexpected consequences of the physicalist alternative. Consider the couplet that follows the painstaking order to throw the thunderbolt: "My fluttering soul, sprung with the pointed Kiss, / Hangs hovering o're her balmy brinks of bliss" (11–2). If the previous lines stumble over "thoughts," these recover by moving in the other direction. Altering the metaphor of penis and thunderbolt yet remaining within its mock-heroic structure, the couplet attributes to the soul the physical properties of fluttering, hanging, and hovering only then to exclude the mental from the story of causation across the board.[25] The material soul's first action is not so much to refuse to respond to the mind as to act without the mind's influence: "In liquid raptures I dissolve all o're / Melt into sperm and spend at every pore" (15–6). These lines have been read by most (though not all) as a premature ejaculation.[26] I would concur, but only once we move down the poem a bit to the speaker's declaration, on line twenty-five, that he is "the most forlorn lost man alive." That is where a set of mental terms establishes that the ejaculation wasn't at all what the speaker had intended. In the moment of its occurrence, the couplet presents the ejaculation as an event without any relation to properties like intention. It is neither premature, on time, nor behind schedule. It simply is. Only after the response of the speaker and the embedded voice of the woman— "All this to Love, and Raptures due— / Must we not pay a Debt to pleasure too?" (23–4)—does the event take on the meaning of something contrary to what the speaker would have preferred. I strain at this finicky point because the poem will become so concerned with matter that acts without constraints from the mind. In the opening section, the presentation of the soul as a thing that flutters and hovers leads to raptures that are liquid and a melting and spending that simply happen. The image is not yet of the difficulty of harnessing the mind to a physical world. It is rather of matter that has no need of a mind to complete its causal circuit.

My point in putting things first in terms of a closure to the physical—an ejaculation without mist, as it were—is to establish up front how perplexed the poem seems to be by either side of mental causation. There is a certain completion to the melting and spending independent of the "thoughts" that precede them and the forlornness by which they are followed. Were thoughts to be appended to melting and spending, they might seem either tacked on or just to do the same thing from above.[27] The idea that mental states are irrelevant or redundant with respect to actions will return at the end of the poem in the account of the wayward erection. At this point, it sets up the view that actions proceed even after we subtract consciousness from them. It leads to the possibility that consciousness is at best a free rider on top of the physical and at worse a kind of obstruction. With the arrival of anguished mental states, then, the earlier ejaculation not only becomes premature but the ensuing flaccidity turns impotent. Unlike in the first instance, however, impotence immediately attaches to the state of affairs. Where the ejaculation was separated from the forlornness by ten lines of verse, remaining limp is instantly at odds with what the speaker would like to be doing.

> But I the most lost forlorn man alive
> To shew my wish'd obedience vainly strive:
> I sigh alas! and Kiss, but cannott swive. (25–7)

This first of two consecutive triplets distends in contrast to the matter it describes. Along the way, it tacks states of mind to the mere presence of something that is flaccid. Striving in vain is different from melting and spending because it adds a thought to act otherwise onto the description of events. This seemingly obvious point is vital for the next triplet, where thoughts become quite loose and ambiguous:

> Eager desires Confound the first intent,
> Succeeding shame does more success prevent
> And Rage at last Confirms me Impotent. (28–30)

Having dipped into his language of the mind, Rochester liberally splashes the triplet with emotions and attitudes. Mental properties do not simply ride on top of actions, as a kind of will-o'-the-wisp;

they also confound and prevent them. The result is impotence, for two reasons: first, because the mind gets in the way of success; and second, because it is only in the presence of mental states that impotence has any sort of meaning or is "confirmed." This confirmation occurs not in virtue of just any mental state. The second triplet is especially hectic and packed because it distinguishes between having emotions like shame or rage and having intentions to perform an action.[28] Emotions put a tint on conscious experience, while intentions formalize a relation to an outcome. There is something that it is like to be angry, and something one wishes to do when having an intention. The design of the triplet then is to set the first against the second, with desire, shame, and rage keeping the intention to swive from being realized. If mental states seem not only irrelevant but costly in this triplet, that is because it places to one side what states of the mind feel like and to another the causal role they play in initiating behavior. Intent holds out the idea of a purely formal version of thinking, stripped of the extra hum of conscious emotion. Were that all there were, the lines suggest, mental to physical causation might not have gone so awry.

The view is not so different from what we saw in *A Satyr against Reason and Mankind,* except that intention seems locked to emotions that get in the way of its functioning. Also, where the *Satyr* stops with mental states reduced to their causal roles, *The Imperfect Enjoyment* wonders whether causation could go about without the presence of the mental at all. I've paused over the famous failure of mental to physical causation at the midpoint of the poem. It is worth recalling, however, that this moment is bracketed on either end by episodes more physical in their concerns: from the material soul to the melting and spending to the insolent erection. In these episodes, the question is whether and in what way matter can act on its own. The question arises moreover from the commitment to the physical with which the poem begins. Given that the soul (along with everything else) is physical, specifying its physical properties should explain its physical effects.[29] No work ought to be left for mental properties except, as we have seen, to go along for the ride or gum up the works. Even properties that merely specify formal relations, such as intention, might be redundant on their physical supports. That being so, the poem is left to ponder what a world without minds might look like.

Enter the scabrous drollery of the runaway erection. Where earlier the mind-body problem concerned the difficulty of willing oneself to erection, the second half of the poem (roughly, lines thirty-seven to seventy-two) frets over the priapic disregard erections have for the mind. At the end of the first of several invectives, the speaker asks his "wither'd flower" to disclose the sources of its actions: "Through what mistaken Magick doest thou prove / So true to Lewdness, so untrue to Love?" (48–9). The couplet at once describes the present imperfection as a surfeit of emotion and leaves past actions as ably physical. The speaker has thus answered his own question with the alliterative conjunction of "mistaken Magick." There is little to mistake and even less of magic in words joined by consonance: the one relates to the other in virtue of a shared phoneme. Like the withered flower, words do the work on their own. Physical causation is like alliteration in the sense that a cause does not have to appeal to anything outside of matter to yield its effect. The prick proves true to lewdness but not to love. Why? Because lewdness has a kind of roughness that seems like matter while love seems like the very example of an emotion. The poem reaches for an analogy, that is, between kinds of words and kinds of being. The analogy is sustained in part by cadence, with rough sounds betokening physical things, and in part by reference, with the concreteness of one noun standing against the abstraction of another. For this reason, we might read the coarsening of language in the second half of the poem as an attempt to realize the physicality of causation. The erection has been "False to my passion, fatall to my Fame" yet true to any "Oyster, Cynder, Beggar, Common whore" it happened to meet (46, 50). In remaining so true, the erection has been the very emblem of cause-effect efficiency:

> When Vice, Disease and scandall lead the way
> With what officious hast doest thou obey!
> Like a rude Roaring Hector in the streets
> Who scuffles, Cuffs and Justles all he meets. (52–5)

The nouns fall into a tidy contrast. Flat and assonant terms like love, passion, and fame wrestle with dissonant counterparts linked in a string, first the oyster, cynder, beggar, common whore, then the vice, disease, and scandal. Nouns of the mind dissipate in vowel likeness to one another. In contrast, not a single stressed vowel sound repeats itself in the listed causes of action. The implication wrought by sound is that jagged clatter is like to something physical and thus like to something one could imagine as a property relevant to causation. A similar resting on the solid occurs in the objects to which the nouns refer. With the exception of vice and scandal, the sources of action are all items one might point to or hold in one's hand. Were passion or fame or love somehow to enter the story, they would do little more than repeat the work already done by the more gristly nouns, work indicated by the truculent ease in which the erection roars and scuffs without supplement or interference from mentality.

The possible exclusion of all mental states from the story of causation is less something to celebrate, however, than something that makes the sort of resolution reached for in poems like *A Satyr against Reason and Mankind* untenable and suspect. It would for this reason be misleading to see *The Imperfect Enjoyment* as a salute to the physical, as is suggested near the end by an image of stasis as perfect as it is scurrilous:

> Worst part of me and henceforth hated most,
> Through all the Town a Common Fucking Post,
> On whom each Whore Relieves her tingling Cunt
> As Hoggs on Gates doe rubb themselves and grunt. (62–5)

The language is abrasive even for a poem marked by escalating roughness. Yet the portrait is one of indolence rather than action, as the erection freezes and avails itself to the rubbing of others. Melissa Sanchez reads these lines to be "severing the penis from the body as Cartesian dualism would sever the body from the immaterial mind."[30] I would too, up to a point. Given a chance to elaborate his metaphysics, Rochester rarely pays heed to dualism.[31] The problems with mental causation, as I have been presenting them, take place amid a somewhat chaotic attempt to remain within a physical conception of mind and world. The trouble is not how one substance interacts with another. Mental properties are, after all, properties of matter. The trouble concerns how mental properties might enter into causal relations once physical properties have done all the work. What Sanchez observes in this respect is not so much a lingering sense of the immaterial as a familiar worry about actions, as if the difficulty of conceiving how mental states might enter into them becomes at the end a difficulty of conceiving how they might ever occur. Sanchez is right to say that "[l]ove is anything but natural because it relies on 'commands' that encumber instinctual drives rather than satisfy them."[32] The point I've been pursuing here is that the poem's reluctance to locate emotions like love as a source of behavior leads first to a sense of mechanism as a complete course of action and then to a world bereft of acts, a roar and jostle and then intransigent stiffness.

The shifting sense of what it means for something to lack properties of the mind occurs within a rhetorical structure of apostrophe and, since the address is to a piece of flesh, an apostrophe that creates a relation of part to whole, of "Worst part" to "me." The result is a different sense of parthood, and especially parthood over time, from what we observed in *Love and Life*. In that poem, the speaker established a three-dimensional model of identity in which part-whole spatial relations do *not* correspond to part-whole temporal relations. Past versions of the speaker are not part of him in the way that parts of his body are. In *The Imperfect Enjoyment*, by contrast, part-whole temporal relations hold strong as their analogous spatial relations break down. Past, present, and future versions of the object all reduce to one thing across four dimensions: once it was "Stiffly Resolv'd," now it is a "Dead Cinder," soon (or so the speaker threatens) it will "in Consumeing weepings wast away" (41, 33, 68). The dead cinder is one part, the fucking post another, the consumed in weeping still another, *of* the same entity. Considered in succession, these are three stages of a single object. The poem makes a great deal of the coherence of identity over time, as each interval provides a reason for the speaker's rage. What time gives, however, space takes away. Just prior to the apostrophe, the speaker uses the first-person pronoun for the last time: "Trembling, Confus'd, Dispairing, limber, dry, / A wishing, weak, unmoving Lump I ly" (35–6). From this identifying of a spatial part with its whole, the poem moves to a gradual splitting and finally to a wish for a future in which the part is beset with "Ravenous Shankers," consumed by weepings, and beset by "stangury and stone" (66, 68). One effect of the address is thus to stretch parts into the future while pushing them away from the person who might own or care for them. To the extent that the speaker wishes harm upon his worst part, in other words, the part is temporally relevant while spatially extraneous.

The separation of the penis from the person established by the apostrophe suggests that if actions happen at all, they happen independently of the mind, or, more strangely still, that if minds exist at all, they extend outside the head. One problem that remains therefore is how to relate this familiar reliance on things external to a model of agency. If mental content is externally located or determined, as many of the poems seem to suggest, then how can it enter into a person's behavior? If the woman's tongue orders a throw of the thunderbolt, then how does throwing become the speaker's intention? Few poems are more interested in these problems than *A Ramble in St. James's Park*. Told in brusque and raspy tetrameter, the story concerns the behavior of a former lover, Corinna, who has abandoned the speaker for the fops and parvenus gathered in the park. In keeping with its gruff form, the poem is all about actions,

about the coming, going, and intermingling of Corinna and her partners. Yet the hectic pace is intriguingly unmatched to any accompanying states of mind, with sex appearing to be something one does
on a specific sense of keeping up with appearances. I'll wrap up this
section of the chapter, then, by looking at the twin commitments to
desire as the source of behavior and the outside world as the source
of desire. On the reading I'll pursue, *A Ramble* locates the shape
as well as meaning of actions first in the physical composition of
the park—its trees and pathways—and then in its assembled social
milieu. I'll be particularly interested in the way that, in a poem committed to following one sex act into another, comparatively little
attention is paid to the intentions or pleasures of agents except as
these derive from an environment always in view.

Although seldom remarked upon, it is telling that the poem
begins with a momentary subtraction from the presence of other
people. The speaker leaves a tavern where "Much Wine had past
with grave discourse, / of who Fucks who, and who does worse" in
order, as he puts it, "to cool my Head, and fire my heart" (1–2, 8).
Somber chatter about action (or doing) belongs to a fired head, just
as actual doings belong to the heart. Yet when the speaker leaves his
company and takes a stroll through the park, he encounters first not
active agents in their actual doings but rather foliage, as "There by
a most incestuous *Birth*; / Strange *Woods*, Spring from the teeming
Earth" (11–2). Before it is represented as a space of social gather-
ing, the park is encountered through impersonal and outward form,
as if the speaker needs to leave the presence of others in order for
woods to show him how copulations are done. Literally inseminated
by ancient Celts, the woods provide something of a husk around
actions, prefiguring them in outline before they actually occur:

> Whence Rowes of *Mandrakes* tall did rise,
> Whose lewd Tops Fuck'd the very Skies.
> Each imitative Branch does twine,
> In some lov'd fold of *Aretine*. (18–22)

Shrubbery provides a visible proxy for agents to pattern their actions on the venerable principle of imitation. The park is not a place where forms are abandoned so that desire may be expressed at will. It is rather a place where forms recruit and shape desire. Branches are "imitative" because they look like erotic illustrations from Aretino, which are in turn imitations of sexual postures.[33] The trail of imitation concludes when humans perform acts first limned in silhouette, when "Nightly now beneath their shade, / Are *Bugg'ries*, *Rapes*, and *Incests* made" (23–4). James Grantham Turner is therefore right, I think, to describe Rochester's version of the park as "a quintessentially libertine space . . . populated by adventurously promiscuous aristocrats," but only once we place a pause between the space and the populating.[34] The poem soon fills the park with all sorts of agents, yet these seem to occupy slots provided in advance.

When persons take on the form of plants, they bring with them additional features of social difference. The postures set by mandrakes are overlaid by postures set by status, profession, and type. The "All-sin-sheltering Grove" turns into a place of profligate mingling, where

> Great *Ladies*, *Chamber-Maids*, and *Drudges*,
> The *Rag-picker*, and *Heiress* trudges:
> *Carr-men*, *Divines*, great *Lords*, and *Taylors*,
> *Prentices*, *Poets*, *Pimps*, and *Gaolers*;
> *Foot-Men*, fine *Fops*, do here arrive,
> And here promiscuously they swive. (27–32)

This is Rochester at his most Juvenalian.[35] Rome has been replaced by London, but the image of urban chaos remains the same; the satirist recoils in fascination from a cityscape of promiscuous intercourse, as a cross-section of the social order blends at its most sensitive points of contact. Forms once more create conduct but differently from the way they do in the emptier moments at the beginning of the poem. The lines rely on the trope of *concordia discors* to show how social muddling might be confected into formal harmony.

The speaker does not so much approve of all the swiving going on between aristocrats and commoners as enjoy bringing them together with meter, rhyme, and alliteration.[36] While social forms precede agents by defining in advance the roles they might play (from heiress to ragpicker), literary forms precede agents by setting the kind of relations they enter into. In either case, agents discover whom they would like to have sex with after it is made clear to them by one or another kind of causal relation, whether with respect to a status role one is meant to occupy or a sound one is supposed to make.

Corinna's activity should raise few questions. When she throws herself into the whirl of forms she ought to discover the intentions they realize. But that is not exactly what happens. The problem for the speaker is that Corinna has not found her place in the clutter of lines twenty-seven to thirty-two, but rather waited eleven lines for the arrival of "Three *Knights* o'th'Elbow, and the slurr." These knights represent the least valued type of social actor in the Rochester universe, those aspiring courtiers and not-quite aristocrats who always seem to miss their mark. The "vain, affected pretenders to social standing," as Marianne Thormählen puts it, replace the order of the *concordia discors* with a more fluid set of relations: ambition, upward mobility, fraud, impersonation.[37] The result is somewhat curious. Corinna appears to act without intentions or desires at all, as if these attitudes were not only solicited by forms but also made superfluous by them. Whatever states of mind she might have are so unrelated to her behavior that they first appear to be beside the point and then to go without mention.[38] The version of externalism most at issue in this poem thus seems to imply that mental states may not so much dangle off actions as not even exist, that agency only requires entering into a causal relation with one's environment, not the environment creating any desires, intentions, or feelings.

In putting things this way, my account of the agency ascribed to Corinna is at some odds with the drift of recent criticism. "Corinna retains initiative," according to one reader; hers is a "considered female libertinism," according to another.[39] Given this consensus view, it is worth taking another look at the moment of apparent volition.

> One in a strain 'twixt Tune and *Nonsense*,
> Cries, *Madam, I have lov'd you long since,*
> *Permit me your fair hand to kiss.*
> When at her *Mouth* her *Cunt* says yes. (75–8)

Startling and disquieting as the final line may be, it is difficult to sustain a reading of it on behalf of expression. Turner has described the line as a "grotesque inversion of bodily hierarchy" that leaves Corinna "wholly sexualized."[40] Yet the poem does little to establish a top-down hierarchy that could be so deposed and less to set up Corinna as "sexualized," if by that term one means (as Turner seems to) suffused with a desire that comes from below. The relation of cunt to mouth is neither of part to whole nor bottom to top; the relation instead is of part to part. One implication of the line therefore is to deny a special intimacy that parts might have with each other. No sexualized initiative wraps pieces into a bundle. Parts meet other parts according to literary and social form: doggerel puts a cunt at a mouth while a volatile town has it say yes. The leap into public sex that follows is, fittingly, one into a swarm of parts that refuse to stand still.

> And with these Three confounded Asses,
> From *Park*, to *Hackney-Coach*, she passes,
> So a proud *Bitch* does lead about,
> Of humble *Currs*, the Amorous rout;
> Who most obsequiously do hunt,
> The sav'ry scent of Salt-swolne *Cunt*. (81–6)

Whereas the earlier *concordia discors* puts one actor in unlikely relation to another, the arrival of the faux knights turns sex into a roundabout chase, an image the poem insists upon so strenuously as to make it difficult to see how bodies stop moving long enough to come into contact. In either case, a structure of relations comes first. Because he has described a social scene in terms of instability and motion, the speaker then has Corinna move with considerable speed.

Corinna slips into her environment in such a way that seems to leave her actions indistinguishable from nearby events.[41] The speaker does not so much condemn the recklessness of what she does, therefore, as its independence from mental causes he could assign to her:

> Had she pickt out to rub her Arse on,
> Some stiff-Prick'd *Clown*, or well hung *Parson*,
> Each job of whose Spermatick Sluce,
> Had fill'd her *Cunt* with wholsome Juice,
> I the proceeding shou'd have prais'd,
> In hope she had quencht a Fire I rais'd:
> Such nat'rall freedoms are but just,
> There's something gen'rous in meer Lust.
> But to turn damn'd abandon'd *Jade*,
> When neither *Head* nor *Tail* perswade;
> To be a *Whore*, in understanding,
> A Passive *Pot* for *Fools* to spend in.
> The *Devil* plaid booty, sure with thee,
> To bring a blot on infamy. (91–104)

Across their accumulating list of obloquy these lines contrast one sort of action with another. Were Corinna to have "pickt out" her partners, she would have acted from the "gen'rous" and "nat'rall freedom" of lust and so would have "pleasure for excuse" (124). She is a "Whore, in understanding," however, because neither head nor tail has any persuasion in the sequence of events. The first presents an alternative and, on the view of the speaker, preferable kind of action, while the second presents an unusual type of passivity. The speaker would have "mere" lust continuous with its surroundings and so sufficient to act as a cause. As it turns out, however, objects and events don't so much enter into a person's reasons for acting as make the person and her reasons irrelevant.

Court and Town

When the speaker enters St. James's Park to clear his head, he discovers that heads are filled with (or set by) forms at turns physical, social, and literary. This insight leads to some concern about whether heads, tails, mouths, and cunts compose whole entities and, if they do, about what ties them together over time and across space. On the face of it, the blurring of the boundaries between parts and their environment ought to make causation easier to imagine. The closer one property is to another the fewer complications there should be in locating a relation between them. Yet what turns out to be the case is a reduction that makes such relations superfluous. The poem seems to say that external forms recruit parts and draw their connections to each other and, this being so, that there is no point in asking what role Corinna plays in her actions. Something similar happens with respect to agents and their parts in the notorious poem on King Charles, although there the trouble with reconciling the two takes place against a more overtly political model of the external. The portrait of sovereignty in the poem balances a runaway desire with an extreme pliancy. According to the speaker, the king has become won over to a French mistress who is an agent of a Catholic conspiracy from abroad.

> Peace was his Aime, his gentleness was such
> And Love, he lov'd, For he lov'd Fucking much,
> Nor was his high desire above his Strength:
> His Scepter and his Prick were of a length,
> And she may sway the one who plays with t'other
> Which makes him litle wiser then his Brother. (A5–13)

As readers have long observed, these lines disturb the expected synecdoche of scepter and sovereign in order to introduce the royal prick as an example of causation run amuck.[42] The scepter stands in for the institution of monarchy only to show how monarchy is subject to sway. Desire is in this respect a curious property, at once establishing a reason for acting in the body of the king and tracking internal reasons to the peripheral sources of lovers and nations. It is interesting therefore that one version of the poem, found in four separate manuscript copies, substitutes "designs" for "desire" in line 10.[43] The effect of the substitution is less to desexualize or censor the poem—the "fucking" of line 9 is retained—than to emphasize the proximity between reasons for acting and contexts in which actions occur. "Designs" adds to "desire" a sense that the tarse, prick, ballacks, and arse of the poem compose a king only when they are arranged just so, while at the same time retaining the meaning that the king acts out of preferences. The switch from the one to the other, in other words, draws upon the twin meaning of design as form and design as intention to emphasize a certain blurring or uncertainty: the desire that seems directed at objects is designed by setting.

As Harold Love's definitive Clarendon edition of Rochester's writings has shown, designs and desires alternate across the history of this poem because of the particular way it was made public.[44] Like all of Rochester's poems, the scandalous portrait of the king circulated first in manuscript before it was rewritten by friends or scribes, entered into commonplace books, and included in miscellanies. As legend has it, this particular poem was accidentally handed to the king before radiating outward, retaining along its movement a special intimacy between the language of agency and the place of reading. Love identifies two communities and periods of circulation. Initially the poem circulated "within Whitehall as a 'court satire,' that is, as part of an ongoing factional battle between alliances of grandees over how personal closeness to the sovereign could be used for purposes of factional self-interest." Later in the decade, the poem entered into "miscellanies with 'country' satires directed at the king and the court," collections that were "addressed to an audience outside Whitehall for whom the king's malleability was not a court-factional but a nationally significant issue."[45] Either might rewrite the king's intentions, from an eroticism one might have an interest in being nearby to policies one might wish to critique. One virtue of Love's scholarship then is that it shows how the circumstances of the poem's reception rewrite its language of intentions. The king likes fucking, to be sure, but whether this is a design or a desire is a matter of where the poem is read. In this respect, the history of the poem provides an example of its model of agency, as it is the lattice of circulation that puts in place the state of mind.

The form of mental causation described by the scepter poem concerns the relation between desire and action, a wanting of something and a behaving in such a way that might secure the having or doing of that thing. Attitudes like desire and intention have a special place in Rochester's poetry because their role is solely to establish these sorts of relations. There is no need for a desire or an intention to be felt, let alone to be embellished into something like an emotion.[46] Indeed, felt mental states tend to be difficult to work into the story of causation, as the *Satyr* and *The Imperfect Enjoyment* in their different ways explore. One way of clearing the distracting feints of mist, as we have seen, is to locate causation in some sort of external structure. Persons sometimes have feelings; towns rarely do. The last of Rochester's poems I will look at in this chapter, the urban satire *Artemiza to Chloe*, takes up this kind of causation specifically with the emotion of love. *Artemiza to Chloe* is an epistle from a woman "in the Towne" to a woman "in the Countrey" about the gossipy goings-on back home. As befits its locale, the poem was among the most widely circulated of Rochester's poems, reproduced in collections by three scriptoria and printed twice.[47] The pattern of transmission according to Love radiates from court to town, with the perspective throughout of a courtier looking askance at the new social habits of the metropolis.[48] The poem "is *about* the Town" but "not *of* the Town."[49] One interesting feature of this model of textual circulation, however, is that it is in some tension with the model embedded within the poem, according to which texts move from the town to the country. Seen this way, Artemiza's writing to Chloe triangulates a movement begun with the circulation of manuscripts at

Whitehall. If the first movement presents town habits to court, the second movement presents the town to itself, as when for example the printed copy adds to the title that the letter is "concerning the Loves of the Town."[50] The problem in all these cases is how to get love to end in an action, and the worry (if we can call it that) is that love requires the habits of town to complete its causal circuit.

Readers of *Artemiza to Chloe* have often wondered whether Artemiza articulates a certain norm around love at the beginning that is then lost when she recounts all that has transpired since Chloe has left.[51] Setting herself for a pause before getting into the recent news, Artemiza writes that she is sad to report that "love" has become "soe debauch'd by ill-bred Customes here" (39).

> *Love*, the most gen'rous Passion of the mynde,
> The softest refuge Innocence can fynde,
> The safe directour of unguided youth,
> Fraught with kind wishes, and secur'd by Trueth. (40–3)

If these lines set a norm, they do so by establishing a wished-for portrait of causation, in which a generous passion of the mind directs the actions of unguided youth. To account for the generosity of love in this fashion, however, is to describe it as something other than an emotion, at least so far as Artemiza nowhere makes love seem like something one feels and everywhere describes it as a reason for behavior.[52] Love serves as a reason in other words because it has the lean properties of an intention with none of the messy or misty properties of consciousness. In the perfect order of things, love would control otherwise wayward actions. The only feature additional to intention it might supply would be the constraining of actions according to safety and truth.

In other poems by Rochester, the difficulty with passions like love is that they cannot be reduced to a causal role and so therefore are an extra something that interferes with behavior. Artemiza's project (and her lament) is to show how one might get from love to directions or, put another way, have love do the actual guiding. The logical form of the project would have there be something about love that gives rise to actions or has them come out in a certain way. Without love, youth are unguided; with love they act with truth and safety. Try as she might, however, there is little Artemiza can say about love that would put it in this position. Twist and turn the passion as you will—show it to be a "Cordiall dropp" thrown in our cup from heaven—and love will still not reveal why and how it serves as a cause (44). For love to direct youth it needs to work as a connective to guided behavior; emotions swept in its train are a kind of surplus or get in the way. Stripped to this logical form, the sentence "love directs youth" leaves Artemiza to search for a bridge from the one to the other. Yet the more she tries to say what it is about love that puts it in the role of direction—the passion's affinity to a cordial drop from heaven, its "Subsidyes of Prayse" or making us feel "blest"—the further she gets from whatever makes actions happen (47, 49).

From the perspective of Artemiza, the solution is a melancholy one. The properties that connect love to youth are not set or held by a person who is in love but in the structure of town living. The result is that it is everyone in town, not just Corinna, whose actions are shaped on the periphery. Artemiza's description of her neighbors will soon turn to individual depravities of one or another extreme. She begins, however, with a general account of how citizens relate to events, and, again, the role played by love:

> To an exact perfection they have wrought
> The Action *Love*, the Passion is forgott.
> 'Tis below Witt, they tell you, to admire,
> And e'ne without approving they desire.
> Their private wish obeys the publicke Voyce,
> 'Twixt good, and bad Whimsey decides, not Choyce.
> Fashions grow up for tast, att Formes they strike;
> They know, what they would have, not what they like. (62–9)

The opening couplet has a prickly relation to the discussion of love that has only just finished. Love is no longer a passion, and so the difficulty of reconciling extraneous properties of mind with causation falls out of the description. Yet along with these superfluous properties go the rest of mental state terms, as if to connect love and action one must imagine them as events or as things. Once the passion of love is forgot, in other words, all that is left is something that happens and something that exists, or, "the action love." From this reshuffling of the deck, a neat series of comparisons emerges: admiration and wit, approval and desire, private and public, choice and whimsy, liking and having. The second of each paired item locks onto the practical and external context of language, society, custom, and habit; the first subsists in a left-behind or frail state of the internal. Perhaps the most curious placement is desire, which like intention names a formal relation (*P* wants *Q*) that needn't come with extra baggage. Yet according to Artemiza even this bare relation tacks one *event* to another, in the absence of internal approving. The causal entailment skirts on the surface, like a marble on a desk. The rest of the action relations either sustain this flatness or go in the reverse direction from the earlier ideal. The two paths are at some odds with each other: in the one case, events cause events with no involvement of mental states; in the other, mental states are the aftereffect of events. In the first case, desire happens without approval, while in the second, the private wish obeys the public voice. What draws the account together is an aversion to mental causes so extreme as to make their reverse possible while in all other respects sustaining a sense that nothing mental exists. Elsewhere the poems suggest that mental states might be prior to action once they are reduced to their causal roles (when, for example, the *Satyr* says that right reason ties together certain facts about the environment with certain behaviors of the body). In Artemiza's world, either there are no mental states or, if there are any, they come along after external objects and events have done all the work, filling in spaces carved for them in advance.

The Afterlife of a Couplet

The portrait of causation provided by Artemiza is only one among others in the poetry and, like the one in *A Ramble*, is perhaps best considered as an extreme presentation of not always compatible premises. Try as we might, we would have a hard time locating a single perspective on actions in Rochester's verse. Even so, the couplet with which Artemiza begins her tirade presents its concerns in neatly crystalline form: "To an exact perfection they have wrought / The Action *Love*, the Passion is forgot." Lifted out of the poem, the couplet might seem to ponder how anything happens once causes have literally been put out of mind. I've tried to show how these concerns move in several directions in the poetry and its environs. In the present section, I'll move out of Rochester entirely to his reception in the early eighteenth century. However, I will keep focus on this one couplet, which seemed to hold a certain fascination for its later readers.[53] In 1709 alone, the couplet was cited twice by Steele in the *Tatler* (nos. 5 and 49) and in the opening pages of Delarivier Manley's *New Atalantis*; soon it cropped up in the oddest places. My concern will be with tracking the meaning of the citation across the radical alteration of its circumstances.

Rochester's poems circulated in close quarters among courtiers and in the distant reaches of town and country, in individual manuscripts, scribal miscellanies, and printed separates. By the time Steele selected the action-passion couplet from *Artemiza*, Rochester had been drawn into a more uniform public. The poems had twice been assembled into printed collections under his name, the first in 1680 and the second in 1691.[54] His life had become the subject of Bishop Burnet's widely sold potboiler about libertinism, conversion, and redemption.[55] The Rochester of the early eighteenth century had become, in other words, part of a national print culture in the making, two central architects of which were, as reputation has it, Addison and Steele. When, for example, Rochester writes of the "publicke" in *Artemiza* (the only time the word appears in his poetry), he does not seem to mean the audience of the poem.[56] When the *Tatler* does the same, audience seems very much to be its concern.[57] The public whose actions of love put passion in peril has become one that consumes print daily and enjoys discussing small chestnuts of the national literature, like several lines from *Artemiza to Chloe*. These lines from "long ago," as Steele puts it, sit atop number 5 as an epigraph instructing readers how to talk about love and so find their place among "the Discourses of the young Fellows of this Age."[58] Should his readers require any further help, they need only turn to a certain well-known lady: "[A]sk Mrs. *Meddle*, who is a Confident, or Spy, upon all the Passions in Town, and she'll tell you, that the Whole is a Game of Cross Purposes. The Lover is generally pursuing one, who is in Pursuit of another, and running from one that desires to meet him" (1:46). The importance of the address is as much in its form as its content. Writing directly to his readers, Steele puts anyone who picks up the paper in the position of shared listening and thus implicitly in the possession of shared meanings. Any one reader can ask Mrs. Meddle as well as any other, and all should get the same response. To accept the address from the voice on the page is thus to discover one's place in a community of usage.

When Steele returns to Rochester's couplet three months later, he clarifies that his concern is with the "Imposition of honest Names and Words upon improper Subjects" (1:347). Steele engages such matters because he would like to diminish any lingering "Confusion among us" about what words mean, especially when they carry with them ideas of some moral importance (1:347). The question then is how the journal might refer to common meanings and at the same time correct for principled usage. Steele would both characterize the way his audience understands names and alter this understanding for the better. Looking back at the Rochester couplet, for example, we see that it assigns the name "love" to two passions of unequal moral weight: "Of all the laudable Motives of human Life, none has suffer'd so much in this Kind as Love; under which rever'd Name, a brutal Desire call'd Lust is frequently concealed and admitted" (1:348). Love has become so elastic in usage that it names two different reasons for action. The confusion doesn't lie in the description of the action, however, but in the reference to the passion by which the action is caused. Steele's readers should have no trouble discerning a difference between gallant and rakish behavior, in other words, even though they have become a little confused about the states of mind corresponding to each. No better example of this problem is to be found than in *Artemiza*. "*Philander* the other day . . . upbraided me for having some Time since quoted these excellent Lines of the Satyrist:

> *To an exact Perfection they have brought*
> *The Action love, the Passion is forgot.*

How could you (said he) leave such an Hint so coldly?" (1:348). The hint is cold, Philander thinks, because it assigns rakishness and gallantry to a single name. In response, Steele explains that the passion of love should hold on to to its familiar title while "the action love" ought to be called lust. Each name refers to distinct and opposing intentions as well as distinct and opposing actions. Love has no "Design or Direction" and so looks for others with the "Concern and Fondness" of "Benevolence" (1: 348). Lust "tends chiefly to prey upon Innocence, and has something so unnatural in it, that it hates its own Make, and shuns the Object it lov'd, as soon as it has made it like itself" (1:348–9). Steele's effort at lexical clarification thus swerves away from the feeling itself—the qualities that describe what it is like to experience love or lust—and moves toward the different relations love and lust have to their objects. Lust eagerly consumes, love respectfully shies from the beloved: "Love . . . is a Child that complains and bewails its Inability to help itself, and weeps for Assistance, without an immediate Reflection or Knowledge of the Food it wants: Lust, a watchful Thief which seizes its Prey, and lays Snares for its own Relief; and its principal Object being Innocence, it never robs, but it murders at the same Time" (1:349). Despite the claim that a name should be locked to its subject, therefore,

Steele defines love and lust in terms of relations, as if the associated feelings were irrelevant or impossible to describe. A state of mind reveals itself in the kind of relation it creates.

The importance of this turn in the argument is that each relation models a kind of social interaction. An agent's feelings make themselves evident in the way she treats other agents. Proper naming is for this reason important for establishing polite relations within a society of readers. Steele understands the "passion of love" Artemiza had found so lost on the world as the basis of civility, as a surrender of personal appetite that marks true concern for others. At the same time, he understands the "action of love" Artemiza found so defining of life in town as an antisocial and destructive concern for oneself. "We may settle our Notion of these different Desires, and accordingly rank their Followers," because individual behavior indicates an underlying reason for action (1:349). Some reasons make civil society; others destroy the same. Consider Aspasia:

> In this accomplish'd Lady, Love is the constant Effect, because it is never the Design. Yet, tho' her Mien carries much more Invitation than Command, to behold her is an immediate Check to loose Behaviour, and to love her, is a liberal Education: For, it being the Nature of all Love to create an Imitation of the beloved Person in the Lover, a Regard for *Aspasia* naturally produces Decency of Manners, and good Conduct of Life, in her Admirers. (1:349)

Lacking in design is like lacking in command; each describes a benevolent relation to the beloved. Aspasia is both a model citizen and creator of model citizens, since "Love is the happy Composition of all the Accomplishments that make a Fine Gentleman" (1:349). In contrast, devoting oneself to lust leads to the murder of innocents and the shunning of bonds. So while it may be difficult to discern the feelings named by love and lust, the behavior they cause may be individuated with some care. "The Motive of a Man's Life is seen in all his Actions," and those that are motivated by love "have a Simplicity of Behaviour" conducive to the society of gentle getting along fashioned by the journal (1:349). Just as the meaning of words, for good or ill, is to be found in a community of usage, motives in mind come into view through visible actions. Steele's public discussion would have the second part of the externalism correct the first: we know how people feel in virtue of how they act and therefore we should reconsider what we mean by the word "love."

Steele's rival Delarivier Manley published her scandal novel, the *New Atalantis*, a month after the *Tatler*'s first citation of Rochester. Her exposé of the intimate lives of prominent Whig politicians begins with the goddess Astrea's return to Atalantis and reunion with her neglected mother, Virtue. Virtue's first words to her daughter on the sad state of affairs at home include the following:

> Innocence is banished by the first dawn of early knowledge. Sensual corruptions and hasty enjoyments affright me from their habitation. They embellish not the heart to make it worthy of the God; their whole care is outward and transferred to the person. By a diabolical way of argument they prove the body is only necessary to the pleasures of enjoyment; that love resides not in the heart, but in the face, and as certain of their poets have it,
>
> To an exact Perfection they have brought
> The Action Love, the Passion is forgot.[59]

Rochester's couplet has become an occasion of party politics. On Steele's Whig reading, the passion of love allows us to imagine a society built on the pleasant concern for others. Manley's Tory response concentrates on an action of love set loose on a fallen world. In many respects, Manley's novel is nothing other than a series of instances in which desire takes shape from politics. The various examples of debauched court life follow the careers of crafty citizens who manipulate sexuality for personal advancement. Soon after the Rochester citation, for example, we are told how Fortunas and Germanicus plot their ascents at court by surrendering to the desires of others, Fortunas to the Dutchess, Germanicus to the Prince. Neither has "desire" to speak of, but each burns with insatiable "ambition."[60] The distinguishing feature of ambition, on Manley's view, is that it requires an adjustment of what she calls the heart, by which we are to understand love, desire, intention, and the like, to what she calls the face, by which she seems to mean all "outward" or political meanings. Whereas for Steele this adjustment was finally to be celebrated as the discovery of communal language and shared meanings, for Manley it is to be decried as the rapacious character of modern politics.

Steele and Manley twist the Rochester couplet to fit their different allegiances. The twin citations reveal how ideological argument made use of rival models of action. Four years later, Jane Barker further twists the couplet to explore minds at work in the new form of the popular novel. Barker's *Love Intrigues* begins by establishing itself as a pleasing retreat from the sort of party conflict that embroiled Steele and Manley. The "little Novel," as she calls it in the dedication, recounts the ill-fated courtship of Galesia and Bosvil, two lovers who never quite manage to understand each other's intentions.[61] Framing the narrative is a discussion between Galesia and her friend Lucasia, who meet in the St. Germains Garden while war rages abroad and political conflict percolates at home. Exhausted from discussing "the Several Adventures of the former and late War, and what they had to hope or fear from the Success, or Overthrow of either or both Parties," Lucasia "desired *Galesia* to recount to her the Adventures of her early Years, of which she had already heard some Part, and therefore believed the whole to be a diverting Novel" (83). Barker does not simply shift away from Manleyan political allegory; she stages this shift as the essential importance of her novel.

The diversion offered by the novel lies in its switch from politics to psychology, from the war and party conflict to Galesia's "most secret Intentions" or "interiour Thoughts" as they are conveyed in the intimacy of personal disclosure (89, 94). Barker's embedded reflections on her own method thus have to do with the first-person style she develops, a style that often seems to place the "interior" or "intentions" against the customs and expectations of the external world. Galesia was unable to express her thoughts in public because to do so would violate the norms of propriety. She will instead retail them to Lucasia, who stands as a proxy for the reader. One doesn't have to nudge the novel too much to see this strategy at work; "tho' in *Bosvil's* Presence I made a shift to keep up this Outside of a seeming Insensibility of Love," she says, for example, to Lucasia, "but interiorly I was tormented with a thousand Anxieties" (87). The revelation is then followed by a homily: "Thus a Mask is put on, sometimes, to conceal an ill Face, and sometimes to preserve a good one: And the most part of Mankind are in reality different from what they seem, and affect to be thought what they are not" (90). Novels show people as they really are, apparently, by attaching passions to actions or worrying about their split. Novels do what they do, moreover, by developing forms like first-person disclosure to open up seemingly hidden states of mind.

Since Galesia is in a position to instruct us on how to read the novel, it is no surprise that she thinks she has finally learned how to read Bosvil's mind. When Bosvil discovers he has a rival for Galesia's affection, one Mr. Brafort, he asserts the priority of his claim. Brafort easily complies and slinks away, causing Galesia to reflect:

> To an exact Perfection he had brought
> The Action Love, the Passion be forgot. (91)

The Rochester couplet helps to explain Brafort's bluff indifference, compared with which Bosvil's recent attention appears genuine: "This Transaction . . . gave me a strong Belief of *Bosvil's* Sincerity and made me interpret every little dubious Word, which he sometimes mixed with his fond Actions, to be Demonstrations of a real Passion" (91). Soon thereafter, Bosvil again forsakes Galesia, and she is forced to admit that his real intentions were never in her grasp. The same model of reading that would place authority in Galesia's private experience thus places Bosvil's mind at a considerable remove.[62] The story would validate first-person authority over one's own mental states, thus leaving Galesia's mind open for the reader/Lucasia while closing off Bosvil's thoughts, unless of course one were to write his novel or become his friend.

Barker cites Rochester on one of those occasions when the peculiar intentions of the early novel rise to a point of didactic articulation. In this respect, she relies on the notion that forms of courtship and contract continually misrepresent what people are really feeling, that passion is one thing and action another, and that it is often difficult to read backwards from the second to the first. At the same time, however, she also relies on the notion that certain kinds of writing express these intentions and so make external what is ostensibly on the inside of characters. But despite the genre's seeming commitment to the first person, as the embedded form of narration to Lucasia as well as the privileged means of access to states of mind, various kinds of third-person formalization are relied upon throughout. Galesia, for example, introspects in couplets—on "solitary Walks" her "rolling Thoughts" often just "turn'd themselves in to these Verses"—or in gobbets of Scripture or fable (88). Even as the novel asks to be read as the communication of private thoughts, therefore, these thoughts take the form of public convention, from rhymed couplets to Jesus's parables to bits from Ovid (98, 103). Barker's version of private experience and language, that is, at once suggests that this experience and language exist in advance of the public forms they create *and* that they come into existence after they are set by these forms.

To bring action to an exact perfection while forgetting passion articulates an externalism that resonates across Rochester's poetry and beyond Rochester's time. Once more, the distinction between actions and events turns on mental states and causes. An event is an action when its causes include some sort of mental state. An event is simply an event when it is a mere happening. Taken on its own limited terms, the couplet suggests that actions have no passions in train and therefore are difficult to distinguish from other events. This conundrum applies throughout Rochester's verse: from the more theoretically elaborate poems like *A Satyr against Reason and Mankind* or *Love and Life* to the more roughly worded sexual verse like *A Ramble* or *The Imperfect Enjoyment*. The poems seem alternately to fit mental states to actions after they have already happened or to get rid of both entirely; they imagine a world in which mental states exist without persons or persons don't exist in time or parts don't make wholes. When Steele and Manley cite a couplet from one of these poems, they take it to distinct but not entirely different ends. Manley's interest in politics is perhaps the more evidently Rochesterian. Yet Steele's interest in public language is preoccupied with establishing rules for language and behavior, neither of which place authority in inner meanings or private usage. Like Steele, Barker is interested in linguistic behavior, but in her case the names apply to the experience of passion. She lines up this experience with terms we associate with inner life, yet at the same time marks its expression with rule-bound public forms. Thus even the "interior thoughts" lurking below masks turn out to be one or another convention or story. In these ways, Rochester's couplet helped to work through problems of action in several different kinds of writing. In the final example, the question is how to represent one character's thoughts and another character's actions in a genre professedly committed to first-person experience. The result is an early excursus into the problems and limits of this commitment in written form. Barker would like to write of what something is like for her character and devises forms to capture this or that experience. But she also seems to acknowledge that these forms are finally shared and external. Whether there is something that it feels like to do something and whether this feeling plays any sort of causal role remain intriguing difficulties. The next chapter will continue this particular thread into Locke's long-revised account of actions and, once more, a related response in novelistic fiction.

4   Uneasiness, or Locke among Others

To ask why someone did something is to inquire into observable events: a theft of a bundle, a riding in a coach, a cutting of some hair. I've argued so far that writers like Hobbes and Rochester drew these kinds of events into a science of causes. I've also emphasized the concern many took either to blur or to etch in stone the line between objects and events outside the head and the workings of mental states themselves. Are persons that different from other objects? How does the intention to do something or a reason for acting in some way take shape from the external environment? This chapter pauses over a major statement on the topic from a major philosopher. In the first edition of the *Essay Concerning Human Understanding*, Locke devotes a short chapter to actions. In the second, he revises the chapter thoroughly and allows it to grow to considerable length. In between, he engages in an intense correspondence with the Irish philosopher William Molyneux about the topic of actions and about the importance of conscious experience in coming to an intention to do something. In order to do something, Locke argues, one must not only have a desire to achieve some end, one must *feel uneasy* in the absence of this end. His painstaking revision of the *Essay* thus consists in adjusting the argument from an emphasis on the form that actions might take to an emphasis on the experience with which they are accompanied.

Locke's revision brings his account of consciousness into the theater of actions. One's theory of actions is incomplete to the degree to which it neglects *what it is like* to perform them. In putting things this way, Locke leans on a topic he devotes considerable time to elsewhere in the *Essay*, as we've seen. This chapter will therefore return to the problem of consciousness during the period, and it will do so with particular attention to how the experience of what something is like becomes attached to a discussion of reasons for acting. I will begin by discussing Locke's theory of action in the first edition, where all salient features of an agent's behavior may be understood from the outside and where the arc of any given action may be described in rigidly formal terms. I'll then show how this theory came under review in the Molyneux correspondence and how Locke placed the account featuring uneasiness into the second edition of 1694. I will close with some attention to the migration of Locke's category into the early novel, a genre sometimes concerned to attach what something is like with why things are done.

Action in the First Edition

Locke's theory of action is spelled out in the twenty-first chapter of book II of the *Essay*, entitled "Of Power."[1] "Every one," he there writes, "finds in himself a power to begin or forbear, continue or put an end to several Actions in himself."[2] What then causes a person to choose one action over another? In the first edition, the answer is plain: "Men are always determined by Good, the greater Good; and are constant, and in earnest, in matter of Happiness and Misery" (127). At bottom, everyone is moved to act by what they see as good for themselves, which, if they understood things correctly, would be exactly what society or God has chosen for them. At a first pass, the question of what causes an agent to choose one action over another has a simple and invariable answer. "If willing be but the being better pleased, as has been shewn," Locke argues, "it is easie to know what 'tis determines the Will" (123). "Good, then, the greater Good is that alone which determines the Will" (124). The trouble is that not all people are able to judge what is ultimately in their long-term interest, so while the wise choose to protect their souls for the afterlife, the foolish choose present pleasure over later rewards. This is not a problem of reckless desires overtaking reason. Rather, the source of the problem is the "*wrong Judgment* that *misleads us*, and makes the Will often fasten on the worse side" (127). When actions go astray and agents choose poorly, it is because of the "weak and narrow Constitutions of our Minds" (128). Not everyone's reason is able to calculate things correctly, and so often the good appears to be bad and the bad to be good. These kinds of mistakes happen most frequently "when we compare present Pleasure or Pain with future" and fail to see lasting torment in its proper light (127). Whether choosing well or poorly, however, the logical form of the action remains the same: one always uses reason when acting, even when reason provides the wrong sort of information.

Our fallible minds often leave us to predict consequences improperly and to neglect what is truly the greater of several goods or the lesser of two evils. The positive account lies in the contrasting situation, according to which the mind, after contemplating its options, prefers the object that really does present the greatest pleasure. Acting to acquire the greater good is, moreover, the foundation upon which agents join their individual wills to a moral order, whether that is the binding relations of civil society or the transcendent realm of the afterlife. "This is not an imperfection in Man, it is the highest perfection of intellectual Natures" because goodness, in the last instance, is always defined in terms of the "future state" of our souls (124).[3]

> To him, I say, who hath a prospect of the different State of perfect Happiness, or Misery that attends all Men after this Life, depending on their Behaviour here, the measures of Good and Evil that govern his choice, are mightily changed. For since nothing of Pleasure and Pain in this Life, can bear any proportion to the endless Happiness or exquisite Misery of an immortal Soul hereafter, Actions in his Power will have their preference, not according to the transient Pleasure, or Pain that accompanies, or follows them here; but as they serve to secure that perfect durable Happiness hereafter. (127)

Locke wants to argue that all reasonable people calmly incline toward the good. No one would choose eternal damnation over endless happiness, so acting wrongly must be the result of poorly executed calculation or dimness of vision. Practical reason alone is sufficient to guide one's behavior. The passage neither refers to the feelings elicited by the prospects of eternal reward or punishment nor seems to want to raise them in the prose. Flatness of style echoes a theory of action. This is especially remarkable given the role played here by pain and pleasure. Even though pain and pleasure are categories of experience, they are important for the story Locke tells as items one thinks about. One doesn't feel and then act. Rather, one calculates the duration and amplitude of future feelings, including those placed at the considerable distance of the afterlife. In other words, pain and pleasure enter into actions not as what we would now call qualia (instances of phenomenal consciousness) but rather as variables in a calculus. Molyneux will later criticize Locke's view as aridly mathematical, and it is not so hard to see why. In the first edition of the *Essay*, all actions may be expressed in formal terms as something like $P(Y) \rightarrow Q$: Agent P would like Q (pleasure in the afterlife). She believes that without Y (good behavior) there will be no Q. Therefore she Y's in view of getting Q. Given all the facts, all agents should come to the same decision. The pity is that not everyone ever has all the facts or can perform all the right calculations.

The mathematical nature of the theory becomes subject to extensive review in the second edition. In light of the changes that Locke will introduce, it is perhaps most important to observe that he deliberately leaves desire out of the causal structure. The word appears only once in the first version of chapter 21, in a dismissive (if revealing) attempt at lexical clarification. Locke is attempting to explain that freedom refers only to a lack of restraint:

> He that has his Chains knocked off, and the Prison-doors set open to him, is perfectly at liberty, because he may either go or stay, as he best likes; though his preference be determined to stay by the darkness of the

Night, or illness of the Weather, or want of other Lodging. He ceases not to be free; though that which at that time appears to him the greater Good absolutely determines his preference, and makes him stay in his Prison. I have rather made use of the Word *Preference* than *Choice*, to express the act of Volition, because choice is of a more doubtful signification, and bordering more upon Desire, and so is referred to things remote; whereas Volition, or the Act of Willing, signifies nothing properly, but the actual producing of something that is voluntary. (125)

The problem with desire is that it has no obvious relation to actions, not that it leads them astray. The prisoner may desire to leave his cell and yet not get up to go. Perhaps his desire to keep out of poor weather is greater or perhaps he has nowhere else to sleep. One might never know. At the very least, one could never read backward from his observable behavior to the litany of desires by which he may or may not have been beset. Even if we were to observe him making his choice and leaving the cell, the content of his desire would be remote. Maybe he wants to see the sun; maybe the kinks in his legs need a turn. Since Locke is concerned with the "actual producing of something that is voluntary" the existence or nonexistence of preceding desires clouds the issue. The mental state that issues into the "actual producing" of an action need only be described as a preference for its being done. An external view of the prisoner's behavior is therefore a complete view of his behavior. Seeing things from his vantage or coming to know the experience that accompanied his behavior is impossible or irrelevant or both.

Locke avoids the word "desire" because it is "remote" and therefore distinct from the more accessible idea of "preference." The prisoner left because he preferred to be out of his cell. He remained because he preferred to stay. Were we to substitute desire for preference in these two sentences, we would need some further information to understand the meaning. To get a sense of why Locke strains at this point—a seemingly baroque distinction between wanting and preferring—we need only turn to the particular definition he had provided for desire in the immediately preceding chapter on the passions. There he writes: "The uneasiness a Man finds in himself upon the absence of any thing, whose present enjoyment carries the *Idea* of Delight with it, is that we call *Desire*, which is greater or less, as that uneasiness is more or less vehement" (114). Our idea of desire is based in part on a certain feel, and without accounting for that feel we lack a sense of what desire is. There is no corresponding feeling for preference. To say that the prisoner prefers to stay in his cell is simply to observe that he has not left. To say that he desires to stay in his cell would make a claim about the uneasiness that the prisoner is experiencing, and the uneasiness of another person is "something remote." This close connection of the idea of desire with the feeling of uneasiness will prove to be significant. The two are flip sides of a single state of mind: desire names a relation to an object, uneasiness what that relation feels like. The more you want something, the more uneasy you feel. In the first edition, however, the proximity of desire to uneasiness seems to inhibit its use in the subsequent chapter on actions.⁴ Like other passions, desire is to be understood as a kind of affliction and therefore as a mode of passivity, one of the "Modifications or Tempers of Mind" that have no clear relation to what one does.⁵

Taken together, the account of desire in the chapter on the passions and the brief mention of desire in the chapter on actions form a tricky complement. The one links the term to the conscious feel of uneasiness; the other says that such feels have no role in a person's behavior, or at least none that are left over once we have finished saying how having a reason to do something derives from its being good for someone. The result is that Locke is left without a word to describe why something is done other than that one understands it to be the right thing to do. He therefore turns his attention to completed actions and away from the experience of choosing. In order to grasp the "actual production of something that is voluntary" we need not have any idea of what the experience of this production is *like*; we need only see that something has happened. One way of considering Locke's move away from this argument in the second edition is to say he discovers a causal role for the passions of the mind. Another would be to say that he switches from the record of something having happened to asking why the action was done. The following section watches these revisions as they begin to be worked out and offers a hypothesis about why they might have been introduced.

Molyneux's Problem

William Molyneux will forever be known for the question he posed Locke about perception: Imagine a blind man familiar with the shapes of cubes and spheres by touch. Were that man to be possessed of sight, and were he then to see a cube and a sphere placed at a distance, would he be able to distinguish the one from the other? Molyneux's problem attends to the role of experience in coming to know external objects. As we will see, the moral was that experience counts a great deal. Before looking at how this is so, and what it meant for a theory of actions, however, I want to place the question in the context of the correspondence in which it was asked.[6] For two years beginning in the summer of 1692, Locke and Molyneux exchanged letters concerning the chapter on actions, letters written, as Maurice Cranston put it, in "terms of unusual cordiality."[7] The correspondence began when Locke stumbled upon Molyneux's book *Dioptrica Nova* (1692) and read that "the incomparable Mr. Locke . . . in his *Essay Concerning Human Understanding*, has rectified more received mistakes, and delivered more profound truths, established on experience and observation, for the direction of man's mind in the prosecution of *knowledge* . . . than are to be met with in all the volumes of the Ancients."[8] In July 1692, Locke wrote to Molyneux that he was pleased that "those who can be extreme rigorous and exact in the search of truth, can be as civil and as complaisant in their dealing with those whom they take to be lovers of it."[9] Molyneux responded in August: "I find by Yours to Me, that My Ambition is not fallen short of its Designe;

But that you are pleased to Incourage me by assuring Me that I have made great Advances of Friendship towards you; Give me leave to Imbrace the Favour with all Joy Imaginable. And that you may Judge of my Sincerity by my Open Heart, I wil plainly confess to you, that I have not in my Life read any Book with More Satisfaction, than your Essay; Insomuch that a Repeated perusal of it is still more pleasant to Me" (507–8). Molyneux begins with crediting Locke for having drawn his truths from experience. Locke responds with pleasure to Molyneux's civility. Each makes reference to the joy of reading the other's work, the happiness in having become close friends, and the delight in collective thought. The letters also suggest that the experience of having such thoughts occurs in the vicinity of actions: in this case, joy accompanies advances, while pleasure comes with encouragement.

Elsewhere in the letters Locke is similarly vivid about what we might call the experience of his friendship or what it is like to read Molyneux and write to him in turn. "There are beauties of the mind, as well as of the body, that take and prevail at first sight," he writes, and "wherever I have met with this, I have readily surrender'd my self, and have never yet been deceived in my expectation" (522). The act of writing to Molyneux has a qualitative feel, an associated quality of experience.[10] Moreover, giving himself over to friendship is an acting out of feelings, in the sense that taking and prevailing pay no mind to a judgment of future pleasure or pain. Were this all there were to the correspondence, it might seem a bit of a stretch to involve the back-and-forth in an account of Locke's theory of action. Surely it is no great surprise that his "mathematical" approach was a bit messier when brought into the give and take of friendly exchange. The language of felt experience in the letters is relevant for the theory of actions, however, because it includes both a working through of the planned revisions and a presentation of the cubes and spheres problem. The feelings Molyneux and Locke write about coincide with a discussion of what feelings are useful for in the first place. "Wonder not," Locke writes, "if having been thus wrought on,

I begin to converse with you with as much freedom as if we had begun our acquaintance when you were in Holland; and desire your advice and assistance about a second edition of my Essay, the former being now dispersed" (522).[11] Molyneux responds in kind: "You are so desirous to Hear the sense of Others, you are so Tender in differing from any Man, that you have Captivated me beyond resistance" (648). Molyneux's advice and assistance will soon focus on chapter 21, but there's a sense in which the topic had already been broached. Each letter situates emotions in some sort of quasi-causal relation to actions. Locke says that asking for help, like deciding to be friends, is something "wrought on" by feelings. Molyneux says that Locke's wanting his opinion is a kind of sensitivity that draws his attention.

In the context of a theory of actions, this personal dimension implies that there is something that it is like for one writer to imagine the other and for both to consider revisions. The two writers thus enact the revisions they are in the process of considering. Consider how the first edition might account for its own revisions in contrast to the account provided by the correspondence. It would say that the appearance of a second edition in objective, printed, and public form completed and fully depicted the arc of revision. Locke's and Molyneux's experience would be irrelevant to the causal story and so nothing that needed to be explained or understood in order to have a full sense of how the second edition appeared. Anyone who noticed the change from the first to the second could simply stipulate the cause as the greater good (in this case, the good of correcting mistakes) and then no longer worry about the matter. And yet this account of the revisions would run counter to the story of actions the second edition turns out to contain. The second edition, as we will see, credits the experience of coming to act on something and tries to work such experience into a story about causation. Before tracking the way that the revisions are discussed by Locke and Molyneux and then put into the edition, therefore, it is worth considering how the question of experience crops up in the line of inquiry that would ensure Molyneux's lasting fame in the history of philosophy.

Molyneux had first posed his question to Locke in a letter sent after receiving a précis of the *Essay* published in Paris in 1688. He returns to the question in the midst of their later correspondence, where he closes the "tedious lines" of one letter with a "Jocose Problem":

> Suppose a Man born blind, and now adult, and taught by his Touch to Distinguish between a Cube and a Sphere (Suppose) of Ivory, nighly of the same Bignes, so as to tel, when he felt One and tother, Which is the Cube which the Sphere. Suppose then, the Cube and Sphære placed on a Table, and the Blind man to be made to see. Quære whether by his sight, before he touchd them, he could now Distinguish and tel which is the Globe which the Cube. (651)

The question takes up mind-world relations by asking what internal repertoire we bring to external objects and what information we gain from interacting with them. Could the mind abstract from the data of touch to fill in the absent data of sight? "Your ingenious problem will deserve to be published to the world," Locke responds, and then does just that in the second edition, where he poses the question to his readers (666).[12] In subsequent decades, Leibniz, Berkeley, Voltaire, Diderot, and others all take a crack at solving the problem.[13] The position one took on the thought experiment tended to coincide with the stance one had on innate ideas. Molyneux, Locke, and Berkeley, for example, all said that the newly sighted blind man would not be able to distinguish between the shapes because he lacked the sensory knowledge to recognize them at a distance. Leibniz said that the blind man would be able to combine reason with what he knew from touch to make the proper deduction. Can the formerly blind man tell the difference by sight? "I answer, Not," responds Molyneux, "for tho he has obtain the Experience of How a Globe, how a Cube affects his Touch. Yet he has not yet attain the Experience, that what affects my Touch so or so, must affect my Sight so or so; or that a Protuberant Angle in the Cube that presd his hand unequally, will appear to his Eye as it does in the Cube" (651). By seeing the objects in front of him, he learns something new. He learns what cubes and spheres look like, which is nothing he could have pieced together from secondhand reasoning on the basis of touch. The blind man suddenly possessed of sight will not be able to recognize the cubes and spheres he has previously touched because visual experience provides information that is additional to tactile experience. No amount of reasoning on the foundation of touch, on this account, may produce what it is like to see something.

One plausible reading of Molyneux's problem would be that the priority it places on experience indicates directions in which more traditionally literary genres will move: not only Pope's interest in the motives of Belinda and the Baron, but, more conventionally, the representation of mental states in works of prose fiction. I will have something to say about this development at the close of this chapter and will explore it at greater length in the two that follow. Another would be that it reintroduces the topic of consciousness that Locke was in the process of tackling elsewhere in the *Essay*. We may see some implications of this move by jumping ahead to our present-day interest in what I described earlier as the hard problem of consciousness. I'll consider this connection now. One influential articulation of the hard problem comes by way of a famous thought experiment in Frank Jackson's 1982 article "Epiphenomenal Qualia." The thought experiment has come to be known as "Mary the color scientist," or simply "the Mary problem," and it has distinct similarities with Molyneux's question to Locke.

> Mary is a brilliant scientist who is, for whatever reason, forced to investigate the world from a black and white room *via* a black and white television monitor. She specialises in the neurophysiology of vision and acquires, let us suppose, all the physical information there is to obtain about what goes on when we see ripe tomatoes, or the sky, and use terms like "red," "blue," and so on. She discovers, for example, just which wave-length combinations from the sky stimulate the retina, and exactly how this produces *via* the central nervous system the contrac-

tion of the vocal chords and expulsion of air from the lungs that results in the uttering of the sentence "The sky is blue." . . . What will happen when Mary is released from her black and white room or is given a colour television monitor? Will she *learn* anything or not?[14]

Jackson's question is a rough updating of Molyneux's in the sense that he wants to know whether one can ever anticipate the kind of knowledge gained from conscious experience. Although Mary already knew everything there is to know about the neuroscience of perceiving blue, the first-person experience of blue is wholly new to her. Does this experience add something to the third-person, objective science of color perception, or does it merely repeat what Mary already knows? Jackson's answer is like Molyneux's. "It seems just obvious that she will learn something about the world and our visual experiences of it. But then it is inescapable that her previous knowledge was incomplete."[15] Jackson's conclusion shares with Molyneux's and Locke's an emphasis on conscious experience. The first-person experience of color provides information that the third-person, physical analysis of color cannot provide. One cannot acquire a conscious experience of one thing based on the experience of something else. Where Jackson differs from Molyneux and Locke is on the question of mental causation. He argues that since qualia cannot be explained in physical terms they consequently have no causal role to play in physical activity.[16] As we shall see, Molyneux and Locke draw the opposite conclusion. The point of their thought experiment for my current purposes is that it draws consciousness into the question of actions. Molyneux will want to know why agents take one or another action. Something is lost, he thinks, if we do not phrase this in terms of the conscious experience of the agent.

Molyneux designs his thought experiment to show that sensory perception provides knowledge that cannot be gotten by reason or intuition alone.[17] It is not simply the case that agents may deduce the shape of things from the facts gathered by other senses, as there will always be some further feature that is left out of the description. This further feature is what Molyneux calls "experience," or the discovery of what some object, event, or action is like. In light of this argument, it is not much of a surprise that Molyneux puts some pressure on the theory of actions he found in the first edition of the *Essay*. In his first letter, he asks Locke to expand on the notion that choosing to do something might be "Demonstrable according to the Mathematical Method" (508). The trouble with this method, he thinks, is that it expresses behavior as a relation among variables. If every *P* does *Y* in view of *Q*, there is little to bind or modify the meaning of each. Proper names for example would seem to require an expression as integers rather than variables. Were we to formalize Eve eating the apple we would want her to remain constant, as say 1 or 0 or 3. We would want this in order to have some way of entering what it was like for her into the equation. What did the apple taste like? Was she hungry? On this view, Locke's method in the first edition lacks a specific account of the experience that went along with and led into any one action.

Molyneux does not attempt to rewrite Locke's chapter, but he does ask him to clarify how its "wonderfully fine spun" account of agency is supposed to work.[18] Locke had written that reasons may always be discerned from the outside as the greater good of the agent. Should a person act in a hurtful manner that is because she has mistaken what is really good for her, in much the same way as another person might make a slip in long division. Experience provides no salient information here because what choosing an action is like is distinct from why the action was performed. For Molyneux this is a bit like telling the blind man he is at fault for not discriminating between cubes and spheres; "[Y]ou seem to make all Sins to proceed from our Understandings," he says to Locke; "Now it seems harsh to say, that a Man shall be Damn'd, because he understands no better than he does" (601).

Locke's response is not so much to explain the position of the first edition as to promise a thorough revision along the lines that Molyneux suggests. "I got into a new view of things," he writes

during the summer of 1693, "which, if I mistake not, will satis-
fie you, and give a clearer account of humane freedom than hith-
erto I have done" (700). He then lists twelve new sections, couched
among which are some startling assertions: "Uneasiness determines
the will"; "Desire determines the will"; "desire is an uneasiness";
and "the greater good in view barely consider'd determines not
the *will*. The joys of heaven are often neglected" (700).[19] No more
complete revision could have been announced. Once remote and
inaccessible realms of the mind, desire and uneasiness now supply
the very explanation of behavior. As if to underscore the new commitment to Molyneux's view, Locke follows the section of his letter titled "The greatest present uneasiness usually determines will"
with "as is evident in experience" (700). One can get a sense of the
role played by desire simply by introspection. Reflect on your experience of acting and you will recollect some antecedent feeling of
uneasiness. "This short scheme," Locke closes, "may perhaps give
you so much light into my present hypothesis, that you will be able
to judge of the truth of it, which I beg you to examine by your own
mind" (701).

The call to examine one's experience raises an interesting distinction between Locke's two new categories. One can only introspect
on uneasiness, not on desire considered as a formal relation. In
other words, Locke outlines something like a double-aspect view of
action, according to which desire determines the will when considered as a kind of function (*P* wants *Q*), and uneasiness determines
the will when considered as an experience. This view becomes clear
in his last letter on the topic, in which he again presents an outline
of his revisions to the chapter. Included in the letter is the following
tricky sentence: "That which in the train of our voluntary actions
determines the will to any change of operation, is some present
uneasiness, which is, or at least is always accompanyed with that
of desire" (722). Locke's categories strain to be pulled apart. He
defines desire in terms of the causal role it plays in behavior and
uneasiness in terms of the felt experience of desire. At the same time,

he attempts to run the two together and say that the experience performs the causal role because it is desire. Almost as an afterthought,
he then clarifies that what we might call the phenomenal and the
functional dimensions to wanting are separate aspects of mind, and
so uneasiness is "always accompanyed" by desire.[20]

If Molyneux was puzzled to see the argument turned toward experience, he might have been equally intrigued to see the word "uneasiness" raised to such prominence. Locke never defines the word in the
letters and gives no clue of its derivation. Whereas "desire" appeared
in the first version of chapter 21 as something "doubtful" and
"remote," "uneasiness" was not in the first version of the chapter at
all.[21] It is only when the experiential side of actions comes to Locke's
attention that a term needs to be invented or called upon to name
what desire feels like. One further feature promised to Molyneux
complicates this process, however. Desire determines the will, Locke
says, but at the same time is subject to an as yet unspecified rule of
reason: "The greatest uneasiness does not always determine the will,
because we can suspend the execution of our desires" (701). Locke
will eventually spend many pages, over years of revision, attempting
to identify the precise relation between the desire that causes actions
and the reason that monitors them. At this point, he merely suggests
that a free agent is one who acts on desires "guided by his own judgment" (722). The mathematical method has not entirely receded, as
Locke suggests that we have the ability to guide or even suspend
desire at the same time that we experience desire as uneasiness. How
this is so awaits the second edition.

Action in the Second Edition

When the second edition of the *Essay* appeared in 1694, the chapter "Of Power" was nearly twice as long, containing twenty-six new
sections and, as was promised to Molyneux, had an entirely new
thesis. The opening discussion of the will and the concluding discussion of judgment and the future state remain (although with several

important modifications), while the middle section on the "greater good" is replaced by a longer reflection on desire. The changes Locke introduces early on in the chapter are subtly indicative of the larger transformation to come. The 1690 version of section 5 defines the will as follows: "[We] find in our selves a Power to begin or forbear, continue or end several, Thoughts of our Minds, and Motions of our Bodies, barely by the choice or preference of our Minds. This Power the Mind has to prefer the Consideration of any *Idea*, to the not considering it; or to prefer the Motion of any part of the Body, to its Rest, is that, I think, we call the *Will*" (117). The 1694 version is the same up until the final clause of the first sentence, where it reads, "barely by a *thought* or preference of the mind ordering, or as it were commanding the doing or not doing such or such a particular action."[22] The second sentence is also revised and expanded, and now reads: "This power which the mind has, thus to order the consideration of any *Idea*, or the forbearing to consider it; or to prefer the motion of any part of the body to its rest, and *vice versâ* in any particular instance is that we call the *Will*" (125–6). As Locke rewrites himself, the prose takes a dilatory form uncharacteristic of the first edition: each sentence wrangles into a multiple devolution of subordinate clauses. The style bears the weight of the revision. Locke appears to burrow within the prose, to slip one clause behind another, in order to say that mental states and attitudes have a causal role to play in a person's activity. Even as the sentences seem to buckle, however, the point is to secure a sense of order. The effect is a tension between content and form, as Locke attempts to show that we have the power to control our actions, and don't merely "prefer" things but rather "order" or "command" them.

Locke soon makes clear that the turn away from preference is to desire and so to an aspect of mind assiduously avoided in the first edition. The shift occurs across sections 29 through 47, each of which is entirely new to the chapter. What is it that "*determines the Will in regard to our Actions*"? For any reader of the first edition apart from Molyneux, the response would be staggering: "[U]pon second thoughts, I am apt to imagine [it] is not, as is generally supposed, the greater good in view: But some (and for the most part the most pressing) uneasiness a Man is at present under: This is that which successively determines the *Will*, and sets us upon those Actions, we perform. This Uneasiness we may call, as it is *Desire*" (134).[23] Whereas the first edition had described preferring as a rational calculation of future pleasure and pain, this new view describes desire as a feeling of uneasiness, the most intensely felt episode of which sets an agent upon some act. Like the opening sentences on the will, that is, Locke's "second thoughts" range over the mind's causal powers only to settle on the role played by conscious feeling.[24] "Good & Evil; present & absent, 'tis true, work upon the mind: But that which immediately determines the *Will*, from time to time to every voluntary action is the uneasiness of *desire*, fixed on some absent good" (134–5). We may call uneasiness desire because it is a feeling that both accompanies and initiates the doing of something. Locke not only says that desire has a certain kind of feel, in other words, he says that this feel is an ineliminable part of acting. In some cases, good or bad qualities may line up with an action, but only the strongest feeling of uneasiness *determines* the will.

To see the causal burden placed on experience we need only look again at how Locke revises himself. In both editions, section 29 attempts to answer the all-important question, "what is it that determines the will." The two editions provide revealingly different answers. Here is the first edition:

> Now because Pleasure and Pain are produced in us, by the operation of certain Objects, either on our Minds, or our Bodies; and in different degrees: therefore what has an aptness to produce pleasure in us, is that we labour for, and is that we call Good; and what is apt to produce pain in us, we avoid and call *Evil*. . . . For the cause of every less degree of Pain, as well as every greater degree of Pleasure, has the nature of Good, and *vice versa*, and is that which determines our Choice, and challenges our Preference. *Good* then, *the greater Good is that alone which determines the Will*. (124)

The nature of the good lies outside the mind, in objects that are apt to cause pain or apt to cause pleasure. Preferring to do one thing or another results from a calculation of the experience these objects will yield, either immediately or at some later moment, perhaps even in the afterlife. The greater good is thus both a contingent estimation, subject to error, and something that lies outside of us, with lasting consequences for our happiness. In either case, the good has a causal role with respect to our actions. Here is the second edition, entirely rewritten:

> To the Question, what is it that determines the Will? The true and proper Answer is, The mind; For that which determines the general power of directing, to this or that particular direction, is nothing but the Agent it self Exercising the power it has, that particular way. If this Answer satisfie not, 'tis plain the meaning of the Question, *what determines the Will?* is this, What moves the mind, in every particular instance, to determine its general power of directing, to this or that particular Motion or Rest? And to this I answer, the motive, for continuing in the same State or Action, is only the present satisfaction in it; The motive to change, is always some uneasiness; nothing setting us upon the change of State, or upon any new Action, but some uneasiness. This is the great motive that works on the Mind to put it upon Action, which for shortness sake we will call *determining of the Will*. (133)

The new version begins with a dramatic turnaround from an order of objects to the mind, as if the mind were able to spring a wanting of this or that thing entirely from its own resources. As the section continues, however, Locke makes it clear that he is not concerned with all of mental life but rather has narrowed his focus to conscious experience and to the particular version of experience he has named uneasiness. Posed this way, the mind-world gap announced in the first new sentence gradually lessens its hold. Since uneasiness is a feeling possessed in response to circumstances, the revision in its favor attempts to place experience into an order of causes that includes "the mind" along with other parts of the world. The question is how and why does uneasiness lead to actions of various kinds.[25]

Locke's most curious moves at the end of the chapter might be explained by this attempt to locate uneasiness among the world's various causes. I've drawn attention in earlier chapters to the difficulty that writers of the period had in fastening down the exact procedures in which the mind *causes* events in the world to happen. We saw in Locke's use of hand movement, for example, that he takes the causal role to be a "matter of fact" yet one completely beyond the reach of his understanding, perhaps one of the great mysteries of nature. The recourse to uneasiness addresses this complicated relation to causation. We may never know the exact procedures by which a mental event like wanting to move his hand results in a physical event like the movement of his hand. That is, we may never know at the ultimate level of "the peculiar Constitution of Bodies, and the Configuration of Parts, whereby they have the power to produce in us *Ideas* of their sensible Qualities" (2nd ed., 152).[26] We may get some sense, however, of how this sort of causation happens at the higher-order level of "sensible qualities" like uneasiness. This is a tricky point worth some consideration. When Locke entertains the fundamental question of how matter can think, whether atoms give rise to experience and the like, he tends to argue that the answer is inaccessible.[27] Higher-order properties of thought and experience, in contrast, are available through introspection and language. Therefore we should look at "sensible qualities" like uneasiness to see what sort of role the mind plays in the production of behavior.

Locke would remain within a causal understanding of behavior, in other words, without leaving the more tractable bounds of the mind. The virtue of uneasiness is that it explains why an agent did one thing rather than another. And yet rather than make agents captive to their feelings, Locke wants to show how we have the "power to suspend the prosecution of this or that desire, as every one dayly may Experiment in himself" (2nd ed., 141). Everyone can recall moments of suspending desires, for everyone has used reason to judge the future consequences of present behavior. Why does this not contradict Locke's new view that actions may be explained by uneasiness alone? Having spent so much time dismissing the role of judgment, why does he come back to it in the end? Nearing the end of his life, Locke returned to chapter 21 for one last revision, published in the fifth and posthumous edition of 1706. The revision consisted of two new sentences that address this very concern: "[A] Man may suspend the Act of his Choice from being determined for or against a thing proposed, 'till he has examined, whether it be really of a Nature in its self and Consequences to make him happy or no. For when he has once chosen it, and thereby it is become a part of his Happiness, it raises Desire, and that proportionably gives him Uneasiness, which determines his *Will*, and sets him at work."[28] At any moment, an agent examines her circumstances and responds with unease; the greatest unease leads her to act. In this respect, the final version of the chapter aims to accommodate both the existence of competing desires and a certain kind of externalism. When Locke comes back to judgment, that is, he draws attention to the environment in which actions occur. One uneasiness is separate from another and one finally greater than another according to factors that lie outside the head: the properties of one object or another, the effects of one doing or another. The upshot of the final revision then is soberly to fasten down procedures of judging one desire from another and at the same time to fold actions into the rest of the world.

So how are we to understand Locke's revised theory of actions in light of the concerns traced thus far in this book? One way to do so might be to say that he examines the conscious dimensions to behavior and lands at the end with a relatively intricate model in which various desires compete for the will. This description would of course need some further clarification and elaboration for it to account for how Locke arrives at his final theory or for it to point to the avenues left open for subsequent readers. According to this theory, a certain experience accompanies and elicits all acts of the will. There is something that it feels like to want something, a kind of background drone of uneasiness. At the same time, this feeling both responds to external objects and leads into the doing of things; it causes actions to happen. These are two prongs of the argument that need not have been related. One could imagine Locke arguing that reasons for acting have a specific feel to them without holding the opinion that such feelings enter into or cause actions. Rochester makes such a point before Locke, and Jackson makes such a point after. Uneasiness would on this view be a kind of by-product or complement to actions, like (once again) the mist off a lake. Locke draws the two together with considerable effort, across more than one series of revisions. There was something that it is like for Eve to eat the apple or for the Baron to cut the lock *and* this something actually played a causal role in the actions themselves.

Consciousness both accompanies and leads into actions. This dual approach is in keeping with what we've seen from Locke thus far. Not only does the argument about personal identity rest on consciousness rather than on bodies, as we saw in Chapter 2, but the part of the *Essay* in which Locke makes this clear was also *added* to the 1694 edition. So there's reason to link the two additions through a set of related concerns around action, responsibility, and experience. Locke would like to bring together his idea that personal identity derives from consciousness with his idea that consciousness leads into actions. There is no reason to assume, however, that this interest in consciousness meant a commitment to what some have represented as a kind of partition of the self from the world on which it acts.[29] Locke's theory of consciousness was his own intricate contribution to the compatibilism of Hobbes, Hume, and the like. Like Hobbes, for example, Locke dismisses the idea of a will free to place its mark on things. "It is as insignificant to ask, whether a Man's Will be free," he writes in both editions, "as to ask, whether his Sleep be Swift, or his Vertue square" (1st ed., 119; 2nd ed., 128). Free will is incoherent because the will is a power to execute one's desires and not the kind of thing that could be free in the first place.[30] Freedom refers to a lack of constraint, not to the ability to choose or do otherwise. Locke's views are in these respects in keeping with the larger compatibilist account of how desires are continuous with external objects and events. The novelty of Locke's position is the effort he takes to distinguish the phenomenal from the formal aspects of desire. What do reasons for acting feel like? Why do we have these reasons in the first place? And how can a physical thing have feelings in the first place? These are exceedingly difficult questions to answer, but they explore on the one hand how consciousness leads into actions and on the other how consciousness takes shape from the environment. I will explore in the next section and then at greater length in the two chapters that follow the kinds of avenues they open up for writers in more representational genres. I want to stress in closing this section, however, that writers take the insight in various directions—toward the bustling world of commerce and sociability or into the realm of intention and deliberation—some do this even within the same work.

A Coda on Uneasiness

When Locke tried to come up with a word that would describe what desire felt like, he decided not to draw on ancient categories of anxiety but rather to employ a term from the seventeenth-century vernacular. While uneasiness has no particular legacy in theological or philosophical writing, it appeared widely in other genres familiar to Locke. We know from his letters, for example, that Locke was a reader of romances, at least in his youth. In his correspondence from the 1650s and 1660s he makes reference to two works by Gaultier de Coste, seigneur de La Calprenède, *La Cleapatre* (1646–47), translated into English by Richard Loveday in 1652–59, and *Cassandre* (1642–45), translated by Charles Cotterell in 1651.[31] He and his friends also had the habit of corresponding under romance pseudonyms, like Atticus, Scribelia, and Urania.[32] During his reading of *Cassandre* he would have encountered this routine description of Prince Cassander's behavior around Queen Statira: "[In] all his actions hee shewed a disquietness which could not proceed only from his zeal, and fidelitie to his King. When hee was near her, his eies were perpetually fixt upon her face, but 'twas with troubles and distractions of minde, which took away part of his understanding."[33] The "disquietness" described in this scene—later translated to "uneasiness"—is a passive state of mild suffering, an ordinary moment in the texts Locke read as a student.[34] If Locke had picked up Aphra Behn's *History of the Nun* (1688) several decades later, he would have encountered a more tempestuous description of uneasiness in the novel's account of how the young Henault trembled with desire for Isabella: "[He] would blush, and burn, and pant with uneasiness . . . . And he would check this Uneasiness in himself, and ask his Heart, what it meant, by rising and beating in those Moments, and strive to assume an Indifferency in vain."[35] Without looking at the details of Behn's story, we may simply observe that uneasiness here names what it is like to desire something or someone and provides an indication that major events in the novel will soon happen. For Locke as for Behn, desire *feels* like uneasiness. The philosopher and novelist alike turn to a certain language of phenomenal experience in the tracking down of the antecedents to action.

One can trace a similar project in Catharine Trotter, a writer I turn to in concluding this chapter because she brings together the empirical and the fictional accounting for actions in a single career. Between the first and second editions of Locke's *Essay*, Trotter published the epistolary novel *The Adventures of a Young Lady*, a loosely told story of the various loves of Olinda written to her friend Cleander. Nine years later she published *A Defence of the Essay of Human Understanding by Mr. Lock*. Given what we know of Trotter's later writing, we may imagine that she was reading Locke when she wrote *The Adventures*, and given what we know of Locke's early reading habits, it is not impossible that he read the letters when they were published.[36] The first letter begins with a weary entreaty: "I hope I need not tell you how uneasie this tedious Absence makes me; for I must confess as troublesome as I find it, and as much as I Value you, I can't but wish you may be able to guess at it by what you suffer your self."[37] Olinda asks Cleander to look inside himself in order to understand what she is now feeling. These are, she says, "uneasie hours" (21). She then takes advantage of the letter form to write down the experience of uneasiness as a new feeling of wanting. Here is one letter in which such coming into knowledge is given a vivid turn. Deceived into believing that her suitor Cloridon has forsaken her for someone else, Olinda becomes rather more troubled than she would have expected. "I found myself seiz'd with an unusual I knew not what" (65).

> As soon as I was alone, I examin'd my self upon the matter. Why shou'd this trouble me (said I within myself) who wou'd not entertain his Love, when it was offer'd me, and I have often Resolv'd never to see him, even when I thought him Constant? How comes it then, that I am so Griev'd and Angry that he loves another? And that I wish with such impatience for his Return? In fine, I discover'd that what I had call'd Esteem and Gratitude was Love; and I was as much asham'd of the Discovery, as if it had been known to all the World. I fancy'd every one that saw me, Read it in my Eyes: And I hated my self, when Jealousie would give me leave to Reason, for my extravagant thoughts and wishes. (66)

Olinda is not unlike Mary presented with color or the sighted blind man viewing spheres and cubes. Presented with the new experience of love, she learns what the passion is like. No amount of advice could prepare her for the feeling; thus she "knew not what" had seized her. The strategy of the letter is to present her mulling over of the associated qualia in close proximity to their occurrence. She knew not what but would like to tell us (through the proxy of Cloridon) what she learned. The effort to reproduce qualia takes the form of a switch of tense and a feigning of internal monologue. The "said I to myself" is in the past tense, while the internal speech is, logically enough, in the present: why should this, how comes it? One imagines this flip into a rushing present tense is as close as Olinda can get to the raw feel of uneasiness. The turning of the experience outward then gets a bit heated when she blurs the line between coming to know her feelings and what she imagines as the observation of these feelings by the rest of the world. As she slides back into a past-tense recollection of her new experience, the content of the letter reflects on its form, as if by revealing her love she has made it visible not only to Cloridon but also to everyone else (which of course she has).

I'd like to think about this letter in two ways. Trotter tries out forms to represent conscious experience and so encounters a problem of describing what it was like for her character to have her series of thoughts. As if to highlight the achievement, Trotter comes up with her version of the Molyneux or Mary problem. What would happen to a young woman in love for the first time? Would she learn something new or would her observation of other people's actions teach her all she would have to understand? It so happens that Olinda "knew not what" and thus added to her repertoire of knowledge. Trotter wants to show that Olinda learns something new; she wants to present this learning as best she can. Both amount to a kind of experiment. Near the end of the experiment, the qualia at issue become quite involved. Olinda comes to realize her new feelings are love and then worries that everyone else can see them. To her first new experience she thus adds a second one: the experience of worrying about the experience. This process of recognition and worry could conceivably go on and on (oops, they realize that I realize they see I'm in love, and so forth). Such seems to be the logical consequence of Olinda's coming to an awareness that her behavior is an outcome of her experience and that people might try to reason backward from what she is doing to what she is feeling. The miracle is that such highly involved mental representations can serve as causes of action in the same way as the objects they represent.

Trotter continues to consider this question of the boundary between representations and their external referents in her subsequent writing. When, for example, she endeavored to support Locke against his critics several years later, she returned specifically to a trio of concerns around representations, consciousness, and actions from the vantage of an established theory. "Whatever we can know at all," Trotter argues, "must be discoverable by Mr. *Lock*'s Principles; For I cannot find any other way to Knowledge, or that we have any one Idea not derived from Sensation and Reflection."[38] "Sensation and Reflection," she continues, allow one "to know things are as they are, appear, as they appear, and that doing a thing, differs from not doing it, that an Apple, for Example is not a Horse, that Pain, is not Pleasure, and that performing our Promise is not breaking it" (24). Writing in the manner of a defense, Trotter quickly combines an account of mind and the account of agency. All ideas derive from experience. Included among these must be the "Motives of our Actions," the ideas that lead to "Doing, Willing, or Chusing" (8). Trotter's point is that we come to acquire our conceptual and ethical stock through interaction with the environment; therefore having a concept like "apple" is not so different from having a motive, like "wanting to eat an apple" or having a belief, like "it's good to keep promises."

Trotter's polemical style unites in a single stroke the having of ideas and the making use of them. To be able to think "apple" is to be able to form ideas about eating them and about why it might be good to share with those who are hungry. At the same time, Trotter adds to these functional notions of representation and action the further feature of conscious experience. "Whatever Substance there is without *Consciousness*," she writes in a quick defense of Locke's categories, "there is no *Person* . . . and no farther than the same Consciousness extends, can there be the same Person" (29).[39] Persons are in this respect not unlike letter series: collections of consecutive and causally arranged experiences, like the crisp bite of an apple or the redness of its skin. "I am thinking," Trotter writes, "of a Horse; his Beauty, Strength, and Usefulness: Does this thought preserve in my mind, the Idea of a Church, of Happiness or Misery?" (33–4). Or are these things pushed out by new ideas? Because I still have the idea of a church somewhere in my mind when I think about a horse, she continues, or because I can preserve the idea of happiness when I think of an apple, I am able to string different ideas into single thoughts. And because some of my thoughts come with uneasiness, I choose to take one step or another. I'm the sort of thing that might write letters and have adventures.

Reading Trotter alongside Locke thus brings us to a cluster of categories and forms: experience, persons, uneasiness, actions, narratives, letters, and consciousness. The cluster will look different depending on the story one wants to tell. Perhaps Trotter uses the form of the letter to explore what it is like to ponder events and be a person; perhaps she calls upon empirical philosophy to help craft the epistolary novel at an early moment of its genesis. The story I would tell concerns the appearance of uneasiness as a category of feeling across separate genres interested in the antecedents to action. Trotter's philosophy, like her fiction, understands persons to be agents in narratives and provides a language and form for connected experience. How would this fill in the work of the *Essay* as Locke imagined it? Locke's revisions suggested that one cannot really form a complete picture of actions until one comes to understand the feelings that lead into them: the uneasiness that accompanies desire. The next two chapters will follow separate attempts to account for and locate these antecedents to action. The first will examine a case of one novel's intriguingly externalist model of action, elaborated around no less compelling a topic than erotic consent. The second (and last) will look at an elaborately staged crossing between this view and several others in a novel that doesn't so much take a position on things as let stand the important differences of the age.

5   Haywood and Consent

Few words cut so neatly across social and intimate relations as consent, a category central to modern democracy and sexuality alike. One consents to be governed or taxed, to have sex or marry, and in so doing one yields to an outside entity or another person, at least for as long as consent lasts. Anything else would be injustice or a crime, a violation of deeply held ideas of political rights and personal autonomy. The assumptions that lie beneath these ideas are sometimes hard to see, precisely because they are so foundational for modern living. It is difficult to imagine existing in a social or sexual order that is not founded on consent, on a willingness to be governed or to partner with other people. But what kind of mental state is consent, and what kind of action is consenting? The question bedeviled seventeenth- and eighteenth-century writers because it tested the ability to understand how thoughts could be revealed in practice. To argue that the political order ought to be founded on the consent of the governed assumes that one can grasp the eagerness of a people to be ruled. Similarly, to argue that marriage or sex should be voluntary assumes that one can understand what passes in someone else's mind (or in one's own). And yet in either case, the internal state of consent may only be inferred from outward signs and actions.

The problem of consent is, in this respect, one way to focus the concerns around action that have preoccupied this book from the beginning. For example, no concept might seem more immune to external shaping. The meaning of consent would seem to depend solely on qualities of the mind. But as it happens, the situation on the ground of usage is more complicated. Just when we expect to proceed from mental states to the world they inhabit, we find ourselves moving in the opposite direction. Actions are things one sees, while states of mind can only be surmised. How wrong then are our intuitions about consent in the period? After all, government based on the consent of the governed, as it is devised in Locke and elsewhere, seems to invoke a psychology of individual agency as the ground of political authority. Marriage and sex based on the voluntary wishes of both partners, as they become foundations of the modern novel, seem to turn into matters of psychological as well as narrative intrigue. It would be hard to deny, in other words, that liberal theory and the early novel draw upon and help to create a language in which the internal deliberations that feed into acts of consent may be articulated with appropriate weight and significance. Yet this chapter will do just that. Sort of. I will look at a particular problem in some works of philosophy and fiction: in order to know whether someone has consented, one must understand what someone is thinking, and in order get a sense of what someone is thinking, one needs to examine closely what someone is doing. Once thoughts move into actions, they become part of the world of objects and events. So for some the process of representing consent was in equal parts a rendering of mental states on the page and a close look at the forms and locations of behavior. Sometimes the two got interestingly confused. I'll begin with the canonical treatment of consent in Locke's *Essay Concerning Human Understanding* and *Second Treatise* and then move to two now familiar novels by Eliza Haywood, *Love in Excess* (1719) and *Fantomina* (1725).[1] Haywood provides something of a case study of the language of consent as well as notions of mind and mental states in eighteenth-century fiction. However, the case is intriguingly oblique. One reason that criticism has been so drawn to the kind of novels Haywood wrote, I'll argue, is that they present consent and related states precisely where we might not expect to find them.

The Consent of the Governed

The language of consent appears early on in the *Essay Concerning Human Understanding*, when Locke attempts to locate the provenance of moral virtue. We have no innate ideas of how to act morally, Locke argues; simply look at the world around you, and you will see that is so: "[T]he Actions of Men are the best Interpreters of their thoughts," and "since it is certain, that most Men's Practice . . . have either questioned or denied" the moral principles alleged to be common to them, it is "impossible to establish an universal consent . . . without which, is it impossible to conclude them innate."[2] Were we to find a common adherence to a set of principles, we should call that adherence consent. Looking at human action, however, it appears that no such consent exists. There are too many "Outlaws and Robbers" and too much "Fraud and Rapine" for there to be some universal consent to a set of moral truths in the minds of humans (66, 67). Considering the importance of the term in Locke's political philosophy, this use in the *Essay* is somewhat curious, especially since it is meant to show that consent to innate moral ideas does not exist. Were such consent to exist, it would hover somewhere between an idea one has and an act one performs. One would possess an innate idea of, or disposition toward, certain moral truths (kindness to strangers, not killing or stealing). At the same time, this possession would be manifest in one's active agreement to a set of behaviors. The result is a dual legacy. Consent is what we bring to relations with other people or abstract institutions and is perceivable in what we do.

Locke's account of consent in the *Essay* is in this respect an attempt to peel back the layers of men's actions to access what does or does not exist in their thoughts. If men were to consent to a set of principles, their consent would be readable in their behavior. Since their actions violate these principles, we can assume that there is no consent in their minds. The nature of this assumption reveals something important about the status of consent as a kind of mental state. One could not, after all, easily make this claim about all states of mind. Were one to watch "Outlaws" and "High-way-men" at work one couldn't, for example, infer automatically what beliefs or desires they possess (66). Consider an outlaw we observe stealing a purse of money. Perhaps he feels above the law; perhaps he is opposed to private property. There is no way to get to the belief just from the action (or the desire, for that matter; perhaps he wants money, perhaps he thinks the purse is pretty). One thing the action does clarify, however, is that the outlaw has not consented to the principle that it is wrong to steal. In other words, our observation of his action has yielded some knowledge of one mental state (consent) but not another (belief/desire). On Locke's view, consent is rather unique in being so situated. Not only do we lack access to the beliefs connected to the theft, but it is likely that the outlaw has all sorts of other beliefs seemingly unrelated to the theft at all. He may believe that carrots taste better than potatoes or that rain on Tuesdays brings luck on Thursdays. One cannot make analogous statements about consent. Try to create a sentence about consent unrelated to an external set of facts and you will be baffled. "'Tis very strange and unreasonable," Locke writes, "to suppose innate practical Principles, that terminate only in Contemplation" (67). It is strange because, unlike other mental states, consent has no meaning apart from the "Conformity of Action" it produces (67). To ask if a person has consented is to inquire into her mental states, but it is also to place these states in "Operation" with something else (67). One consents *to* something or someone. In so doing, one also brings one's consent to something or someone. Consent is intimate and personal, on Locke's view, even as it is not something that exists prior to any singular application. One does not consent and then enter in relations with others. One consents *as* one is in relations with others.[3]

This dual nature of consent is especially significant in the political writing, including the influential discussion in the *Second Treatise of Government* (1690). However, one important difference here comes into play. In the *Essay*, the treatment of consent focuses on the absence of a mental state, in order to prove the nonexistence of innate ideas. In the *Second Treatise*, the argument moves to show the existence of consent in certain kinds of political and social relations. Locke's goal is to figure out how one might prove that agents have agreed to the authority of the polity in which they live. He begins with the ubiquitous and comparatively simple relation between persons and money. Experience shows that not all agents have consented to a code of moral behavior. But experience also shows that all agents have consented to the value of money. No one would say that a certain coin isn't worth a certain bundle of goods. But how did this sort of consent come to be, and what is its structure? Locke answers this question through a kind of historical sociology: it is part of our uneasy character, he argues, to labor and create things out of nature. Over time, this activity leads to the founding of states and societies. Industry mixes labor with the natural world, and thus creates private property.[4] Private property increases the general store of goods and improves the land of a nation but needs a state for its protection. Rather ominously, the chapter on property ends with the notion that all men have agreed to the "inequality of private possessions" because they have agreed to find value in money. Since money does not spoil, it may be amassed in great quantity, which leads finally to the "disproportionate and unequal *possession of the earth*" (29).

Some have plenty while others have none, and it is one task of the state to ensure that this is always the case. In what sense, however, have men consented to the value of money? Clearly no one ever quite says that a certain coin will be worth a certain figure. One need not do so because the consent is contained in the practice. We use money and therefore accede to its expression of value. The turn to the actual existence of consent in the *Second Treatise* thus marks a further change from the model of thinking in the *Essay*. While the *Essay* tends to focus on mental states one experiences, and goes so far as to say that all thinking must be conscious, the *Second Treatise* makes a contrary move and pays primary attention to mental states that are implicit. This is Locke's influential notion of *tacit consent*:

> But since gold and silver, being little useful to the life of man in proportion to food, raiment, and carriage, has its *value* only from the consent of men . . . it is plain, that men have agreed to a disproportionate and unequal *possession of the earth*, they having, by a tacit and voluntary consent, found out a way how a man may fairly possess more land than he himself can use the product of, by receiving in exchange for the overplus gold and silver, which may be hoarded up without injury to any one. . . . This partage of things in an inequality of private possessions, men have made practicable out of the bounds of society, and without compact, only by putting a value on gold and silver, and tacitly agreeing in the use of money. (29–30)

By participating in a money economy, we consent to the capacity of money to express value; and, once we consent to the value of money, we also consent to a society of unequal wealth and power. Yet one never declares an agreement that a pound is worth a basket of goods or writes down a commitment to inequality. It is likely that one never thinks too much about such things. Rather, one's behavior reveals a tacit consent to forms of exchange and systems of inequality and so validates both. Money extrudes thought into practice, and consent dissolves into the welter of daily life.

The further we read in the *Second Treatise*, the more we realize that Locke builds his model of political legitimacy on this notion of unspoken and implied consent. A just government, he famously argues, takes its authority from the consent of the governed. This incipient mainstay of liberal theories of democracy hardly needs to be underscored except to say that it indicates the weight placed upon a single mental state in the self-conception of modern society and politics. As Locke elaborates what kind of mental state consent to a political system is, he divides the concept into two kinds: the express consent in which we actually contract to obey the laws of a government that does not infringe upon our rights, and the tacit consent in which our actions entail our consent to be governed. Express consent is a relatively rare item, involved in founding covenants or at the upper reaches of political society. In contrast, tacit consent reaches every level of the social order and is something repeated every day in practice. By reaping the benefits of an established state—freedom from violence, protection by law—we consent to its legitimacy merely by living our lives. Here is Locke's influential argument, at some length:

> *Every Man* being . . . *naturally free*, and nothing being able to put him into subjection to any earthly power, but only his own *consent*; it is to be considered, what shall be understood to be a *sufficient declaration* of a man's *consent*, *to make him subject* to the laws of any government. There is a common distinction of an express and a tacit consent, which will concern our present case. No body doubts but an express *consent*, of any man entering into any society, makes him a perfect member of that society, a subject of that government. The difficulty is, what ought to be looked upon as a *tacit consent*, and how far it binds, *i.e.* how far any one shall be looked on to have consented, and thereby submitted to any government, where he has made no expressions of it at all. And to this I say, that every man, that hath any possession, or enjoyment, of any part of the dominions of any government, doth thereby give his *tacit consent*, and is as far forth obliged to obedience to the laws of that government, during such enjoyment, as any one under it; whether this his possession be of land, to him and his heirs for ever, or a lodging only for a week; or whether it be barely travelling freely on the highway; and in effect, it reaches as far as the very being of any one within the territories of that government. (63–4)

In one way or another, we declare our consent to be governed; our consent cannot be imposed by those who rule over us. "Nothing" other than this consent grants legitimacy to a government. Even so, consent is one of the mind's more tricky acts. Locke begins with actions that we can all presumably agree constitute a declaration of consent, the noncoerced acts of stipulation that come with the founding of nations or that bind courtiers and statesmen. He then moves to the acts of consent that are never quite marked as such.

Owning property seems to stake out one's consent because material well-being is annexed to a system of law. So does a short-term lodging or even passing through a nation. Any time we freely accept the protection of our government, we are consenting to its having power over us. Consent thus burrows into our "very being." As John Dunn puts it, "[If] a government is legitimate almost any adult behaviour within the boundaries of the country—that is, all behaviour except emigration—constitutes consent."[5] Express consent has aspects of conscious experience. I realize that I am consenting as I sign a document or state an oath. Tacit consent has aspects of an unconscious belief. I do not realize I consent as I walk along a highway, much as I might not realize that I believe in gravity until asked. I act as if I consent, and that is sufficient.

Tacit consent in this respect adds an important dimension to the idea that the actions of men are windows into their thoughts, since it seems by the logic of Locke's argument that action creates as well as discloses states of mind.[6] We may formulate our desire to buy property or to travel a certain distance, but we do not always formulate the political consent thereby incurred. Consent is not always prepared with detachment and calculation; it is often entailed while we are busy doing other things (things that may in fact be thought out with great deliberation). I walk to the store to buy some apples. I pay for the fruit with some money in my pocket. I expect and receive some change for the bill I hand the merchant. All of these acts are done with intentions. According to Locke's argument, the gravest consequence of them, however, is not the product of an intention at all. From leaving my house to returning home, the entire action has proceeded under the background assumption of consenting to be governed. Never once has this consent been present in my thinking. Every time I do anything, however, my consent comes along for the ride. The implications of this model go in several possible directions. One might be to say that a system of state and civil society is built from the actions of self-willing agents. My consent isn't a result of deliberate intentions but everything else I do is, and so consent is a kind of by-product, like the mist off a bog (to return to Rochester's metaphor). Another might be to say that consent is a kind of external scaffold: a contract made without our thinking, by the way our lives are led, by what we do. In either case, political obligations are attached to the small acts of daily living, to private as well as public life, while consent becomes a matter of interpreting and reading another person's behavior.

The Measures of Consent

To put things in terms of daily life and other minds is to begin to see how ideas of consent make their way into the worldly genres of romance and the novel, where intimacy, desire, and actions are at turns interpersonal and societal. It is worth further observing, in this respect, that when Locke uses the term "men," he means either all humans or just men, depending on the situation. Women and men have the same minds, the same way of perceiving the world, the same operations of consciousness and willing.[7] At the same time, consent presumably means one thing in civil and another in domestic society, where women are placed in a role subordinate to men, who are accordingly likened to the state. Such has been the familiar critique of Locke, from Mary Astell in the eighteenth century, to Carole Pateman in the twentieth.[8] I will want to adopt and dissent from this critique by attending to Locke's double-aspect view of consent: a concept rooted in minds and entailed by actions, an index of personal autonomy and something above and apart from individuals. One reason that Haywood has become recently interesting to us, I suspect, is that her fiction is concerned with strong feelings without having a concern for individual persons.[9] She seems, that is, to take one half of Locke's formula and leave the other. Locke and Haywood are both interested in how actions might reveal states of consent to moral or political systems; Haywood is much less interested in confining these states to the head or even body. At the extreme, this sort of argument runs the risk of anachronism, of finding in

Haywood a fragmentation of character or self she could never have imagined as whole in the first place.[10] I will instead look at this dimension to her novels as a particular feature of the third-person style she was in the process of developing, a feature that might be considered as her distinctive contribution to the compatibilism of her time. Haywood takes great liberty in telling us what her characters are thinking and feeling, threading the experience of one over the experience of another in ways that on occasion seem to trouble ordinary English grammar. But her representation of thought from the third person is less a burrowing into her character's mind than a kind of turning of thought outward into the external world where it can be observed by the narrator. Once there, a state of mind like consent might be a property of what one is doing, or where one is, or whom one is with.

The expression "measures of consent" appears in an early episode in Haywood's first novel, *Love in Excess*, when the long and digressive story of romantic intrigue pauses over a nighttime tryst. The rakish D'elmont has conceived a passion for the young Amena, who returns his desire even in the face of the "religion, reason, modesty, and obedience" that would insist he first become her suitor.[11] Alone in the garden of the Tuilleries, the lovers hover at the brink of a lushly described intimacy:

> The heat of the weather, and her confinement having hindred her from dressing that day, she had only a thin silk night gown on, which flying open as he caught her in his arms, he found her panting heart beat measures of consent, her heaving breast swell to be pressed by his, and every pulse confess a wish to yield; her spirits all dissolved sunk in a lethargy of love, her snowy arms unknowing grasped his neck, her lips met his half way, and trembled at the touch; in fine, there was but a moment betwixt her and ruine. (63–4)

This passage acquires its peculiar urgency from the tying together of a mental state ("consent") with a state of the body ("her panting heart"), and both with the surrounding milieu (the heat of the day, the empty park at night). In Haywood's louche syntax, thought and feeling, action and passion, seduction and submission, pursuit and retreat, cascade over each other within a sustained balance.[12] Amena's heart, pulse, and breast chase after D'elmont, while her lips meet him halfway. Her arms embrace his neck, yet are still "unknowing." The passage maintains a commitment to experience, in the sense that it tries to reveal to the reader what it is like to be in the throes of passion. At the same time, it is equivocal about who, if anyone, is having these experiences. Written from an unsteady third person, the passage focalizes first through D'elmont, who is receiving the embrace and feeling the pulses throb their measures of consent; it then turns after the "yield" to focalize through Amena, whose spirits fall into a lethargy of love. At the end, the passage arrives at a moralizing omniscience, which presents the action as a near disaster. The effect is a kind of wobbling, as we move from his perspective to hers and finally to no perspective at all. If we think of consciousness following Nagel and Chalmers as what an experience "is like" for whoever is having it, then we would have to conclude on the basis of this passage that Haywood establishes the consciousness of no one in particular.[13]

The blurring of point of view is a kind of externalism in the sense that it moves the qualities and qualia of erotic passion from one person to another and then finally outside of persons entirely. Criticism has long noticed this sort of strategy in Haywood's fiction, but has typically accounted for it as a residue of older styles of characterization, in particular those of the heroic romance. Thus William Warner says the characters in *Love in Excess* "are defined less by anything they bring to the narrative before their appearance in it than by their position in the plot."[14] I would modify this assessment to say that plot also conveys terms and categories of the mind. So Haywood's novel becomes a particular example of mental-state language inhering outside of individuals, in stories and settings and interactions. Or to put the point another way, Haywood comes up with strategies and forms (like multiple and fractured focalization) to represent thinking as a type of acting, and, in the process, often to move thoughts between or around bodies in motion. The proximity of thinking and acting is especially thorny, of course, with respect to the consent thrumming on the skin of Amena. Were one to say that consent is something Amena "brings to the narrative," then the pulse should express an eagerness that belongs to her. Haywood chooses instead to have the consent experienced by D'elmont, who is able to read a state of mind off the surface of Amena's body. This turning outward might be said to be a version of tacit consent writ small in the domain of sexuality. Amena's actual behavior, not her hidden thoughts, constitutes her interest in D'elmont. But if Haywood describes a version of tacit consent in sexual relations, she also shifts the meaning of that consent. For Locke, the importance of tacit consent was to attach un–thought out actions to a variety of obligations. Haywood's response is to suggest that putting the "measures of consent" outside the head might not separate them entirely from deliberation. Consider the double meaning of "measures": the repetitive beating of the heart (as in a metronome) and the meaningful act of judgment. Each encloses the other. That Amena's consent must repeat itself in time means that it is subject to withdrawal as soon as her pulse no longer quickens (as in fact happens). Of course, that withdrawal may be misperceived or ignored by D'elmont, which is one reason why, as Haywood will go on to suggest, consenting to other people is different from consenting to abstractions like the government or money. At the same time, were Amena to consent to D'elmont's advances, she would experience the measures of ruin evoked at the end by the narrator.

Shifting points of view thus track the movement of consent, as Amena discovers a yielding and then a disapproval someone else has experienced for her. This movement responds after a fashion to Locke's idea of tacitness because it implies that some actions bring consent along with them. Whereas for Locke the mind at issue belongs to the person who is acting, however, for Haywood actions are crowded by mental states that trace back in several directions.

Consider the shift at the end of the passage to a perspective distinct from either of the bodies present in the scene. To whose mind may we assign the expression "In fine, there was but a moment betwixt her and ruine"? The sentence presumes the distance of Amena (and presumably D'elmont) from such worries; she is in peril because she has forgotten not to be ruined. The thoughts ostensibly belong to the narrator, who brings up the gravest of possibilities as a kind of warning. The turn at the end of the passage is therefore not so much to a view from nowhere as to a view from the community of the concerned: those who see her at risk of losing a place in polite society, the marriage market, and the exchange of property and titles. These thoughts at once belong to no one who is there and represent an impersonal, public opinion we come to know without its assignment to a single body marching its way across the story.

The thoughts of the community of the concerned become one of several perspectives filling the scene and competing for attention.[15] Trouble arrives when the competition sets one against another, when in this case the warning voice of public opinion becomes at odds with the eager thrumming of consent. This is made clear when the lovers are interrupted at the moment of consummation by the arrival of Amena's maid, whereupon "Amena's thoughts were wholly taken up with her approaching shame, and vowed she would rather die than ever come into her father's presence, if it were true she was missed" (64). Once again, Haywood's syntax seems crowded by mental states. The nominative position in the second clause belongs to shame, the thought of which does the actual stating. This abrupt transition is significant, as shame was considered by many to be the singular point of connection between sexual desire and social expectation.[16] Shame "incite[s] us to Vertue," in the words of Descartes.[17] Or, as Bernard Mandeville, the eighteenth century's most voluble writer on the topic, put it: "Shame make[s] us sociable" because the "Greediness we have after the Esteem of others, and the Raptures we enjoy in Thoughts of being liked, and perhaps admired, are Equivalents that overpay the Conquest of the strongest Passions, and consequently keep us at a great Distance from all such Words or Actions that can bring Shame upon us."[18] On these accounts, shame is the passion of sensing that one's behaviors might be known and disapproved of by others. To experience shame is to imagine a community judging one's character according to "religion, reason, modesty, and obedience." As the maid enters the scene, therefore, we witness the blank third-person "ruin" trigger a shift from one state of mind to another.

The shift roughly coincides with a turn from the narrator's perspective to Amena's, except that the shame remains sufficiently detached to take a verb on its own. So while shame might be expected to move inward, here it remains curiously alongside the rest of the events at the park. One could make a good case that this is so for all terms of mind in this episode. My point in doing so, however, would be to emphasize the ease in which this identifying of mind with the motion and circumstances of bodies solves some abiding concerns about action. Haywood's novel does not wonder how consciousness might or might not lead the body to move, or might or might not be understood correctly by others. Rather, it wonders whether there is any real distinction among body, environment, and mind in the first place. Consider again the grasping of D'elmont's neck. We might ask of this motion a question posed much later by Wittgenstein: "[W]hat is left over if I subtract the fact that my arm goes up from the fact that I raise my arm?"[19] Wittgenstein's answer was "nothing." "*Doing* itself seems not to occupy any volume of experience . . . the phenomenal happenings only to be consequences of this acting."[20] The point is relevant to the situation in the garden because in both cases there is no state of desire or intention prior to the movement of arms. Were we to subtract the fact that Amena's fingers touch D'elmont's neck from the fact that Amena clasps his neck we would also be left with nothing. Amena doesn't know that she touches D'elmont's neck because she doesn't have to. It is necessary for the clasping that fingers touch his neck. It is also sufficient for the clasping; no further facts or deeper causes need be added.

This close fit between mental and physical causes is one part of what I want to keep from my quick dip into *Love in Excess*; the location of these causes is another. Haywood is interested in the framework and contexts of actions. She is also interested in languages of mind and passion. She tends, however, to run the two together rather than set them apart. The measures of Amena's consent blend into their surroundings to such an extent that one suspects that framework and context *are* desire and consent. These surroundings will eventually include the structure of expectation, custom, and decency experienced as shame. Conflict and complexity emerge not so much from the thwarting of inwardly held desire, therefore, as from separate forms of the external. Haywood's prose does not ask us to suppose Amena culpable, nor does it suggest that her private experience will be misunderstood by the world of social custom. Rather, we are to experience in the sentences themselves the alternating pulse of consent and shame.

In England, around 1725

Love in Excess repeats this convergence across its many pages, as one or another moment of passion comes up against the inopportune knock at the door. Bodies and parks do all the necessary work until the intrusion of social expectation in the person of the maid puts the measures to an end. Something similar happens in *Fantomina*, except that the measures don't so much stop as repeat themselves time and again. Whereas *Love in Excess* takes place in a romance setting and time far away from its reader, moreover, *Fantomina* tells its story in the byways and locales of a recognizably contemporary London and Bath. For both reasons, the novel has attracted a critical attention and a place in the eighteenth-century teaching canon that likely outstrips its initial notice.[21] As is now well known, the story concerns a young, unnamed woman of considerable rank and means who, after observing prostitutes at work in the theater, disguises herself in such a manner in order to experience what it is like to receive unalloyed male desire. Soon she falls for one Beauplaisir, a young libertine who knows her only under the newly begotten alias Fantomina. In order to keep his easily distracted attention, the young lady adopts a series of alter egos (prostitute, maid, widow, aristocratic libertine), each of which protects her from shame as she seduces the inconstant lover. Carefully balancing the audacity of her masquerade with the prohibitions it mocks and overturns, the lady's plot becomes an extended fantasy of activity outside of the rules of modesty. Like others, I will focus on *Fantomina*'s attention to erotic behavior within a delimited social setting. I will also be interested, however, in the novel's consideration of sexual consent and use of third-person grammar in the representation of mental states. How far do acts of consenting extend? How far do narrated minds—"she felt," "he thought"—move outside the head?

Haywood begins with an examination of the young lady's patterns of thought and habits of observation. Unlike the other fashionable ladies at the play who are "not of a Disposition to consider any Thing very deeply," our unnamed heroine watches masculine supplication with detached fascination: "She perceived several Gentlemen extremely pleased themselves with entertaining a Woman who sat in a Corner of the Pit, and, by her Air and Manner of receiving them, might easily be known to be one of those who come there for no other Purpose, than to create Acquaintance with as many as seem desirous of it."[22] The perception then lingers in her mind: "She still thought of it, however; and the longer she reflected on it, the greater was her Wonder, that Men, some of whom she knew were accounted to have Wit, should have Tastes so very depraved.—This excited a Curiosity in her to know in what Manner these Creatures were address'd" (41). Haywood's account of the young lady's thinking looks first at the men and women in the pit and then at the operations of the lady's mind. The description curls from objects beheld to the beholder, whose response then becomes part of the story itself. This attention at once to the qualities of external objects and the workings of minds is something of a microcosm of relations within the novel, as an appetitive and calculating desire combines with an impersonal, self-evacuating protagonist. Haywood's trick is to show how the young lady's boundless desire can be so tightly fit to the objects around her that it comes to seem like a part of the world it acts upon.

Haywood manages this trick through a loosening, often at the local level of sentence grammar, of mental states from their ostensible subjects. Consider the thoughts that follow the young lady and Beauplaisir parting for the first time. The difference in response is telling: "[T]hey took Leave of each other; he to the Tavern to drown the Remembrance of his Disappointment; she in a Hackney-Chair hurry'd home to indulge Contemplation on the Frolick she had taken, designing nothing less on her first Reflections, than to keep the Promise she made him, and hugging herself with Joy, that she had the good Luck to come off undiscover'd" (44). Haywood's lopsided prose reflects the different versions of mind in play. The only difficulty in Beauplaisir's mind is that what he wants has yet to match with what he has, a fully sanctioned if temporary part of his narrative. Haywood indicates the relative tedium of this state of mind by obliterating his consciousness in alcohol. In contrast, the young lady dives into the available language of mental life: contemplations, reflections, and momentarily, the passion of joy. These states of mind seem almost to overflow the sentence, in marked excess of the pronoun to which they belong. The effect is that the grammatical subject of the clause seems to traipse after her own mind. In the case of the hugging, the joy of coming off undiscovered almost announces a gerund without a noun, as if joy floats loose of any happy person, one hugging herself and perpetually about to do something. Haywood's style aims less to capture the intensity of the young lady's thoughts kept safe from raucous behavior, in other words, than to obscure the distinction between an inner world of experience and an outer world of expression and so between having a thought and completing an action.

Haywood's third person presents the young lady's mind as if it were in a constant tumble of thoughts, some more closely tied to pronouns, others more loosely dangling off sentences, still others placed in adjacent clauses. Following the trip back to her home, for example, the joy elicited by the episode in the theater runs into and then alongside the gendered decorum voiced by the narrator. What follows is a kind of maelstrom, in which the lady's heated thoughts jostle for space with the voice of admonition:

> But these Cogitations were of a short Continuance, they vanish'd with the Hurry of her Spirits, and were succeeded by others vastly different and ruinous:—All the Charms of *Beauplaisir* came fresh into her Mind; she languish'd, she almost dy'd for another Opportunity of conversing with him; and not all the Admonitions of her Discretion were effectual to oblige her to deny laying hold of that which offered itself the next Night. —She depended on the Strength of her Virtue, to bear her safe thro' Trials more dangerous than she apprehended this to be, and never having been address'd by him as Lady,—was resolv'd to receive his Devoirs as a Town-Mistress, imagining a world of Satisfaction to herself in engaging him in the Character of such a one, and in observing the Surprise he would be in to find himself refused by a Woman, who he supposed granted her Favours without Exception.—Strange and unaccountable were the Whimsies she was possess'd of,—wild and incoherent her Desires,—unfixed and undetermined her Resolutions, but in that of seeing *Beauplaisir* in the Manner she had lately done. (44)

To say this remarkable passage is narrated entirely within the mind of the young lady is to expand the term "mind" to its breaking points. Terms of mind splatter over the sentences only to become the actions they represent or consider. The young lady may or may not refuse the inevitable advances of Beauplaisir. She may just want to engage in amorous conversation; she may want more of his charms. What seems clear as the passage continues, however, is that it hardly matters. No amount of discretion can keep her from "laying hold of that which offered itself the next Night." The antecedent to "that" would seem to be the amorous conversation initiated earlier in the day. But the language of palpability and grasping inclines the sentence to the body of Beauplaisir, as if to think about doing something were already to have done that very thing. The collapse of thought and action would help to explain the erotic charge fastened to the conversation itself, the "world of satisfaction" that lies in tomorrow's banter. So much is clearly feared or encouraged by the narrator, who finds the cogitations themselves "ruinous" and who seems to suspect or insinuate that "Virtue" has failed even as it makes its first appearance, followed soon as it is by the resolution to receive Beauplaisir's "Devoirs." The collapse is so thorough, finally, that when the paroxysm of erotic passion arrives near the end, the result is not so much the unfixity or confusion of agency suggested by the narrator as a steely resolve. "Bent, however, on meeting him whatever shou'd be the Consequence," the young lady arrives early the next day and rents a room in a public house (45).

The episode that follows is among the trickier accounts of action in the Haywood canon. Margaret Case Croskery has argued that the scene raises "the deepest questions surrounding the definition of consensual sex."[23] I would agree but also observe that Haywood's understanding of these questions may not be ours, and that her answers are rooted in the period's conflicted notion of consent as at once a state of mind and a kind of act. The young lady has at this point taken the matter entirely into her own hands. At the moment when supper is concluded and she finds herself alone with Beauplaisir, however, Haywood presents us with the difficult situation of consenting agency between two minds: "It was in vain; she would have retracted the Encouragement she had given: —In vain she endeavoured to delay, till the next Meeting, the fulfilling of his Wishes:—She had now gone too far to retreat:—*He* was bold;—he was resolute: *She* fearful,—confus'd, altogether unprepar'd to resist in such Encounters, and rendered more so, by the extreme Liking she had to him" (46). Croskery and Ros Ballaster both describe the scene as a rape, and both shore up this reading by cutting the final clause, the "extreme Liking," from their citations—a revealing nervousness, I think, around the novel's ambiguous treatment of consent.[24] Either the young lady's behavior has been misunderstood by Beauplaisir and she was never consenting at all, or she had consented up to a point in time and now attempts to draw back, or she is unable to separate her will from the world it inhabits and wants what she doesn't want. Haywood seems to suggest all three at once and to suggest thereby the difficulty in isolating the mind from the activity or both from the setting. Consider the temporal markers of the passage. The young lady is unable to retract past actions that have been read (rightly or wrongly) as indications of consent, attempts to delay until the future the act to which she has perhaps intimated her interest, and has difficulty withdrawing because of her ongoing desire, her "extreme Liking." At each moment, the experience and presence of another person, and the world for which he or she stands in, obscures a clear pattern of volition. If Beauplaisir has misread the implied meaning of the young lady's actions and found consent where there was none, that is because of the "vast deal of amorous Conversation" already between them and because of the mysterious, unspecified "Liberty he had taken with her, and those he still continued to prosecute" (46). If the young lady attempts to postpone her consent by revealing the deception, she can do so only up to a point, since she has already committed acts (the conversation and the allowing of "liberties") that would bring with them "the Danger of being expos'd, and [having] the whole Affair made a Theme for publick Ridicule" (46). Finally, if the young lady's actions seem at odds with each other and her intentions obscure, that is because of the social disapprobation that would follow her lost "Honour" and thus complicate her "Liking" and the liberties to which it has led (46).

All of this leaves the question of the young lady's behavior unanswerable in the terms in which Ballaster and Croskery have framed it. The language of mental states is too shifting in time and too inextricable from conflicting social forms to land on one or the other side of consent. Haywood intimates this again by her choice of perspective. Whereas she had previously been attending to the fine gradations of the young lady's thoughts, now she switches to those of Beauplaisir, who appears to enjoy an unusually prolonged bout of reflection:

> Thus much, indeed, she told him, that she was a Virgin, and had assumed this Manner of Behaviour only to engage him. But that he little regarded, or if he had, would have been far from obliging him to desist;—nay, in the present burning Eagerness of Desire, 'tis probable, that had he been acquainted both with who and what she really was, the Knowledge of her Birth would not have influenc'd him with Respect sufficient to have curb'd the wild Exuberance of his luxurious Wishes, or made him in that longing,—that impatient Moment, change the Form of his Addresses. In fine she was undone. (46)

The young lady's mind falls into abeyance during "that impatient moment," perhaps signaling her protest, perhaps registering the ambiguity of the scene, perhaps signaling that we should turn to Beauplaisir's view of the events. He still understands her to be a willing agent, or he ignores her attempts to withdraw consent, or he is puzzled when she ends the scene in tears: "He could not Imagine for what Reason a Woman, who, if she intended not to be a *Mistress*, had counterfeited the Part of one, and taken so much Pains to engage him, should lament a Consequence which she could not but expect, and till the last Test, seemed inclinable to grant; and was both surpris'd and troubled at the Mystery" (46–7). The lastness of the "last Test" would seem to suggest a final statement of nonconsent, one that might or might not have been perceived at the moment by Beauplaisir. Even so, Haywood obscures the lament and confuses the blame. What we are to understand as sexual penetration is euphemistically referred to as conversation, a "Form of his Addresses" that has brought the young lady a "world of Satisfaction" up to this point.[25] Her tears follow "the ruinous Extasy," an experience of cleverly ambiguous provenance, one neither his nor hers but rather the subject of an indeterminate definite article.

As we saw in Locke, consent is something personal and yet has meaning only in relation to other persons and to impersonal contexts. One can never consent alone. *Fantomina* explores the resulting uncertainty, with its complicated relays of transparency and opacity, communication and deafness, volition and compliance. The young lady, now called Fantomina, learns to exploit this uncertainty, and proceeds to seduce and trick Beauplaisir for the rest of the novel. Lest we approve too quickly of what will follow, the narrator presents the resolution through a sort of despairing, delighted response. As she pauses to look closely at the mind of her main character, she sees a mottled combination of Fantomina's thoughts and her own:

> She had Discernment to foresee, and avoid all those Ills which might attend the Loss of her *Reputation*, but was wholly blind to those of the Ruin of her *Virtue*; and having managed her Affairs so as to secure the *one*, grew perfectly easy with the Remembrance, she had forfeited the *other*.—The more she reflected on the Merits of *Beauplaisir*, the more she excused herself for what she had done; and the Prospect of that continued Bliss she expected to share with him, took from her all Remorse for having engaged in an Affair which promised her so much Satisfaction, and in which she found not the least Danger of Misfortune. (49)

The dash marks would seem to indicate a shift from what the narrator is thinking about Fantomina's thoughts to what Fantomina is actually thinking. The effect is the by-now familiar slide between public opinion and personal desire: the one set next to the other as joint states of mind tethered in some fashion to the character. On the one hand, we are invited to think about the mistakes that Fantomina is about to make. On the other, we are invited to see Fantomina as a subject of sexual agency that would claim Beauplaisir as an object of future bliss. The ensuing flurry puts all of these thoughts into a mix. But it does so with an important change. "Her Design was once more to engage him, to hear him sigh, to see him languish, to feel the strenuous Pressures of his eager Arms, to be compelled, to be sweetly forc'd to what she wished with equal Ardour, was what she wanted, and what she had form'd a Stratagem to obtain, in which she promis'd herself Success" (51). The narrator's admonishing thoughts give way in this unusual sentence, but not exactly to the impetuous desire of Fantomina. They cede rather to Beauplaisir as his imagined desires give shape to hers. Her wish is to submit to his wishes, to be compelled to what she already wants. In a certain sense, the question of consent is clearer in this assignation than the first. All the intransitive verbs of action point to her will. Yet that is because Fantomina has discovered how to thread her "wishes" and "Stratagem[s]" through his desire and actions. The young woman has consented to have her consent decided by someone else. She therefore imagines that her wants don't so much belong to her as to the entire framework of seduction. She will be sweetly forced by arms that carry an ardent wish.

The rest of the novel is preoccupied with excavating her desire and placing it elsewhere, in scenes that repeat an essential pattern. Here, for example, is their next meeting, in which the young lady has traveled to Bath and taken her second disguise as a servant at Beauplaisir's lodgings: "His wild Desires burst out in all his Words and Actions: he call'd her little Angel, Cherubim, swore he must enjoy her, though Death were to be the Consequence, devour'd her Lips, her Breasts with greedy Kisses, held to his burning Bosom her half-yielding, half-reluctant Body, nor suffer'd her to get loose, till he had ravaged all, and glutted each rapacious Sense with the sweet Beauties of the pretty *Celia*, for that was the Name she bore in this second Expedition" (53). This passage only appears to concentrate more on Beauplaisir's passion than Celia's, for we know by this point that she has carefully planned her seduction and that her passion is bound up with his. Capture is precisely her design, the balance of yielding and reluctance the form her desire takes. Beauplaisir's "wild Desires" burst out in the movement of his body, allowing Celia's experience of them to consist in a certain inference. She feels how he experiences her half-yielding, half-reluctance in *his* ravages and glutting, in the external signs of the experience of seducing a servant girl. The young lady's fourth and final persona, the wealthy libertine Incognita, explains how this is so through a rare use of internal monologue:

Had he been faithful to me, (*said she, to herself,*) either as *Fantomina*, or *Celia*, or the Widow *Bloomer*, the most violent Passion, if it does not change its Object, in Time will wither: Possession naturally abates the Vigour of Desire, and I should have had, at best, but a cold, insipid, husband-like Lover in my Arms; but by these Arts of passing on him as a new Mistress whenever the Ardour, which alone makes Love a Blessing, begins to diminish, for the former one, I have him always raving, wild, impatient, longing, dying.—O that all neglected Wives, and fond abandon'd Nymphs would take this Method!—Men would be caught in their own Snare, and have no Cause to scorn our easy, weeping, wailing Sex! (65)

I have been arguing that Haywood is interested in consciousness but not exactly in personhood, that she keeps experience at a distance from agents of experience, and that the intriguing game of masquerade in the novel provides an occasion to modulate thoughts according to locales and types. The monologue would seem to strike an alternative to this pattern. What does the parenthetical and italicized statement "said she, to herself" provide an example of, in other words, if not interior thoughts, spoken in privacy, in advance of place or relation? The mind would seem to represent rather than extend into the world. Haywood's style is at some odds with this picture, however, and slides the direct speech from an internal monologue to a variety of impersonal statements and then back. "The most violent passion" clause, for example, shifts to an indicative that knocks the entire first sentence off-kilter, as if to imagine oneself as an object one must write as if one were an object. Helen Thompson has observed that Haywood presents the young lady as "a succession of different objects" in the imagined view of Beauplaisir.[26] Along these lines, we might say that Haywood deploys a form of internal quotation in order to pin down the view of oneself as experienced by someone else and so to make another's view of oneself an object of conscious experience. I would only add that, depending on where you are in the passage, this view occupies the thoughts of Incognita or no one in particular. For all its capacity to represent the "raving, wild, impatient, longing, dying" of another, Incognita's spoken first person starts and stops, announces itself and then gives way. As elsewhere, Haywood smudges the distinction between one person and another, as the plea moves from the mouth of Incognita to Beauplaisir to all men to all women.

Thompson argues that the imagined sense of objecthood proceeds without any "subjectivizing residue."[27] By this I take her to mean that there is no self that binds moments of experience into a person apart from the "rigorous discontinuity" of circumstance.[28] So much would seem to be in keeping with the sequential pattern of *Fantomina*, including the causal relation it draws between context and experience. How might we understand this account of action in relation to others? I cautioned earlier against the view that Haywood merely subordinates character to plot, or at least to a plot absent of mental states and vocabularies. Perhaps a greater risk than reducing Haywood's variety of characterization to older styles of the romance, however, is the converse argument that she resists norms of character that hadn't yet been invented or anticipates their later deconstruction.[29] In the place of this sort of argument, I would submit that Haywood's externalism responds after its own fashion to ongoing concerns about how to apprehend consent and how to represent minds in works of fiction. Without the sort of expository obligations of Locke, she moves toward an unusual approach to each. For Locke, a person is "a conscious thinking thing" relatively distinct from its living body. In these terms, the young lady's story joins several persons to one life, a matter of some consequence when the pregnancy is revealed at the end. Whereas Locke argued that personal *identity* consisted in the relative continuity of experience over time, however, Haywood presents "conscious thinking" together with the motion and place of bodies. Thus even the most significant of mental states stretches into the broader ecology of acting. For the purposes of the story, it matters less if the same person, in Locke's sense, is having the experience than if the experience fits to a place and a kind: *what is it like* for a widow in a coach or a servant girl in a parlor or an aristocrat in a park or, for that matter, a young rake?

I've focused throughout on the category of consent because it presents such a clear challenge to this kind of externalism. Consent is, after all, a term that would seem most securely locked to interior or private states of being. And yet, as we've seen, theories and representations of consent turn out to be significantly more complicated than this. For Locke the term at once provides the basis for legitimacy by linking individual agents to state and social authorities and only exists in relation to one or another action or set of circumstances. One cannot consent alone or to nothing. The importantly tacit varieties of consent, moreover, were not something one had to experience. They were rather a kind of by-product of the actions one takes. The same is true in a different sense for Haywood. In the two novels I've featured, consent is something that is intensely felt. Yet it is not something that is always felt intensely by the one who is consenting, or at least not first or not at the same time. Rather, consent hovers in the world or on one's skin or between bodies or over different slices of time. I've attempted to show how this understanding of consent and other related states—passion, yielding, shame—linked up with a certain formal style in Haywood's early fiction. When states of mind are outside the head they may be described and evoked with greater ease by the narrator, who picks and chooses varieties of consciousness like items on a shelf. The result is an infusing of the prose with qualities of mind, as the sentences themselves seem to take on the passion or perform the action stirred in this or that episode. The next chapter will discover a version of Haywood's model in one thread of a very different kind of fiction. There the idea will be that a state of the world might stand in for a state of the mind, and what one believes about external circumstances might explain or lead into what one wants to perform within them.

6   Action and Inaction in Samuel Richardson's *Clarissa*

A young woman refuses to marry a man chosen by her family; at the same time, she corresponds with a known libertine and agrees to meet him at the gate of the family estate. The libertine spirits her away to London, where she is raped and dies. Some of these items are actions taken by the young woman; others are events that befall her; still others are refusals to accept what life or the world offers. Together they compose a series of questions around agency: Must I intend to do something if I am to be held responsible for its outcome? Have I acted if I do not do anything at all? Do I get to define the meanings of my actions, or will they be defined by the world in which I live? I will close this book by looking at how these questions are set forth in the period's most involved novel of examined behavior. I'll do so from what some might consider an unusual angle. Criticism has tended to consider actions in *Clarissa* in terms of psychology, of how a frustrated mind expresses itself to others or escapes a world of difficulty. I'll be concerned instead with what might be called the ontology of actions: when they start and stop, whether they have parts, how they realize intentions or entail responsibility. The basic ontological question about actions is whether one has happened. I will therefore be interested in how the novel presents rival accounts of whether an agent may be said to have done anything and, if so, in what that doing consists. My point in ending with *Clarissa* is not to argue that the novel sorts out or completes some accounting for actions in eighteenth-century literature. All things have not led necessarily to this pass. Rather, the unusual attention the novel pays to the role of the mental in various kinds of behavior seems to me to draw together many of the problems with causation and agency I've looked at since Hobbes.

Clarissa's Intentions

One way of describing Clarissa's own account of agency is to say that she holds fast to intentions. She believes that actions may be explained by an agent's reason for acting, and that reasons for acting have no dependence on external circumstance.[1] She further maintains that reasons for acting carry a moral force, and therefore that one's behavior must be reasonable in light of a set of internally held convictions of right and wrong.[2] These ideas will be recognized by anyone familiar with Clarissa's habit of referring to her guiltless intentions precisely at those instances when it appears that she has done one or another horrible thing: from rejecting the will of her father, to leaving and living with Lovelace, to dying from grief. "Let me wrap myself about in the mantle of my own Integrity, and take comfort in my unfaulty intention," she writes to Anna Howe soon after the kidnapping, voicing a sentiment that will be repeated at pivotal instances later in the novel as well.[3] Clarissa maintains that one ought to be held responsible for the actions one has intended; as a corollary, she also believes that one shouldn't be blamed for things one did not mean to do. In the initial volumes of the novel, this means that Clarissa is not to be blamed for the ill fortunes that would allegedly befall her family should she refuse to marry Solmes, for she has no intention to do anyone harm and thus has not acted at all. Later, this means that she is not to be blamed for her lost honor, because she had no intention to fly off with Lovelace and live as his mistress. Unconscious during the rape, moreover, she could not have formulated an intention to have sex. Still later, this means that she is not guilty of suicide as she lies dying, for she has not intended her demise or acted to shorten her life. Seen this way, we can understand why so much of Clarissa's self-validation consists of rendering herself inactive. Most of the time, her intentions are to do nothing or to keep one or another event from happening.

The novel's steady movement away from Clarissa's happiness is marked by her difficulty in sustaining this account of actions. What then does it mean for Clarissa to say that her intention is blameless even as she has left home with a libertine enemy to the family? I will try to answer this question by shuttling ahead to a lineal descendant of the eighteenth-century philosophy of action. "Intentional actions," writes Elizabeth Anscombe in her famous study of the topic, "are the ones to which the question 'Why?' is given application."[4] When we say why such an action happened, Anscombe argues, we provide its intention by describing the action in a certain fashion. "To call an action intentional," is therefore "to say that it is intentional under some description that we give (or could give) of it."[5] On this view, a single action might be intentional under one description and unintentional under another. Clarissa writes to Lovelace, and her quill makes a certain noise as she is doing so. "Writing a letter to Lovelace" describes an intentional action, while "tapping a rhythm with a quill pen on sheets of paper" does not.[6] The point can take on ethical significance as well. Given the information Clarissa has, for example, "meeting Lovelace at the gate" describes an intentional action, while "meeting a liar and scoundrel at the gate" does not. Clarissa's taking of comfort sticks close to the kind of description that would leave the intention unfaulty. As she soon finds, however, the description continually slides away from her. In part this is because other people—her family, Lovelace, Anna, the neighborhood and community of the concerned—are as interested as she is in describing her actions, and their descriptions are not always of the variety that would leave Clarissa blameless. Thus criticism has often focused on the interpretation and misinterpretation of Clarissa's thoughts and behavior, and often suggested that the effort to know her intentions is also an effort to describe her actions in a certain way. In Terry Castle's influential formulation, Clarissa becomes "a sort of text, unfortunately open to the wild and unconstrained interpretations of others."[7] In part, however, the description slides away from Clarissa because her intention tends to be some kind of negative: I didn't want him to harm the family (my intentions were for something not to happen); I was tricked or forced (I had no intentions). Her intentions in either case are not so much attached to actions as attempts to keep actions from happening. The question for me is therefore not the epistemological one of whether we know what is on the mind of Clarissa so much as (again) the ontological one of whether or not she has done anything.[8] For Clarissa, a great deal will depend on keeping the two apart.

It is slightly easier to use Anscombe's model to account for Lovelace's behavior. Were we to ask, for example, why Lovelace bribed Leman to make it appear that Clarissa was writing to him more frequently than she was, the answer might put a single action "under description" from several points of view.[9] Lovelace bribed Leman so the family would be angered. He angered the family so they would force the marriage with Solmes. He pushed the marriage so Clarissa would have only him as a refuge. In this account of the bribery, "there is one action with four descriptions, each dependent on wider circumstances, and each related to the next as description of means to end."[10] Therefore we may "speak equally well of *four* corresponding intentions, or of *one* intention," if the one intention is the last in the series and provides the intention "*with* which the act in each of its other descriptions was done, and this intention so to speak swallows up all the preceding intentions *with* which earlier members of the series were done."[11] The "one" intention in this case is to abscond with the virtuous Clarissa and to make it appear (to her family and herself) as if this was *her* intentional act, as if she had written to Lovelace with the one intention of eloping with him.

This is surely not the comforting intention Clarissa wraps herself in after she's left home. That intention rather seems unattached to any action. She presumably intended to remain single or to keep

Lovelace from fighting with her brother, James. In either case, there is no completed action to which we could assign a comfortable intention. And this seems to be the point. Clarissa takes comfort in going over what Donald Davidson would call her "pure intending"—that is, "intending that is not necessarily accompanied by action."[12] Intentions of this order involve mental states that are not only prior to but also conceivably uninvolved with actions of any consequence. Such intentions are notoriously hard to infer, which is one reason that Anscombe tends to avoid them.[13] They are nevertheless important for Clarissa's sense that no one quite understands what she would or would not like to do. The slowly moving nightmare of the first third of the novel thus consists in intentions remaining in one place while actions move to another. Clarissa intends to stay at Harlowe Place yet finds herself in a coach with Lovelace. She intends not to marry Solmes yet fears a ceremony forced by her parents. She intends to remain a good daughter yet finds herself unable to comply with her father's demands. Whether her intentions are blocked, conspired against, or changed matters less to our current purposes than the fact that these are not intentions "*with which*" anything is done. In contrast, Lovelace's intentions rarely make reference to mental states in the absence of doing. As is often remarked, Lovelace's designs seem to change as they develop or as the plot takes him in this or that direction.[14] His intentions nevertheless remain immutable because they may always be read off the surface of his behavior.[15] Lovelace's intentions are "intentions with which," while Clarissa's are "intendings to do." The first refers to actions under a description; the second to mental states on their own. Since the novel seems to validate the perspective of Clarissa, it has often been understood to validate the privacy of mental states in advance of forms, events, or objects they encounter. This reading depends on a certain inflation of intentions to the status of mind as such. As we'll see, Clarissa's goal is often to make sure that only her intentions and no other state of mind are at stake.

From the beginning, Clarissa's few intentions frequently go

unmet. "I have been hindered from prosecuting my intention," Clarissa opens a letter to Anna in order to explain the delay in "continu[ing] to write . . . as minutely as we are used to write to each other" (1:29, 27–8 [54, 53]). This small example of thwarted intention—Mrs. Harlowe has fallen ill and Clarissa's time nursing has kept her from the pen—is important not only for auguring the sad events to follow but also, in a more analytic vein, because it flatly states that intentions may exist without consequent actions. She would have written but couldn't. One may be free to have an intention yet constrained in seeing the intention completed. Since intentions are one thing and actions another, it follows (Clarissa thinks) that one may have a good intention and still witness bad results. Clarissa's correspondence with Lovelace is for her a case of this point. The letters began so Lovelace could provide advice for a Harlowe relation about to travel abroad. The correspondence then had "every one's consent" (1:17 [47]). The letters continued as an effort to pacify Lovelace and keep the quarrel with James from flaming into violence; she was "obliged to go on corresponding with him for *their* sakes" (1:86 [84]). Later still they provide some hope that she might "extricate" herself from the family clutches if she offers to end the correspondence as "a condition of being freed from Mr. Solmes's address" (1:149 [117]). Keeping the family safe and herself apart from Solmes are both laudable goals and so, she thinks, worthy intentions behind acts of writing that might otherwise seem quite dubious. They are examples, as she says in another context, of how one might "take a wrong step, tho' with ever so good an intention" (1:125 [105]).

Clarissa's letters to Anna are in this respect documents in her defense, as they batten down her intentions in what Richardson calls "*instantaneous* Descriptions and Reflections" (1:viii [35]). Unlike, say, Moll Flanders, whose spiritual autobiography is subject to the distortions of memory and conversion, Clarissa relates her intentions in close proximity both to their occurrence and to the actions that do or do not follow. Such epistolary contrivance is of course something of a touchstone in *Clarissa* criticism. "The letter form," Ian Watt famously argued (echoing Johnson), "offered Richardson a short-cut, as it were, to the heart, and encouraged him to express what he found there with the greatest possible precision."[16] On this view, Richardson saw the punctual structure of letter writing as the best way to realize the moment-by-moment perturbations of desire and feeling, and, in so doing, to reach toward "something that may pass for the spontaneous transcription of the subjective reactions of the protagonists to the events as they occur."[17] The half-century since the publication of Watt's book has seen several revisions of this view, most notably perhaps by Thomas Keymer, whose study of Richardson's epistolary style questioned whether *Clarissa* presents "the relation between writing and the self [as] simply descriptive" and "the conscious mind [as] in full possession of its own internal processes."[18] The goal of epistolary disclosure, Keymer argues, is to persuade a reader of a particular perspective or version of events. The overall point of this revision seems to me to be indisputable; even so, one does not have to view letters as shortcuts to the heart to see the use that Richardson makes of them to examine the component parts of an agent's behavior. On Watt's view, Richardson uses letters to provide a document of "private experience" before such experience is misrepresented or manipulated by others. On Keymer's, letters are written by "engaged parties to describe, make sense of, and often advance particular purposes in, their world."[19] The difference between these accounts turns on whether readers are justified in believing the content of a letter. I will argue, however, that these epistemic worries do not matter so much for an action's causal structure, at least so far as Richardson understands that structure. The letters ponder background reasons and record instantaneous intending; the sequencing of letters allows some intentions to reach into actions and others to be curtailed. Once we recognize that intendings may never be realized, we are in the position to see that pure intending may be separated from acting: that one may intend without doing, even though one cannot do without intending. Much will hinge on whether this distinction can hold, yet comparatively little on whether the description of intentions captures the truth or appears to be feigned.

So it is right to say I think that Clarissa's letters provide a vivid record of intentions—above other states of mind—and it is also right to say that the record is meant to advance a version of the events. Consider the following letter sent amid the early struggle with her family. "I have been down," Clarissa writes after a gloomy encounter in her sister's parlor; "I *am* to be unlucky in all I do, I think, be my intention ever so good. I have made matters worse instead of better: As I shall now tell you" (1:141 [113]). What follows is an account of how she meant to apologize to her mother and then to seek her mother's help in pleading with her father. Instead, she finds herself introduced again to Solmes, who is brought into the room for an awkward parley. She had planned a private entreaty and in its place found more rage against her intransigence. As she describes the set of events to Anna, it becomes clear that the letter describes a single, unlucky doing. The action has borne out Clarissa's intendings: she does speak to her mother with a mind to plead her case. The trouble is not that the intentions are thwarted, as they sometimes are; it is rather that they are met with contrary behavior on the part of her family, who, as we shall see, have another take on how actions ought to be described and individuated. The important point for Clarissa, again, is that her intendings are prior to her doings, and, again, ever so good despite having made matters worse. This notion is repeated at the end of the letter when she chooses banishment to her room rather than conversing with Solmes, saying as she leaves, "God help me indeed! for I cannot give hope of what I cannot intend" (1:146 [116]). Were intendings merely cocooned in doings, her future refusals of Solmes might not be so certain; yet, she says, she is now in possession of an intention not ever to be his wife, so the giving of hope is a kind of metaphysical impossibility, like a five-sided triangle.

Clarissa tends to argue that her intentions were faultless or that she had no intentions. And this theory of actions serves her well, up to a point. Her claim that one is culpable for the actions one intends provides solace and a defense when for all outward appearances she has acted poorly: I did not intend to elope, to live with a libertine, to have sex, to die, and so forth. The argument provides considerable discomfort, however, when Clarissa believes herself to be at fault for actions whose intentions are perhaps questionable. One pivotal instance of this occurs just before the kidnapping. "I have done, as far as I know, the most rash thing that ever I did in my life" (2:253 [337]). So writes Clarissa to Anna in perhaps the clearest account of her own understanding of what an action is. The "thing" that Clarissa has done is having agreed to meet Lovelace and seek refuge with his relatives. Accepting for a moment Clarissa's own terms, we may say this is perhaps the first time in the novel that she really does anything of consequence. She thus feels the need to uncover and reveal her intentions so we may forgive, if possible, her behavior: "But let me give you the motive, and then the action will follow of course" (2:253 [337]). What follows is an intensive reflection on the motive and the action, both an involved representation of her thoughts and a notable repetition of the verb "to do":

> I revolved after she [Mrs. Hervey] was gone all that my Brother and Sister had said. I dwelt upon their triumphings over me; and found rise in my mind a rancour that was new to me; and which I could not withstand.—And putting every-thing together, dreading the near day, what could I do?—Am I in any manner excuseable for what I *did* do?—If I shall be condemned by the world, who know not my provocations, may I be acquitted by you?—If *not*, I am unhappy indeed!—For This I did. (2:261 [341])

Clarissa strains in this passage to depict what had risen in her mind so that we may have her motive and, as far as possible, excuse her action. She presents not only the past and present of her thoughts, but also, staged within their depiction, the very process of evaluating intentions itself: if the world, who knows not of what has passed, condemns me, she asks, will you forgive me who do know?

The attempt to represent "provocations" is desperate because Clarissa is convinced that she has in fact acted. Interwoven with her past and present thoughts are three repetitions of a single "doing." The first two are in the auxiliary form: in the first case, a modal expression of duress ("what could I do?"), in the second, an emphasis that an action was taken ("what I did do"). If Clarissa intends the modal auxiliary to justify the action, she at the same time repeats the event in the final and devastating understatement: "For This I did." Were one to want to make the sort of argument that locates in *Clarissa* a particularly textured model of subjective experience one could do worse than to look at passages such as this. What I would want to add to such an account, however, is that the effect of depth is achieved along the way of providing background contexts for observable behavior. If letters like this aim to reveal intensely felt, conscious experience, in other words, that is because, as Keymer points out, they hope to advance a version of the events. The passage is rife with distinctively mental content. The triumphing of her brother and sister, along with the feelings of rancor and dread, exists in the letter only as she represents them to herself (and to Anna and the reader). At the same time, this content is dredged up precisely to provide antecedents to verbs of action.

Let us then summarize what we've observed about Clarissa's theory of intentions before we look at the theories of her rivals. When she initially writes to Lovelace, she intends to secure advice for a cousin about to go on the grand tour. Her act of writing is explained and rationalized by an intention to get advice. When she continues to write to Lovelace, she intends to keep him from brawling with her obstreperous brother James. While everyone else—from her family to her close friends—seems to think she harbors a secret desire for Lovelace, she claims that the correspondence is intended to keep the peace. Whether or not Clarissa "withhold[s] her sexual feelings from Anna Howe, and even from her own consciousness," is for our current purposes immaterial.[20] The important point is that the novel establishes Clarissa's sense of her intentions as a particular match to the world, as a way to achieve or refrain from arrangements as Clarissa understands them. Clarissa appears to have acted in all sorts of horrible ways while remaining nearly faultless throughout. We have access to these faultless intentions because we read her letters and understand her motives. I shall suggest in a bit that this is not the only account of action provided by the novel, but it is important nevertheless to register how much it achieves. The achievement is not exactly, I think, to establish an individual's psychology against its misperception by others, at least if we define psychology in terms of an interiority that surpasses what is available to the reader or, even, to the person herself. Subtract all the modal verbs and one is left with a distinctively mental content. Even so, this content is not as wide as one might think. Clarissa might conceivably "revolve," as she oddly puts it, over a great many things, from the temperature of the tea in her cup to the feelings of the shoes on her feet. Only some of these things would fit into actions, however; only some, that is, are reasons, motives, or intendings. The mistake she wants to guard against is the spilling of this content into the whole of mental life. She may exert control over the one, she thinks, but the other is always subject to being misread or manipulated.

The Harlowe Family among the Philosophers

Clarissa's attempt to explain why she agreed to meet Lovelace stands out because it records an action. Most of the time when she "revolves" over intentions, she considers episodes when nothing happens—or rather, when she would like to insist against her detractors that she has not acted even when they insist that she has. This drift toward a posture of inaction is facilitated by two related parts of her argument: first, that intentions are prior to actions; and second, that intentions are only a fraction of the mind's content. Against the idea that she has done something to harm others, Clarissa usually asserts that she has not acted in ways that are wrong. Against the idea that she harbors desires for Lovelace—or could if placed in the right circumstance—Clarissa asserts that intending is only one part of an agent's thinking and not a feature of psychology broadly construed. One comes to have intentions, possesses them, or realizes them in actions. While something could prevent her from doing what she intends, nothing could make her do something if she had no intention (and if she had no intention she cannot be said to have done anything). The challenge Clarissa faces amounts in no small degree to an argument against this account of actions. I'll take a look in this section at how the Harlowes respond to her notion that refusing Solmes is not an action against their interests.

One important feature of the quarrel between Clarissa and her family concerns the individuation of actions: deciding on the moment when one action starts and another stops or parceling a given act into its several parts. Clarissa imagines her refusal of Solmes as not acting at all, as a kind of internally held separation of her intention from a world that assaults her sense of propriety and order. Her family considers her refusal to marry Solmes as an action taken against them. Whether or not Clarissa believes she has intended to hurt them is ultimately not their concern. The effect of her refusal is. Clarissa sees herself not as acting; her family sees her as acting all the time. "On your single will," writes her mother, "depends all our happiness" (1:281 [188]). The demand that Clarissa act in "compliance with their wills" and the constraints placed upon Clarissa's freedom of movement are, on this view, defensive moves taken against her prior attacks (2:183 [300]). Clarissa's response is simply to say again that she has not acted at all. When it becomes clear that the Harlowes interpret her refusal of Solmes as a step against them, she repeats sternly that she wants "but my *Negative*; not my *Independence*," as if to suggest that she may refuse and yet remain entirely under their authority (2:234 [327]). The result is a prediction—"I will say nothing but No, as long as I shall be able to speak"—which, depending on how you enumerate acts, promises either not to do anything or to assault continually the family's happiness (2:307 [365]).

When Clarissa says no, she does not intend to bring about or influence any state of affairs. On her view, intention has what we might call, following Anscombe, a world-to-mind direction of fit.[21] To intend to do something is to imagine the world changed to fit one's likings. Saying no to Solmes is, in contrast, an effort to keep the world in its place. As we have seen, her family considers her withholding of consent as an assault on their authority and an act against their interests. Their point is not precisely that intention should have a mind-to-world direction of fit; Lovelace will make this argument, as we will see. Rather, they quarrel with Clarissa over how to count actions. For the Harlowes the withholding of consent to the marriage is an attempt to fit the world to Clarissa's likeness and not theirs. They think *she* is the aggressive party. The quarrel at Harlowe Place, in this respect, turns on whether saying no (or refusing) is to be understood as doing something. We might gain some purchase on this quarrel by recalling Locke's first definition of the will: "[We] find in our selves a *Power* to begin or forbear, continue or end several actions of our minds, and motions of our Bodies, barely by a thought or preference of the mind ordering, or as it were commanding the doing or not doing such or such a particular action" (236). Locke here couples the negative to each kind of action. We begin or forbear, continue or end, do or do not do things. Forbearance is in this sense essential to what it means to be an agent. We are always doing one thing and, at the same time, not doing something else. This is important because Locke makes it clear that we sometimes feel a desire for one thing and choose another, hence our ability to act in a manner best for our future state. What Locke does not clarify in this murky sentence, however, is whether forbearance is or is not itself an action. His further reflections clarify the issue only somewhat. "This *Power* which the mind has, thus to order the consideration of any *Idea*, or the forbearing to consider it; or to prefer the motion or any part of its body to its rest, and *vice versâ* in any particular instance is that which we call the *Will*" (236). The sentence would appear to offer some help because it attends to the problem of what counts as action within one's thoughts and to establish an analogy in the second clause with physical movement. According to this analogy, considering is to moving as forbearance is to staying at rest. At the same time, however, Locke makes it clear that forbearing is an important power of the mind and not simply the absence of taking an action. So the ontological status of forbearing remains uncertain. If we can say that actions exist and may be counted, are we to include among them the not doings of things, or are such episodes to be considered a separate category of events?

The Harlowes would like to say that forbearing is a subclass of acting and that Clarissa's not consenting to Solmes is as bad an action as would be her consenting to Lovelace. Clarissa would like to keep the two apart. Each might find some support in Locke, who seems to say, on the one hand, that refusal allows one to avoid bad choices and, on the other, that refusal might still have consequences for oneself and others. "They have begun so cruelly with me," Clarissa writes early on in her trial, "that I have not spirit enough to assert my own Negative" (1:44 [62]). When she soon finds the spirit to refuse her family, she still thinks that she has not acted: "But let *my* actions," she says to her mother, "not *their* misrepresentations (as I am sure by the disgraceful prohibitions I have met with has been the case), speak for me" (1:103 [93]). Clarissa implores her mother to inspect her actions because she sees herself as exerting only a negative and feels that it would be a misrepresentation to claim that a negative is an action against anyone. Her family in turn suspects that her refusal will inhibit their plan to elevate their status and augment their estates. Clarissa sees her refusal as one with no effect on the world outside herself. "Why should I be denied the liberty of *refusing*?" she asks James; "That liberty is all I ask" (2:32 [221]). The question implies that refusal importunes the life of no one and does not alter any external relations. "The liberty of *refusing*," James responds, "is denied you, because we are all sensible, that the liberty of *chusing*, to every one's dislike, must follow" (2:35 [223]). The exchange is revealing because of the way that James translates refusal into a choice. For as much as Clarissa tries to explain to her family that she wants only to refuse and not to choose, that she will "never . . . marry without [her] Father's consent" and "seek no relief that should be contrary to his will," her family consistently presents her refusal as a choice, and consistently endeavors to decode her negatives into intentions that do not exist (2:292, 312 [194, 200]).[22] So the tally of actions would be zero according to Clarissa and one or many according to her family, depending on whether saying no to the Solmes proposal accumulates every time it is done. Clarissa says she has done nothing to fit the world to her intentions; the Harlowes see her negative as a violation of their wishes and a prelude to choosing Lovelace, as both an action and a ground for future actions.

If Clarissa's forbearance is on her own account not an action, it is not by that measure a form of passivity. Criticism has long misunderstood Clarissa as, in Peggy Thompson's words, a "passive, defenceless moral martyr."[23] One does not have to read like a Harlowe to see how Clarissa (and perhaps *Clarissa*) strains to distinguish forbearance from passivity.[24] While her tally of acts remains at zero, she nevertheless strives for a kind of liberty, one that would (again) find some support in Locke, though perhaps toward different ends. "The *Idea* of *Liberty*," writes Locke, "is the *Idea* of a Power in any Agent to do or forbear any particular Action, according to the determination or thought of the mind, whereby either of them is preferr'd to the other" (237). His example is a man tumbling off a bridge who doesn't want to fall but is unable to stop his descent: "[T]hough he prefers his not falling to falling; yet the forbearance of that Motion not being in his Power, the Stop or Cessation of that Motion follows not upon his Volition; and therefore therein he is not *free*" (238). Freedom dwells here in the ability to stop a deadly motion, a saving of oneself from a precipitous crash. The extremity of the example would seem to have something to do with making forbearance elemental to personal integrity. We ought not to be compelled to act when we do not want to. Like Locke, Clarissa understands refusal to be necessary to freedom. She is considerably less ambiguous, however, about the role that refusal plays in what she calls, at several points in the novel, her "free will."[25] I discussed in the first chapter how some philosophers argued that free will was either incoherent or impossible, while others thought it was essential for what it meant to be an agent. Locke was among those who considered the term to be a category mistake, since it ascribed to a power a condition that could belong only to actions.[26] Critics of free will from Hobbes to Hume tended to believe that free actions were unimpeded and so compatible with external determination, while those who wrote in defense of the term tended to see the two in conflict. One plank of the defense of free will is especially relevant to Clarissa's case. Writers who wanted to say that freedom was incompatible with determination, like John Bramhall and Samuel Clarke, maintained an overall weariness toward causal explanation, since such explanation could render the will subservient to something else—from one's desires to environmental stimuli. Bramhall, for example, viewed reason as a sort of advisor to the will and the will as a sort of motor for acting, yet neither, strictly speaking, as a cause of anything else. Later in the period, Clarke argued that it is agents who are free to act not their faculties. When we talk about reasons for acting, Clarke said, we tend to leave out the distinctive role of the agent, who is, Clarke thought, more than the sum of her parts. Once we concede that agents are involved in acting, not merely reasons and intentions, we no longer have to worry about where causation starts and stops or how one can be free in a determined universe.[27]

Clarissa's account of her free will inherits this sense that it is agents who initiate and complete actions, not reasons or intentions or wills, and thus that it is agents who are free or bound. One can get a sense of this not just in the expression "free will"—which after all she says in the context of trying to get out of the marriage to Solmes and later the confinement in Sinclair's bordello—but also in the resistance she shows to causal accounts of her own behavior. She believes that her negative is elemental to her free will because it prevents her from having to act. Her family (again) believes that she is acting all the time. They understand refusing as a cause of all sorts of pernicious effects. She doesn't think her refusal causes anything. When Clarissa refuses Solmes to his face, she asks of her uncle Anthony, "I must not be allowed to have any free-will in an article that concerns my present and future happiness?" (2:192 [304]). Anthony can only understand her will as a decision that he does not like. On his account, refusal is a cause in its own right, one already despised by the family, and so he responds, "You have had your will in every-thing till now; and this makes your Parents wills sit so heavy upon you" (2:192 [304]). The logic of equivalence Anthony establishes between Clarissa's will and the will of her family makes it impossible that hers can only be a refusal and not a choice, since, according to him, the will is something that weighs upon another, like a cause into an effect. At the same time that Anthony insists that Clarissa's will *is* a cause he says it must *have* a cause, either a perverse interest in thwarting her family or an unacknowledged desire for Lovelace.[28] Hence he is led to unwrap her refusal to reveal what he understands as her secret decision: "You know *our* motives, and we guess at *yours*" (2:192 [305]).

The premise of the Harlowe argument is that one can perceive actions as the result of intentions even when agents claim otherwise. The Harlowe position thus has something of a philosophical pedigree, if one distorted to their advantage. I argued in the first chapter that Hume viewed the causal relation between will and action as one best intuited by other people. We feel that we are free, but our actions may be predicted by other people's surmising of our "motives, temper, and circumstances." The very attention to how complicated agency and intention often are leads Hume to view the will, as it were, from a third-person stance, where causal relations have the same probability as anything else one views in nature. I based this reading of Hume entirely on the chapters on liberty and necessity in the *Treatise* and the sections that revisit them in the *Enquiry*. Of equal relevance to the Harlowe theory of action would be the chapters of the *Treatise* on justice, where Hume writes that, although "when we praise any actions, we regard only the motives that produced them," we nevertheless "cannot do [this] directly; and therefore fix our attention on actions, as on external signs."[29] In the first case, Hume discusses the problem of attributing necessary causes for an agent's behavior; in the second, he discusses the assigning of blame or praise. In either case, inward or private causes like motive are important yet also in some basic way inaccessible except by means of probable inference. *Clarissa* depicts this process of inference gone horribly awry, as the Harlowes are constantly attributing motives to what they see as the extremity of Clarissa's actions.[30]

Lovelace and Consent

Clarissa's response to her family is to divest herself of causation; she repeats to Anthony that she will never marry without her father's permission, will never marry at all, will not claim her grandfather's estate, will not, as far as possible, take any actions (2:192–3 [304–5]).[31] As a corollary to this model, she believes she should not have to choose what she loathes to do. "If consent of heart, and assent of voice, be necessary to a Marriage," she writes to her aunt, "I am sure I never can, nor ever will, be married to Mr. Solmes" (2:225 [322]). Clarissa here fastens the question of mental states and their relation to action to one particularly consequential state, in such a way that establishes a connection to the events after the plot leaves Harlowe Place and moves to the Sinclair bordello and beyond. Whereas the quarrel between Clarissa and her family turns on whether the withholding of consent is an action, the quarrel with Lovelace turns on where, precisely, consent might be located. Clarissa and her family both maintain that the term reaches from the heart outward, that consent has a world-to-mind direction of fit.[32] Lovelace's designs are of quite a different order. I argued earlier that

Lovelace's intentions are (mostly) intentions "with which" certain actions are done, not intendings "to do" some future thing. For all his shifting patterns of behavior, his intentions remain the same because they are part of a given action or set of actions. As Frances Ferguson has put it in the brilliant essay "Rape and the Rise of the Novel," "form for Lovelace implies a mental state," and so therefore, according to him, "the forms of actions—however fictitious—carry mental states like intention and consent within them."[33] The argument about implying and the argument about carrying, I would add, are not exactly the same thing; the second, stronger thesis has a temporal predicate that the first does not—namely, that intentions are coincident with actions and not before them. What this means in the early going of the novel is that Lovelace's intendings are always part of his acting—he is Xing with a view to something contained in X and no further. Later in the novel, this turns into a strained attempt to produce Clarissa's consent by arranging for a certain presentation of her behavior. The idea is that if she has behaved in a certain way—run away from home, lived with him as his wife, lost her virtue—then her actions must have been *with* intentions, and these intentions must be those to his liking. So if in the first case Lovelace provides an account of his own actions, in which the form of an action carries the mental state "with which" the action was done, in the second case he provides an account of Clarissa's, both that she has in fact acted and that her intentions are what they must seem to be from an external perspective.

Ferguson credits this strategy to Lovelace's posture of "aesthetic detachment," his having "appeared in the role of the artist" who "assumes different parts at the will of the imaginary text that he is elaborating."[34] Thus the discovery of intentions in the act of doing turns out to draw from the primacy of artistic form and from the capacity of artworks to back-project the intentions of whoever ostensibly made them. This account of aesthetics is, however, itself taken from a broader understanding of form as any a priori establishment of meaning.[35] Lovelace's formalism belongs to a certain

view of aesthetics, but also to a view of society and, most importantly, a view of the law. The priority of social form says that rank
and status precede individuals who come to occupy positions on a
fixed gradient. The priority of legal form says that rules are based
on universal maxims irrespective of circumstance or personality. Fixed as they may seem, aesthetic and social forms are at least
somewhat fungible with respect to time and place and, appearances
to the contrary, evolve over history. In contrast, the law represents
something close to pure formality, like the truths of geometry. Ferguson's reading thus continually equates form with law in order
to show how forms "stipulate" mental states.[36] For example, eighteenth-century rape law says that not being conscious or not having
reached a certain age makes it impossible to consent to having sex,
and common-law rules of marriage say that it is impossible *not* to
consent to sex with one's husband (even one's future husband, as
the case may be).[37] The salient point in these instances is that one's
conscious experience matters not at all for the psychology at issue.
One may feel like one has consented, but if one is under ten the feeling of consent does not represent one's psychology. The fact of one's
age does. Likewise, it may appear as if a woman has lost her honor
with a libertine, but if she's been drugged into delirium her consent
is forever out of reach. The law fastens on mental states yet these
states are not so much experienced as declared. States of mind both
are and are not integral to whatever case is it at hand.

Ferguson's point is at least in part to trouble the reading of
Clarissa as a novel committed to inwardness, interiority, and the
authority of the first-person as it is written to the moment in letters.[38] Yet her conclusion does not simply emphasize the formal
antithesis. Rather, what she calls "psychological complexity" lies
in the coming into conflict of stipulated and experienced mental
states, "what one must mean and what one wants to mean."[39] In
this respect, the double epistolary structure—Clarissa's correspondence with Anna, Lovelace's with Belford—represents not only two
perspectives on the same series of events but also two accounts of

how to understand actions: Clarissa's commitment to the first person and free will and Lovelace's commitment to the third person and necessity. Putting things this way I alter the terms slightly of Ferguson's argument. Where she emphasizes an idea of form modeled ultimately on the law and a particular reading of rape law, I emphasize an idea of the external modeled ultimately on philosophy and a particular reading of the period's ontology of actions and events. On my view, Lovelace's externalism has roots in the problem of will and determinacy that extends from Hobbes to Hume, although as I will attempt to show, it is, unsurprisingly considering Richardson's moral, fraught with difficulty and ambiguity. According to James Grantham Turner, Lovelace takes his cues from "a sensualist, materialist and determinist philosophy that denies intellect and freedom altogether."[40] I have argued in previous chapters that the materialist account of the will tends not so much to deny what Turner calls "intellect and freedom" as to make them compatible with a world understood according to the movement of physical bodies. Lovelace's externalism in this respect lies in the commitment to seeing how minds and actions might fit into the world's causal structure. Where Clarissa seeks to deny causation in order to make a case at once that her will is free and that she hasn't done anything, Lovelace tends to agree with the Harlowes that she has already made up her mind and already acted, not because, as the Harlowes thought, she makes the world accommodate her wishes, but rather because the world always does the intending and consenting for her. We might think of this again in terms of a direction of fit. On the reading shared by Clarissa and her family, intentions like consent have a world-to-mind direction of fit; they make the world fit to the mind, in the sense, for example, that consenting to Solmes would leave both of them married, join her estate to his, make her family happy, and so forth. On Lovelace's reading, consent has a mind-to-world direction of fit; it adjusts the mind to the world, in the sense, for example, that Clarissa's leaving home, passing as his wife, and moving to London means that she has already consented. Thus

Lovelace's strategy is not only to cloak mental states within forms, as Ferguson argues, but also to substitute one kind of mental state for another. He aims to make states of desire, intention, and consent seem like states of belief, so that when external circumstances make it appear as if one has already consented one's mind ought to change (or be changed) accordingly. I believe that it is raining, yet when I step outside I see that it is not; my belief changes with the extra information. I desire to leave home, so I arrange to take a coach the next day. The ordinary absence of coaches outside my door makes me change things to my needs. The Lovelacean view turns the second kind of relation into the first. I find I've left home, so I must have wanted to do so, and so forth.

This reversal of fit between consent and context is similar in certain respects to what we observed in *Fantomina*, and so an example in a different register of Margaret Doody's claim that Lovelace "often speaks and thinks in a Haywoodian manner."[41] For Lovelace the reversal falls under "the *libertine* presumption to imagine, that there was no difference in *Heart*, nor any but what proceeded from difference of *Education* and *Custom*, between the Pure and the Impure" (4:327 [702]).[42] Agents do not bring into the world a code of right or wrong. The environment provides the code for them. To the empiricist argument against innate moral intuitions, however, Lovelace adds a further point. When he puts Clarissa in a "*proper place*" with "*proper* company about her," her consent should fall out as a matter of course (3:75 [424]).[43] Lovelace's theory thus presents a double account of experience: mental states are infinitely plastic with respect to the environment; at the same time, mental states are a mere aftereffect of what one does or seems to do. Experience shapes mental states, yet the experience *of* one's mental states doesn't matter. With respect to the seduction plot, the expectation is for the Haywoodian "*consent in struggle*," "*yielding in resistance*," "*reluctant consent*," or "*yielding reluctance*" (4:13–4; 4:203; 4:358 [557, 647, 719]).[44] In this sort of phrasing, consent is a mental term only in the sense of naming a state of mind. It is not a mental term in the sense of referring to something that is private or hidden or felt. So when Lovelace joins the category to behavioral terms like "struggle" and "resistance" the result is that it becomes inseparable from observable events. All he needs for Clarissa to have consented is for things to look a certain way. "A dear silly Soul," Lovelace exclaims after the first escape, "to depend upon the goodness of her own heart, when the heart cannot be seen into but by its actions; and she, to appearance, a Runaway, an Eloper" (5:114 [789]). A description of the facts in which Clarissa appears to have consented should be a complete description of all the important facts. The addition of her felt experience should bring nothing further to the story. This commitment to understanding conscious experience as irrelevant or post hoc, a kind of libertine epiphenomenalism, would then explain Lovelace's early resistance to violence, the "Abhorred be *force*, be the *necessity* of force, if that can be avoided!" stated on several occasions to Belford (4:223 [657]).[45] "*Force* is the devil" because the only mental state with which it may be correlated is refusal, and so the only perspective it would validate is Clarissa's, that consent lies prior to society in the heart (4:223 [657]).[46]

Richardson would thus seem to equate Lovelace's externalism with his disregard for first-person mental states. Consent is like belief because it is set by the physical facts at hand. The mental merely comes along after the rest of the causal relations have been put in place, as a kind of aftereffect or shadow. Or to put the point even more strongly, as Richardson seems to want Lovelace to do, once these relations have been set, a state of mind like consent should follow *by necessity*. Lovelace thus has little interest in Clarissa's talk of "free will," since he thinks the will is not free but necessitated and is so by the external, physical facts in its surrounding. The drama leading up to the rape from this perspective expresses the coming into conflict of two views of causation and the mental. Lovelace attempts to arrange Clarissa's environment to make it appear as if she has consented, or, what is the same, to make it so she *has* already consented. Clarissa responds with feelings against what she has experienced. Consider the dinner party and introduction of Miss Partington. Clarissa has left home, passed under Lovelace's name, dined with his fellow libertines, and still she refuses to share a bed with the woman recruited for her seduction. "I am very much vex'd and disturbed at an odd incident," Clarissa writes to Anna. "Mrs. Sinclair has just now left me; I believe in displeasure, on my declining to comply with a request she made me: Which was, To admit Miss Partington to a share in my bed" (3:338 [546]). "There might be nothing in it," she continues, "and my denial carried a stiff and ill-natured appearance. But instantly, upon her making the request, it came into my thought, that I was in a manner a stranger to everybody in the house: Not so much as a servant I could call my own, or of whom I had any great opinion: That there were four men of free manners in the house, *avowed* supporters of Mr. Lovelace in matters of offence . . . That Miss Partington herself is not so bashful a lady as she was represented to me to be . . ." (3:338–9 [546]). The result is not Lovelace's notion that consent is like belief and therefore responsible to the facts of the environment. What we read, rather, is the Lovelacean view as it is experienced from the perspective of Clarissa—that is, the Lovelacean view as it is *experienced* as such. So what is supposed to elicit a fit between the world and the mind expresses rather a split between the two. The Partington affair shrinks Clarissa into herself, as her experience is at odds with everything about her and she "a stranger to everyone."

I have argued so far that Lovelace understands Clarissa to act out of necessity. Richardson has Lovelace add to this necessity an account of mental states lagging behind their causes. What Clarissa felt as she was leaving Harlowe Place, on this view, matters less than the fact of her leaving. She must have consented to leave. How else could her feet have moved up and down? It is therefore a matter of concern for Lovelace that he has to fall back on drugs and violence, a strategy that reveals, in his words, how Clarissa was *not* "subdued by *her own* consent, or any the *least* yielding" (5:299 [888]). Lovelace had proceeded as if mental states were logically entailed by actions. Subduing should be the rational interpretation any third party would put on the events. Once all mental states have been obliterated by the glass of hartshorn water, however, there is no chance for any to follow the contexts he has provided. Up until this point, Lovelace could always maintain that consent was a free rider on other actions that Clarissa had taken. The circumstances of the rape prove that the plot has yet to be "completed" because "the *consent*, is wanting" (5:300 [888]). For Lovelace's designs to be finished, the action would itself need to be brought to an end with a compliant state of mind. This is not to say that Lovelace becomes interested in Clarissa's conscious experience of consent. He is interested rather in actions that might lie nearby consent: moving a hand, relaxing a grip, falling backward. Without a background framework of consciousness, these actions are hard to imagine and therefore sentences about subduing and yielding difficult to form. Just as lifting one's feet implies intentions to leave, "yielding" in struggle implies consent to lost honor. Inanition and inertia imply neither. This theft of movement attaches special circumstances to the drugging according to Colonel Morden and others, as there is no way to formulate the rape as an action in which Clarissa participated or as anything other than an event that befell her.[47] Even from the perspective of Lovelace, this must turn out to be so. His strategy had depended on mental states coming about after their physical and causal relations had been set. Arrange the world a certain way, and a mental state will follow. This is (again) to imagine that states of desire, intention, and consent have the causal structure of a belief: one adjusts to external facts of the matter and often holds beliefs without knowing so; likewise, one fits in with the world one is presented with and often consents without realizing it. In taking consciousness away from Clarissa, this sort of story becomes impossible to tell. Mental states may not have to be conscious in order to exist or play a causal role or entail responsibility, but consciousness must (it turns out) be somewhere nearby.

Suicide

For her part, Clarissa maintains that belief is one thing and consent another. While a state of mind like belief may depend on features of the environment, a state like consent depends on features
intrinsic to her. This is why what Clarissa believes about Lovelace
varies according to his behavior—or (as he realizes) what she knows
of his behavior—while her consent to the seduction or marriage does
not. For an action to be counted as an action, on her view, it must
be served by a conscious intention. Nowhere is this more at stake
than in her way of dying, to which I will now turn. Criticism has
long taken note of the novel's religious interest in the *ars moriendi*,
especially as it is set forth in the contrast between Clarissa's blessed
departure and the painstakingly observed, unholy deaths of Belton
and Sinclair.[48] Criticism has more recently been intrigued by the
forensic difficulties raised by a death that occurs in the absence of
any clearly stated cause.[49] The first set of concerns relates to the
manner in which Clarissa dies and asks whether this style of dying
imitates the holiness of Christ.[50] The second relates to the reasons
for her death and asks whether these reasons (if there are any) may
be placed under a physical or social or spiritual description. In either
case, the question arises whether Clarissa acts in her own death and,
if so, whether she *causes* herself to die.[51]

Were Clarissa to do so, she would violate a prohibition against
suicide that both dated back to Augustine's interpretation of the
commandment not to kill and was part of a new discussion of
actions and objects in the early eighteenth century.[52] The novel's
delicate treatment of Clarissa's involvement in her own dying is
interesting in both respects, since it addresses the status of mental
causes in relation to physical events as well as the status of persons
as composite entities. We may quickly summarize these as follows.
The dying of a body is undoubtedly a physical event, as Clarissa's
wasting figure seems designed to remind readers. The prohibition
against suicide, however, would separate some states of mind from

other causes. There is nothing wrong with dying. There is something wrong with causing oneself to die. This simple distinction thus lands on the place of minds in the causal order of things and does so precisely to condemn a certain example of mental causation. The prohibition also marks out persons as special kinds of entities. There is something wrong with pulling apart one's body, yet nothing wrong with destroying one's shirt or spilling a cup of water. These claims may seem intuitive, but they rely on premises we've seen under some pressure during the period: not only the notion that persons form a special class of object, but also the notion that any object is more than the sum of its parts.

While the prohibition against suicide is old, therefore, it took on new urgency around the time of *Clarissa* in part because matter, personhood, and mereology began to draw attention. Consider the fate of Alberto Radicati, an Italian materialist briefly living out his exile in London. In 1732 Radicati wrote a short pamphlet in defense of suicide called *Philosophical Observations on Death*. The pamphlet made its way into the salon of Queen Caroline and caused such uproar that the translator and publisher were arrested and Radicati deported.[53] It is not difficult to see why. Radicati begins with a global reduction to the physical. The universe consists only of particles and "exiguous vacuities."[54] What appear to be macroscopic objects are aggregates of simples, whose properties of motion and extension bring into existence the variety of things that populate the world as we experience it. The creation or continuation of life thus amounts to the "modification of Matter, different from what it was before," while the arrival of death amounts to "the dissolution of the Corporal Parts, the which, separating do then assume other forms, and receive different Motions" (10–1). On this view, there is no difference between one object and another except for their arrangements. At bottom, all atoms are the same. So are all things that atoms make. For the situation to be otherwise would presume that something happens in the course from particles to heaps that makes the whole different from the sum of its parts, and that could happen only were we to add something else to the universe. Since this is impossible, Radicati argues, all objects are really identical. Thus it is a "foolish Prepossession, which Men have in Favour of their own Species . . . that *They are the most perfect of all Beings; as being the* lively Images of GOD, *who created all the others purely for their use and Service*" (94). Piles of atoms don't make men; they make piles in the shape of men (and a great many other things).

The point of looking at the smallest units out of which things are made is thus to suggest that persons are no more (or less) than material objects and material objects no more (or less) than their constituent parts.[55] An object is one and the same with its arrangement, with no extra set of causal and moral meanings. This being the case, suicide is perfectly natural when one is in pain or ill or poor or oppressed. "A Man ought not to imagine that, in depriving himself of Life, he any way discomposes the Order of Providence" (92). After all, "the eternal Laws of Motion cannot, in any wise, be varied, or altered, on account of a Creature's living a longer or shorter Space of Time" (92). For a man to kill himself is simply "changing sooner or later the Modifications of its Matter," which then takes a new shape, whatever that might be (92). "It little imports that the Matter which formed the Body of a Man assumes the Form of a Million of Worms, or of other Beings, that of round it becomes quadrangular or multangular" (92). This sort of monism strikes an immediate and stark contrast to the dualism that marks the end of *Clarissa*. Clarissa waits for her body to expire so her soul might ascend to blessedness—a condition uniquely available to humans, the species God created in his own image and invited to an eternity separate from the merely physical. Radicati holds in contrast that eternity belongs only to the matter and laws of the universe, compared with which individual lives are transient and insignificant. "A Man more or a Man less, nay the whole Race of Mankind," Radicati argues, "is not so much, with respect to the Immensity of the Universe, as is a single Drop of Water in Comparison with the vast Ocean!" (93–4). Richardson would write "the history of a young lady" whose death is of singular interest. Radicati would respond with an immensity that makes such deaths invisible and insignificant.

Like Radicati, Hume found writing about suicide to be a source of trouble. His editor refused to include the 1755 "On Suicide" in a collection of his essays, and the piece was published only posthumously, in 1783.[56] The essay remains within Hume's reluctance to describe the ultimate nature of physical reality and so says little about atoms and composition. Even so, his "endeavour to restore men to their native liberty, by examining all the common arguments against Suicide, and shewing that that action may be free from every imputation of guilt or blame," makes an argument similar to Radicati's about the place of agency in a universe structured by causes.[57] As the reference to "liberty" in this sentence makes clear, Hume's point is to situate the defense of suicide within his larger argument that freedom may be compatible with necessity so long as one's actions do not meet with resistance. Agents are asked not to view themselves as the image of God, but rather as a node in the manifold, one "for ever dependant on the general laws of matter and motion," and again this is understood to place limits on the notion "that human life is of such great importance" (10, 11). In keeping with Radicati's aquatic theme, Hume writes that "the life of a man is of no greater importance to the universe than that of an oyster" (11). The prohibition against suicide, on Hume's view, at once raises some agents above others and deprives them of what is provided by nature. In contrast, locating agents in a web of causes returns "their native liberty" to them precisely as it lessens the weight of any one existence.

Hume's argument works by running two kinds of causes together: the "general and immutable laws, by which all bodies, from the greatest planet to the smallest particle of matter, are maintained in their proper sphere and function," and the "bodily and mental powers . . . [the] senses, passions, appetites, memory, and judgment by which [all living things] are impelled or regulated in that course of life to which they are destined" (5–6). Physical laws govern the whole of the universe, yet included among them are the mental causes that push back against the inanimate world. Water runs downhill, Hume says, but not if it is drunk or diverted. The first is an event governed by physical causes, the second an act subject to mental causes, or more precisely a mental to physical route of causation. One might imagine the universe without agents in it, a world structured purely by physical laws of motion. The world we live in, however, contains actions as one of its basic units. That being so, the physical and mental causes of any given act form two threads of a single coil, neither one quite independent of the other: "These two distinct principles of the material and animal world, continually encroach upon each other, and mutually retard or forward each other's operation. The powers of men and of all other animals are restrained and directed by the nature and qualities of the surrounding bodies, and the modifications and actions of these bodies are incessantly altered by the operation of all animals" (6). Applied to the problem of the essay, this dual aspect means that sometimes death is subject to material causation alone, such as in cases of disease or accident, and sometimes to mental causation as well, such as in acts of suicide and murder. Suicide thus presumes that the mental has a causal role and doesn't simply tack along with the physical. Indeed suicide has no meaning without a causal role for the mental. Much depends, therefore, on where one puts the accent. All events are subject to cause, living and dying among them. To forbid suicide is to pick out and distinguish mental causation and life from the natural order of which they are a part.

Hume's essay underscores once again the piety of Clarissa's refusal to countenance suicide, this time in her removal from having a role in causation and in her elevation of her own life above the ordinary flux of matter. Seen this way, the long consideration of a death that she desires but does not cause repeats, in the theater of blessed self-transcendence, her earlier assertion of causal irrelevance to events as they occur. It does so moreover by singling out her physical and spiritual entity from others. "The world is unworthy of her," writes Belford near the end of her days, and readers are encouraged to agree (7:300 [1299]). This lapidary pronouncement has several meanings, not all congruent with each other. First, it refers to the process of reformation Belford embodies. Clarissa's transcendence makes her less of a model for emulation (like Pamela) than a person whose virtues and suffering ought to be considered for one's own improvement.[58] The important actions to pay attention to as Clarissa is dying, in this respect, are not so much Clarissa's as Belford's in turning from Lovelace, Anna's in marrying Hickman, and presumably our own, whatever they may be. Second, Belford's statement indicates the magnitude of difference between the "angelic sufferer" and her environs, not only the sordid brothel and prison-house but also physical places writ large (7:379 [1165]). While the world is subject to the push and pull of actions and events, Clarissa is plucked out for a kind of motionless divinity. Suicide would require mental causes Richardson keeps from the process of Clarissa's dying. This contrast is to such an extent, finally, that the world that is unworthy *of* her begins to have something like a causal role *for* her.

The effect of Belford's statement then is to keep Clarissa's mind and soul apart from causal relations and so to announce a kind of dualism in the same breath as to say that Clarissa has no material influence—and thus no influence at all—on the events that surround and include her as she dies. All causation is physical causation, on this view, and is therefore nothing with which Clarissa's spiritual substance may traffic. We may detect this drift toward epiphenomalism through the series of pronouncements taking up the question of suicide: "O that it were not a sin . . . to put an end to her own life," Lovelace reports Clarissa saying soon after recovering her senses (6:37 [936]). Clarissa voices a similar sentiment to Anna soon after: "What then, my dear and only friend, can I wish for but death?" (6:377 [1117]). These sorts of wishes—the first for a cause to mean something other than what it does, the second for something to happen without having to act as its cause—lead to a third, in the form of a promise: "[A]ltho' I wish not for life, yet would I not, like a poor coward, desert my post, when I can maintain it, and when it is my *duty* to maintain it" (6:377–8 [1117]).[59] The last sentence slightly and subtly changes the terms of her wish so that now she moves away from living at the same time as she sustains her post. One effect is to exaggerate the stillness of her retreat from causation, as Clarissa stands at duty yet apart from life. This stillness is achieved, I would argue, because the wishing not for life is a statement in miniature of a kind of retreat from acting as a cause. Thus this letter's final statement on suicide frames the problem in terms of Clarissa's familiar language of intentions. "I should think it . . . criminal," she writes, "were I now *wilfully* to neglect myself; were I *purposely* to run into the arms of death" (6:378 [1117]). The sentence describes what Clarissa considers to be suicide from two vantages, the first a kind of omission and the second a kind of commission—yet both, on her view, intentional acts. She strains to say that a criminal or unholy dying is one that is willful or purposive, and by implication that her own death will be absent of any such intentions. By subtracting intentions from her dying she also seems to subtract causes, leaving readers to look elsewhere than to herself. "I do so earnestly wish for the last closing scene," she writes early in her illness to Anna (6:187–8 [1018]). Death is "all I have to wish for," she says on her introduction to Mrs. Smith at her final lodgings (6:358 [1106]).[60] Yet, "I shall not die the sooner" for having such thoughts, she remarks upon the delivery of her coffin, because they will remain only wishes and not actions, and because for Clarissa (if not for Hobbes or Haywood or Lovelace or Lucretius) wishes are one thing and actions another (7:309 [1304]).[61]

Clarissa avoids a causal language because acting to end her life would be a sin. How aware she is of the theological history behind the prohibition is not entirely clear, though we are provided some context in the use made of the story of Lucretia, whose rape and suicide lie at the origin of the Roman republic. Lovelace draws attention to the parallel on three occasions, as Pamela had earlier in response to Mr. B's incursion on her chastity; Belford and Clarissa herself make the allusion in separate instances as well.[62] The allusion is significant for my current purposes because the story looms so large in Augustine's epochal declaration that suicide violates the commandment not to kill.[63] He begins with the question of rape: "When a woman's body is overpowered but the intention to remain chaste persists nonetheless, and is unaltered by any consent to evil," Augustine writes, "the crime belongs only to the man who violated her by force. It does not belong to the woman who, forced to submit to violation, did not consent to it by any act of will."[64] Since Lucretia did not consent to her violation, she remains innocent of any offense—a judgment made entirely on the basis of minds and causation. Having excused Lucretia of one crime, however, Augustine goes on to accuse her of another; for it is Lucretia who "slew the innocent and chaste Lucretia," she who is "a murderess of an innocent and chaste woman."[65] On these terms, the story of Lucretia has two implications as a background for the story of Clarissa: on the one hand, it distinguishes between adultery and rape in terms of the mental states of intention, will, and consent, rather than physical states of purity and violation; on the other, it draws a line between the ancient defense of suicide as an acceptable response to suffering or persecution and what Augustine with considerable influence presents as the Christian view of the act as a kind of murder.[66] Lovelace thus describes Clarissa's situation as the latest version of the quarrel between the ancients and moderns:

> Her innate piety (as I have more than once observed) will not permit her to shorten her own life, either by violence or neglect. She has a mind too noble for that; and would have done it before now, had she designed any such thing: For to do it, like the Roman Matron, when the mischief is over, and it can serve no end; and when the man, however a Tarquin, as some may think me in this action, is not a Tarquin in power, so that no *national point* can be made of it; is what she has too much good sense to think of. (7:14–5 [1148])

The end to which Clarissa's death would lead is wholly personal, and cannot serve the public cause of Lucretia. Clarissa is merely a young woman, Lovelace seems to say, not the wife of a statesman, and he is merely a fiend, not a danger to the nation. Yet the drift of her "innate piety" is to accentuate rather than diminish her importance as a private individual. Why, for example, should her "nobility of mind" prevent her from acting in her own death? According to the ontology presented by Hume and Radicati, the world includes a series of causal relations that go by the name of Clarissa (Hume would say we can't really know their particular nature; Radicati would respond with something about atoms). According to the ontology presented by Clarissa and Augustine, the world also includes something over and above these relations; hence Lucretia can be the murderer of Lucretia without redundancy or incoherence.

Lucretia murders Lucretia because she acts to destroy the person who is the image and property of God. This is a kind of dualism shared by Clarissa under the description of strong mind and will, piety and resolve, and so forth. It is also a kind of dualism that leaves physical causation to operate almost on its own. When she asks Anna to "[l]et me slide quietly into my grave," she elucidates as closely as she can the peculiar kind of inactive movement that brings her to her end (6:178 [1013]). Her preferred phrase for culpable action, after all, is taking a "step," as in the "rash step" she took in writing to Lovelace and promising to meet him at the gate to the garden (6:357 [1106]). Where "step" indicates volition, "slide" places agency in the ground beneath her, in Belford's "unworthy" world, where "the loss of my reputation, my disappointments, the determined resentment of my friends" along with "the Irreconcileableness of my Relations, whom I love with an unabated reverence; my apprehensions of fresh Violences [This wicked man, I doubt, will not yet let me rest]; my being destitute of Protection; my Youth, my Sex, my Unacquaintedness with the World, subjecting me to insults; my Reflections on the Scandal I have given, added to the Sense of the Indignities I have received from a man, of whom I deserved not ill; all together will undoubtedly bring on the effect, that cannot be undesirable to me" (6:379, 6:194–5 [1118, 1022]). Such a description might surprise readers familiar only with *Clarissa* criticism. As we have observed, criticism tends either to deny causes for Clarissa's death or to try to ferret them out (from "galloping consumption" to "nervous disorders" to anorexia).[67] The novel lists some causes plainly here, at least so far as Clarissa wants her reader to understand them. The causes are either states of affairs or their mental representations. The novel's rescue of Clarissa from accusations of suicide comes close, in this respect, to the kind of externalism one learns to associate with Lovelace. Her death is not "undesirable" but desire will play no role in its occurrence. Even as the external world appears to do all the causal work in her death, however, the world can only reach her sense and reflections not her intentions, which remain studiously impervious to the environment. The physical matter of body and world is where the action is. As a result, Clarissa's death strikes an odd sort of antilibertine epiphenomenalism. Whereas Lovelace discounted experience in order to say that intentions lagged behind their external and physical causes, Clarissa discounts mental causes to say that intentions watch the world as it passes.

I began this chapter by saying that it was going to be about the ontology of actions and therefore that the relevant question about actions was going to be whether any have happened. Seen this way, how accurately we know the causes of Clarissa's death is less important than the directions these causes point. If the causes point to her, the death is an action as well as an event, an action called suicide. (Likewise if the causes point to Lovelace, as Sandra Macpherson has recently argued, the action is called murder.)[68] Clarissa understands her death to have external causes yet chooses not to locate them with Lovelace, or at least not to blame him for her demise. She also studiously avoids taking a causal role in her death, and calls upon a kind of medical team to ensure that her actions are blameless; "Doctor tell me truly," she says in her final lodgings, "may I stay

here and be clear of any imputations of curtailing, thro' wilfullness
or impatiency . . . a life that might otherwise be prolonged?" (7:256
[1022]). How then are we to take stock of the death of Clarissa?
Richardson takes great pain, of course, to make sure his readers
contemplate the way that she dies. He also draws attention to why
she dies. The why question points away from agents—away from
Clarissa especially, but also from Lovelace and the Harlowes—and
toward the heterogeneous parts of the unworthy world. What
would it mean to consider the death of Clarissa as a major event in
the novel, perhaps *the* major event, but not as an action? It would
mean that Radicati and Richardson have an oblique symmetry. Clarissa dies without any special causal role for her mind. The death
happens in virtue of physical parts not metaphysical wholes.

I started this book with the seventeenth-century insight that the freedom to act could be compatible with necessity. To be sure, Clarissa's
understanding of actions is a long way from this notion. She considers freedom to be independent from necessity. To be a free agent,
she thinks, one's intentions must be able to be completed and must
be held apart from antecedent causes. Lovelace assaults her free will
not only because he holds her prisoner but also because he attempts
to turn her intentions to beliefs, to wrap them in the environment
he creates for her. This is, I think, a pretty close approximation of
what Clarissa means when she declares at several points her belief
in a "free will" under continuous threat from others. Whether
this view belongs to Richardson is beyond our knowing, though
I would make two related points that might complicate how we
understand its relation to other strands of the century-long discussion of actions. First, as I've attempted to emphasize in the layout
of this chapter, the epistolary structure affords competing accounts
of behavior. The multiplying of perspectives allowed by the form of
the letter, that is, keeps any single account of agency from standing apart from another. *Clarissa* is formally committed to conflict;
hence, I think, the interest in *this* novel among others in the period's

ongoing consideration of actions. Second, the overlapping of perspectives on action reveals an important feature of the compatibilist thesis. For the very duress under which Clarissa discovers her theory of freedom shows how even she is bound to an external system that gives meaning to her suffering: from the social rules of personal honor and family responsibility in the first chunk of the novel to the transcendent authority of God in the second. Individuation is in this respect more relational than absolute. At the same time, the Lovelacean commitment to necessity is beholden to some version of the internal, if to nothing other than the realm the environment fastens to and brings into being. The mental is an essential part of his strategy and so can never be eliminated entirely. In their separate ways, Lovelace and Clarissa are each wary of compatibilism: he because it thwarts his plans, she because it thwarts her freedom. Put together, they compose something like the theory of actions they separately resist. I have closed with *Clarissa* because the novel focuses so acutely on questions raised by this theory. I've looked at the problem of counting actions because doing so brings attention not only to the minute consideration of behavior and its component parts but also to the distribution of perspectives provided by the form of this novel. As it considers the problem of suicide, *Clarissa* presents something like a world with events yet no actions. There are still mental states in this world; they just observe events as they transpire. The end of the novel may be an invitation to consider this possible world. It is at the same time, however, a path to the world of actions. Has anything happened? If so, who or what is its cause?

Notes and Index

Notes

Introduction

1. *The Poems of Alexander Pope*, ed. John Butt, vol. 2 (London: Methuen and Co.; New Haven: Yale University Press, 1940), 6–10.

2. My sense of the distinction of actions from other kinds of events is from the twentieth-century theories of action, whose classic statements are by philosophers like Elizabeth Anscombe and Donald Davidson. See, in particular, Davidson's essays "Actions, Reasons, and Causes," "The Logical Form of Action Sentences," and "The Individuation of Events," collected in *Essays on Actions and Events*, second edition (Oxford: Oxford University Press, 2001). Anscombe is often credited with "inventing" action theory in *Intention* (1957; reprint, Cambridge: Harvard University Press, 2000). While Davidson's emphasis on causation makes his work more immediately resonant with the materials I focus on, I rely heavily on Anscombe in the final chapter on *Clarissa*, where the "logical" but not "causal" story about actions has, I argue, a real bearing on Clarissa's own account of her behavior and the account offered by her detractors.

3. A recent example of the novel + empiricism = interiority or "modern subject" thesis may be found in Nancy Armstrong's *How Novels Think* (New York: Columbia University Press, 2005). Armstrong argues that the following is true: "According to eighteenth-century epistemology and moral philosophy, the modern subject came into being as it took in sensations from the outside world and, of that material, composed first the ideas and then the judgment and moral sense that gave it a self-enclosed and internally coherent identity" (1). I will argue in contrast that the taking in of sensations from the outside world and making ideas of them (1) implies neither self-enclosure nor internal coherence and (2) is not the complete

story about philosophy and literature during the period, which begins to look very different when we consider the importance of *actions* along with *ideas*. Because actions bring certain mental states into the world and vice versa (intention to cut hair, for example), they extend rather than "enclose" minds. My point is not, however, to dispute the importance of empiricism to the rise of the novel, classic discussions of which include Ian Watt, *The Rise of the Novel* (Berkeley: University of California Press, 1957), 9–34; Michael McKeon, *The Origins of the English Novel 1600–1740* (Baltimore, MD: Johns Hopkins University Press 1987), 65–89; and John Bender, *Imagining the Penitentiary: Fiction and the Architecture of the Mind in Eighteenth-Century England* (Chicago: University of Chicago Press, 1987), 11–42.

4. John Dennis, *The Critical Works of John Dennis*, vol. 2, ed. Edward Niles Hooker (Baltimore, MD: Johns Hopkins Press, 1939–43), 350. Thanks to Sarah Ellenzweig for this.

5. Pope's description of the cutting seems tilted to the necessitarian reading, both in describing the scissors as a "fatal Engine" (line 149) and, at the moment of cutting, in saying "Fate urg'd the Sheers" (line 151).

6. See, for example, Davidson, "Freedom to Act," in *Essays on Actions and Events*, 63–82; and Susan Wolf, *Freedom within Reason* (Oxford: Oxford University Press, 1990). Hobbes's compatibilism was inseparable from his view of science. Similarly, Dan Wegner, *The Illusion of Conscious Will* (Cambridge: MIT Press, 2002) poses the free will question in terms of the experience and neuroscience of willing actions. Daniel Dennett's two books on the free will problem—*Elbow Room: The Varieties of Free Will Worth Wanting* (Cambridge: MIT, 1984), and *Freedom Evolves* (London: Penguin, 2003)—both combine compatibilism with an emphasis on evolution, Hobbes plus Darwin.

7. Thomas Hobbes, *Leviathan*, ed. Richard Tuck (Cambridge: Cambridge University Press, 1996), 145. Hereafter cited in parentheses.

8. See Quentin Skinner's recent monograph on Hobbes's view of liberty, which he contrasts to the ancient republican view that liberty is incompatible with state power. *Hobbes and Republican Liberty* (Cambridge: Cambridge University Press, 2008).

9. David Hume, *An Enquiry Concerning Human Understanding: A Critical Edition*, ed. Tom L. Beauchamp (Oxford: Oxford University Press, 2000), 72.

10. Among the unities of neoclassical literary theory, after all, pride of place always goes to unity of action: the tying together of what happens in a story into a cohesive structure. Were this a book on seventeenth- and eighteenth-century literary theory and the philosophy of action, this connection would be central.

11. In other words, eighteenth-century theories of mind understood them in terms of what we'd call propositional attitudes. This is Jerry Fodor's definition: "Propositional attitudes should be analyzed as relations. In particular, the verb in a sentence like 'John believes it's raining' expresses a relation between John and something else, and a token of that sentence is true if John stands in the belief-relation to that thing." "Propositional Attitudes," *Monist* 61 (1978): 573.

12. Hobbes is after something like this when he begins *Leviathan* with these words: "Concerning the Thoughts of Man, . . . they are every one a *Representation* or *Apparance*, of some quality, or other Accident of a body without us; which is commonly called an *Object*" (13). Hobbes, like Locke and Hume, held in this respect a "representational" theory of mind. My interest in externalism should not be taken to mean that the period didn't consider mental states in terms of representations. The point has to do with the causal relation between these thoughts and other parts of nature, especially with respect to actions.

13. The term comes from the analytic philosophy of the 1970s, where it refers to how the meaning of certain ideas is set "outside the head." The classic case is made by Hilary Putnam's twin earth thought experiment: on our earth water is H_2O, yet on twin earth water is XYZ; so when we think water here and when twin earthlings think water there the thoughts have a different content even as the experience (of wetness, thirst quenching, and so forth) is identical. See Putnam, "The Meaning of Meaning," in *Philosophical Papers*, vol. 2, *Mind, Language, and Reality* (Cambridge: Cambridge University Press, 1975). A broader case for externalism, about not only content but also thinking and (important for the current case) acting, may be found in the recent work on the extended mind and on enactive consciousness—the idea that the conscious mind reaches around and is involved in the extra-cranial environment; see, for the first, Andy Clark, *Supersizing the Mind: Embodiment, Action, and Cognitive Extension* (Oxford: Oxford University Press, 2008), and for the second, see Alva

Nöe, *Out of Our Heads: Why You are Not Your Brain, and Other Lessons from the Biology of Consciousness* (New York: Hill and Wang, 2009).

14. Here are Fodor's widely quoted, tart words on the subject: "[If] it isn't literally true that my wanting is causally responsible for my reaching, and my itching is causally responsible for my scratching, and my believing is causally responsible for my saying . . . , if none of that is literally true, then practically everything I believe about anything is false and it's the end of the world." *A Theory of Content and Other Essays* (Cambridge: MIT Press, 1990), 156.

15. John Locke, *An Essay Concerning Human Understanding*, ed. Peter Nidditch (Oxford: Oxford University Press, 1979), 629.

16. In this respect he is distinct from Descartes, whose division of the world into mental and physical substances left the causal relation between the two opaque, to say the least. I discuss this briefly in Chapter 2, including the challenge to Descartes posed by Elizabeth of Bohemia and Pierre Gassendi.

17. Jaegwon Kim writes: "[T]he problem of mental causation is to answer this question. How can the mind exert its causal powers in a world that is fundamentally physical?" *Physicalism, or Something Near Enough* (Princeton: Princeton University Press, 2005), 7. Kim's question concerns the place of mental properties in a physical world, not substance. The same would apply to Hobbes and Hume and at moments Locke. Some but not all writers in the period under discussion believed the world to be "fundamentally physical," yet those who stressed a dualism of mind and body were under even more pressure to answer this question, as Descartes discovered.

18. Locke, *An Essay Concerning Human Understanding*, 346.

19. I leave aside religious answers (for example: man is formed in God's image, other entities are not) not only because those answers bring in topics well beyond my interest but also because many of the writers I'm concerned with understood the religious answer to be of a separate order of argument.

20. The expression "something that it is like" is from Thomas Nagel's famous essay "What Is it Like to Be a Bat?" *Philosophical Review* 83, no. 4 (October 1974): 435–50. The point is to describe consciousness as a first-person property, unable to be accounted for completely by objective, third-person or physical description. We might know all there is to be

known about how echolocation works, but we wouldn't know "what it is like" to be a bat.

21. The now popular expression "the hard problem" was coined by David Chalmers. See *The Conscious Mind: A Search for a Fundamental Theory* (Oxford: Oxford University Press, 1996).

22. The seventeenth and eighteenth centuries knew no firm distinction between literature and philosophy or, moreover, between literary and philosophical study. The same is not the case for the present day. So it is with some timorousness that I admit that not all of the philosophers in this book are from my period of study. This sort of thing happens all the time, of course, though usually with a different cast of characters. Readers might be surprised, therefore, to find me citing Anscombe rather than Agamben, Davidson rather than Derrida, Fodor rather than Foucault, Lewis rather than Levinas. What is not merely a matter of taste derives from my interest in sticking to writers concerned with actions and causation, on the one hand, and consciousness on the other. I've found contemporary philosophy of mind and action and, on occasion, contemporary metaphysics and cognitive science to be closer in spirit to the animating concerns of the eighteenth century. Surely I must be crazy.

23. Emergence and panpsychism are at odds with each other, so it is of real interest, I will argue, that the poem keeps them together. Emergent properties come out of base properties that don't have them, as is the case with the poem's view that consciousness emerges from unconscious matter. Panpsychism says that the smallest particles have some sort of experience, a view presented by the poem with respect to will but not consciousness. See Galen Strawson et al., *Consciousness and Its Place in Nature* (Exeter: Imprint Academic, 2006) and Thomas Nagel, *The View from Nowhere* (Oxford: Oxford University Press, 1986), 49–51.

24. Locke, *An Essay Concerning Human Understanding*, 115.

25. The idea of a "temporal part" will be important for my reading of Rochester's *Love and Life*; it assumes that objects have parts of time as well as parts of space, that a given slice of time (for example, Jonathan typing this sentence in October 2008) is part of an object in a way analogous to a section of matter (the hands doing to the typing, for example). See Theodore Sider, *Four-Dimensionalism: An Ontology of Persistence and Time* (Oxford: Oxford University Press, 2001).

26. Anscombe, *Intention*, 19.

27. I use the expression "direction of fit" with respect to Anscombe's theory of actions, as do many others. The application of the term to actions postdates her philosophy, however. See I. L. Humberstone, "Direction of Fit," *Mind* 101, no. 401 (1992): 59–83. For an argument that this expression actually doesn't apply to Anscombe, see Candace Vogler, "Anscombe on Practical Inference," in Elijah Millgram, ed., *Varieties of Practical Reasoning* (Cambridge: MIT Press, 2001), 437–64.

28. I will discuss the person/body question in terms of whether there is something on top of or distinct from the "mereological sum" of irreducible parts or simples. See the discussion of composition in the first section of Chapter 2.

29. I take the initiative to make this statement from David Lewis: "A counterfactual (or 'subjunctive') conditional is an invitation to consider what goes on in a selected 'counterfactual situation'; which is to say, at some other possible world. Partly, the world in question is specified by the antecedent of the conditional: 'If kangaroos had no tails . . .' Partly, it is specified by a permanent understanding that there is to be no gratuitous departure from the background of fact: ignore worlds where the kangaroos float around like balloons, since the kangaroos of our world are much too heavy for that. Partly, it is specified by temporary contextual influences that indicate what sorts of departures would be epically gratuitous; for instance, facts just mentioned may have a special claim to be held fixed." *On the Plurality of Worlds* (Oxford: Basil Blackwell, 1986), 20–1. In the present instance the counterfactual situation is a world without agents and therefore without actions; the background of fact would be the ordinary laws of physics continuing to be in place. The point of the counterfactual would be to see how we discriminate actions from larger classes of events. What drains out of the possible world when we stipulate the absence of actions as an antecedent? It is extremely difficult to imagine a possible world in which there are actions but no events—conceptual evidence that the former is a subclass of the latter and not the other way around.

30. The expression derives from Plato, *Phaedrus* (265e), and is typically used to distinguish between natural kinds.

31. Anscombe, *Intention*, 19.

Chapter 1

1. My use of the term "attitude" in this context refers to the common meaning of mental verbs like believe, desire, intend, and hope as states that connect agents to propositions, which have, in turn, an imbedded "that clause." I believe that it would be nice to finish this book. I desire that it be written, and so on.

2. The title of this chapter invokes Davidson's essay, "Actions, Reasons, Causes" (1960), reprinted in *Essays on Actions and Events*, in which he attempts "to defend the ancient—and commonsense—position that rationalization is a species of causal explanation" (3, 3–21). Recent criticism of Davidson's theory of action has tended to focus on a putative absence for the role of agents. On this view, the belief-desire causal nexus leaves out the agents whose mental states are at issue. See, for example, Jennifer Hornsby, "Agency and Actions," in *Agency and Action*, ed. John Hyman and Helen Steward (Cambridge: Cambridge University Press, 2004), 1–24; and J. David Velleman, *The Possibility of Practical Reason* (Oxford: Oxford University Press, 2000), esp. chapter 6: "What Happens When Someone Acts?" 123–43. For the argument that Davidson has a narrow sense of intention (one that leaves out future intendings, for example), see Michael Bratman, *Faces of Intention* (Cambridge: Cambridge University Press, 1999), 209–24.

3. On the Hobbes-Bramhall debate, see Nicholas Jackson, *Hobbes, Bramhall, and the Politics of Liberty and Necessity* (Cambridge: Cambridge University Press, 2007). Jackson locates the debate within the changing landscape of seventeenth-century politics, in particular arguments about the relative importance of state authority (greater for Hobbes) and church independence (greater for Bramhall). One's actions are guided by authority, Hobbes says, at once aligning himself against the Arminian position on free will and saying it was fine to abolish the episcopacy. Needless to say, these issues extend beyond my more local interest in describing how reasons for acting are debated across the period.

4. Hobbes, *The Questions concerning Liberty, Necessity, and Chance* (London, 1656), 180, hereafter cited in parentheses as *Questions*.

5. Hobbes, *Of Libertie and Necessitie, a Treatise* (London, 1654), 7, hereafter cited in parentheses as *Libertie*.

6. Hobbes, *Humane Nature, or, the Fundamental Elements of Poli-cie, being a Discoverie of the Faculties, Acts, and Passions of the Soul of Man from their Original Causes* (London, 1650), 150. These passions are unperceived because they are mental, not because we are unaware that we are having them.

7. John Bramhall, *A Defence of True Liberty from Ante-cedent and Extrinsecall Necessity, Being an Answer to a Late Book by Mr. Thomas Hobbs of Malmsbury* (London, 1655), 13, noted hereafter cited in parentheses as *Defence*.

8. In his recent account of the free will debate over the course of the eighteenth century, James Harris argues that Bramhall's argument here is particularly influential in later defenses of free will; "It allows, or per-haps appears to allow, the believer in the freedom of the will to distinguish between, on the one hand, the way in which a cause determines its effect, and, on the other, the way in which a motive influences a choice. A motive, according to a believer in the freedom of the will, is not, properly speak-ing, the cause of an act of will. A motive is better thought of as an occa-sion for the agent to exercise his will in a particular way." *Of Liberty and Necessity: The Free Will Debate in Eighteenth-Century British Philosophy* (Oxford: Oxford University Press, 2005), 6–7.

9. The "might have done otherwise" argument is a long-standing main-stay in "libertarian" or "incompatibalist" conceptions of free will—that is, accounts that hold necessity to be incompatible with freedom. The argument dates at least as far back as the Scholasticism of Suarez and is still central to some philosophers today; see, for example, Shaun Nichols's recent attempts to combine incompatibilism with experimental psychology, "The Folk Psychology of Free Will: Fits and Starts," *Mind and Language* 19 (2004): 473–502. For an assessment of incompatibilism, see Randolf Clarke, *Libertarian Accounts of Free Will* (Oxford: Oxford University Press, 2003).

10. The next sentence is important for filling in what Hobbes under-stood to be his orthodoxy: "This concourse of causes, whereof every one is determined to be such as it is by a like concourse of former causes, may well be called (in respect they were all set and ordered by the eternal cause of all things God Almighty) the decree of God" (*Questions*, 80).

11. Hobbes, *Humane Nature*, 150.

12. Thus Sharon Cameron's recent study of impersonality—"a penetration through or a falling outside of the boundary of the human particular"—begins with a quick discussion of Hobbes, *Impersonality: Seven Essays* (Chicago: University of Chicago Press, 2007), ix and passim.

13. My use of the term "externalism" is (again) to emphasize arguments, or dimensions to arguments, that do not locate mental events, states, and processes entirely inside the head or even skin of agents. In particular, it is to emphasize the *causal role* of external objects, events, processes, and the *causal dependence* of the mind on such things external. The relevant texts are cited in the introduction.

14. Hobbes, *Elements of Philosophy* (London, 1656), 306.

15. This is not to say, of course, that Hobbes does not believe in the categories of soul, will, and passions. He just doesn't believe that they belong to a separate, "immaterial substance." Hobbes details his argument for the materiality of the soul in the final chapters of *Leviathan* (part 4, chapter 44, for example), where it becomes important for future rewards and punishment. Without a material soul, he argues, there is no physical basis for the pain of hell or the pleasure of heaven.

16. Hobbes makes a similar point in *Leviathan*, where he argues, in chapter 21, that "Liberty, or freedome, signifieth (properly) the absence of Opposition; (by Opposition, I mean externall Impediments of motion;) and may be applyed no lesse to Irrationall and Inanimate creatures, than to Rationall. For whatsoever is so tyed, or environed, as it cannot move, but within a certain space, which space is determined by the opposition of some externall body, we say it hath not Liberty to go further." A page later, the absence-of-impediments definition of liberty rules out the existence of free will: "Lastly, from the use of the word *Free-will*, no Liberty can be inferred of the will, desire, or inclination, but the Liberty of the man; which consisteth in this, that he finds no stop in doing what he has the will, desire, or inclination to do." Hobbes, *Leviathan*, 145, 146. For an illuminating contrast between Hobbes and other versions of liberty, both the republican tradition of viewing liberty in opposition to sovereign power and the Scholastic tradition of viewing liberty as the rational control of the passions, see Skinner's *Hobbes and Republican Liberty*.

17. According to Skinner (*Hobbes and Republican Liberty*, x–xii and passim), this notion of liberty distinguishes Hobbes from the classical

republican variety which insists that liberty is incompatible with arbitrary power. Liberty on Hobbes's view (again) merely means that one's actions are not impeded.

18. I discuss Locke's position in the fourth chapter of this book. Hume appears later on in this chapter. Kant extends beyond the chronological and geographical boundaries of this book, but this is the full passage from the *Second Critique*: "[H]ow can a man be called quite free at the same point of time and in regard to the same action in which and in regard to which he is nevertheless subject to an unavoidable natural necessity? It is a wretched subterfuge to seek to evade this by saying that the *kind* of determining grounds of his causality in accordance with natural law agrees with a *comparative* concept of freedom (according to which that is sometimes called a free effect, the determining natural ground of which lies *within* the acting being, e.g., that which a projectile accomplishes when it is in free motion, in which case one uses the word 'freedom,' because while it is in flight it is not impelled from without; or as we call the motion of a clock a free motion because it moves the hands itself, which therefore do not need to be pushed externally; in the same way the actions of the human being, although they are necessary by their determining grounds which preceded them in time, are yet called free because the actions are caused from within, by representations produced by our own powers, whereby desires are evoked on occasion of circumstances and hence actions are produced at our own discretion). Some still let themselves be put off by this subterfuge and so think they have solved, with a little quibbling about words, that difficult problem on the solution of which millennia have worked in vain and which can therefore hardly be found so completely on the surface." Immanuel Kant, *Critique of Practical Reason*, trans. Mary Gregor (Cambridge: Cambridge University Press, 1997), 80–1.

19. I will be focusing on the Collins-Clarke debate about free will. Their public debate begins in the very related question of the materiality/immateriality of the soul, as that took shape in response to Henry Dodwell's account of the mortality of the soul. Both published back and forth "letters to Mr. Dodwell" over the course of 1706 to 1708. The liberty-necessity quarrel should be seen in light of these underpinning concerns about matter and spirit.

20. Anthony Collins, *A Philosophical Inquiry Concerning Human*

Liberty (London, 1717), 12, hereafter cited in parentheses. Like Hobbes, Collins ties necessity to causation and motive (47–57), argues that this is the basis of moral action and political obedience (80–94), and questions whether reason provides a bright-line distinction between animals and humans (54–7).

21. Samuel Clarke, *Remarks upon a Book, Entitled a Philosophical Enquiry Concerning Human Liberty* (London, 1717), 19–20, hereafter cited in parentheses.

22. I will discuss in the next chapter the reaction to the seventeenth-century Lucretius revival in similar terms. In either case, Davidson's essay on "Mental Events" (1970) reprinted in *Essays on Actions and Events*, 207–28, is a descendant of Clarke's objection. Davidson's point is that every causal statement, such as token A causes token B, must instantiate a law, such as type Ω causes type π, and there is no way, on Davidson's view, to get mental states to fall under lawlike types—thus the famous "anomaly" of the mental. The difference between Clarke and Davidson is that the former is a substance dualist and the latter is not.

23. Collins has mistaken abstractions for real things, metaphors for entities with causal powers. In "supposing *Reasons* or *Motives* (unless those terms be mere Cant,) to make the same *necessary Impulse* upon *Intelligent* Subjects, as *Matter in Motion* does upon *unintelligent Subjects*," he "is supposing *Abstract Notions* to be *Substances*" (16). Nevertheless, Clarke and Collins argue at length elsewhere about the materiality of the soul, with Clarke taking the dualist and Collins the materialist position. See footnote 19, above.

24. Having such a power is a gift from God: "[T]he *Beginning of the Motion* cannot be in that which is moved necessarily, but in the superior Cause, or in the Efficiency of some Other Cause still superiour to That, till at length we arrive at some *Free Agent*. Which *Free Agent*, may either (which is the case of *Men*,) have *received* the *Power of beginning Motion*, from the *Will* of a Superior Free Agent" (6). This power "inheres" in some physical substance in ways we simply do not comprehend.

25. This is to antedate a development that Frances Ferguson has argued comes to conflict at the end of the century "between individually occupied and socially occupied identity." See *Solitude and the Sublime: Romanticism and the Aesthetics of Individuation* (New York: Routledge, 1992), 98.

26. Two works that have been important in sketching out the context of this distinction in the ethical philosophy of the period are J. B. Schneewind, *The Invention of Autonomy: A History of Modern Moral Philosophy* (Cambridge: Cambridge University Press, 1998), 1–15, 141–64, and passim; and Charles Taylor, *Modern Social Imaginaries* (Durham: Duke University Press, 2004). Schneewind's book is a long conspectus of moral thought from Grotius to Kant; Taylor's combines intellectual history with a sense of the changing institutions in which ideas circulate.

27. Collins, *Philosophical Inquiry*, 56–8.

28. As we shall see, Hume's theory of action is not that people confront a society that precedes them or shapes their intentions in accordance with its rules; it is, as Adela Pinch has written of Hume's theory of the passions, that a person becomes aware of her intentions by encountering them in someone else. See *Strange Fits of Passion: Epistemologies of Emotion, Hume to Austen* (Stanford: Stanford University Press, 1996), 17–50.

29. For three recent and superlative cases, see John Mullan, *Sentiment and Sociability: The Language of Feeling in the Eighteenth Century* (Oxford: Oxford University Press, 1988), 18–56; Pinch, *Strange Fits of Passion*, 17–50; and Lynn Festa, *Sentimental Figures of Empire in Britain and France* (Baltimore, MD: Johns Hopkins University Press, 2006), 22–35. Pinch's chapter on Hume does not take up the question of action or necessity, but her description of the extrasubjective beginnings of feelings is, as we will see, especially germane to the topic. "Hume's *Treatise* tells two different stories about the status of feelings. On the one hand, it asserts that feelings are individual, and that philosophy itself as well as social and aesthetic experience depends on individuals who can rely on the individual authenticity of their own emotional responsiveness. On the other hand, it also contends that feelings are transsubjective entities that pass between persons; that our feelings are always really someone else's; that it is passion that allows us to be persons, rather than the other way around" (19).

30. It is this commitment to what we would now call "folk psychology" that provides his attraction for a contemporary philosopher like Jerry Fodor, whose *Hume Variations* (Oxford: Oxford University Press, 2003) is a sustained reflection on the viability of book 1 of the *Treatise*.

31. Leo Damrosch uses this recourse to common belief as one of several connections between the ostensibly antithetical figures of David Hume and

Samuel Johnson. "Hume and Johnson, for all their radical disagreement that seemed so real to them and their contemporaries, share at a deep level a commitment to 'common life' that is the enabling premise of their writings. The disagreement occurs because Johnson takes common experience as a starting point that is simply given, while Hume reaches it by an elaborate dialectic that leaves a good many traditional assumptions badly damaged along the way." *Fictions of Reality in the Age of Johnson and Hume* (Madison: University of Wisconsin Press, 1989), 44.

32. Hume, *A Treatise of Human Nature*, ed. Peter Nidditch (Oxford: Oxford University Press, 1978), 399. Further references are to this edition and cited in parentheses.

33. Saul Kripke, *Wittgenstein on Rules and Private Language: An Elementary Exposition* (Harvard: Harvard University Press, 1982), 65. Kripke's analysis of Hume is designed to establish a connection to Wittgenstein on the basis of a shared skepticism. Hume's skepticism of private causation provides the basis for Wittgenstein's skepticism about private language, and both provide the basis for Kripke's externalist account of meaning, according to which the meaning of a word lies in its community of use. My point in bringing in Kripke's Hume is thus to establish a connection to externalism. For an internalist reading of Hume, see Bernard Williams, "Internal and External Reasons," in *Moral Luck: Philosophical Papers 1973–1980* (Cambridge: Cambridge University Press, 1981), 101–13.

34. Kripke, *Wittgenstein*, 65.

35. The relevant sections of Hume's famous argument about causation are within book 1, part 3, 73–83, later returned to and expanded in sections IV–VII of the *Enquiry Concerning Human Understanding*. The literature on Hume on causation is vast, to say the least. Particularly useful, I've found, is Don Garrett, *Cognition and Commitment in Hume's Philosophy* (Oxford: Oxford University Press, 1997), 96–136, and Barry Stroud, *Hume* (London: Routledge, Kegan and Paul, 1977), 42–95.

36. Kripke, *Wittgenstein*, 68.

37. Ibid. Kripke's idea of "private causation" is meant (again) to provide an analogue to Wittgenstein's idea of "private language," the argument being that neither is possible.

38. As Garrett (*Cognition and Commitment*, 129) puts it, "It is by projecting observed cases onto unobserved cases that we assign particular

causes to particular effects, and it is by a kind of meta-application of the same inductive procedure that we infer that all events *have* determining causes, on the basis of our experience of events whose determining causes we have been in a satisfactory position to discover."

39. For this reason, Hume claims to be making matter seem more like the will than the will like matter: "I do not ascribe to the will that unintelligible necessity, which is suppos'd to lie in matter. But I ascribe to matter, that intelligible quality, call it necessity or not, which the most rigorous orthodoxy does or must allow to belong to the will. I change, therefore, nothing in the receiv'd systems, with regard to the will, but only with regard to material objects" (410).

40. So Hume would disagree with Hobbes's contention that we are like conscious tops, feeling that we are free while being lashed by unseen hands. Hume would want to make a different sort of point about necessity, and say that we recognize we are spun about as soon as we view in the position of Hobbes, viewing other tops.

41. In addition to the texts mentioned in the introduction, an elaborate account of the rise of inwardness in seventeenth- and eighteenth-century philosophy may be found in Charles Taylor's *Sources of the Self: The Making of the Modern Identity* (Cambridge: Harvard University Press, 1989). "We think of our thoughts, ideas, or feelings as being 'within' us, while the objects in the world which these mental states bear on are 'without.' Or else we think of our capacities or potentialities as 'inner,' awaiting the development which will manifest them or realize them in the public world. The unconscious is for us within, and we think of the depths of the unsaid, the unsayable, the powerful inchoate feelings and affinities and fears which dispute with us the control of our lives, as inner" (111). As Taylor acknowledges (343–7), the example of Hume complicates his tripartite model by maintaining a skepticism of the mind/world opposition, breaking down the self/other division, and finally arguing for the importance of custom and habit in the development of the unconscious. Taylor's argument has recently been challenged by Dror Warhman's historical study, *The Making of the Modern Self: Identity and Culture in Eighteenth-Century England* (New Haven: Yale University Press, 2004), which would both postdate the "the modern self" to the end of the eighteenth century, and make it less a question of philosophy than, as befits a historian criticizing a philosopher,

a series of local and practical developments. My own difficulties with the model are different from Warhman's, however. I am arguing that what we sometimes call inwardness cannot on its own account for the problem of actions. One interesting feature of actions is that they highlight the importance of environment amid all the mind-talk in the seventeenth and eighteenth century, whether in the more externally focused perspective of Hobbes and Hume or the more internally focused perspective of Locke. A comprehensive portrait of private experience as it grows to be distinct from the public realm during the period may be found in Michael McKeon's *The Secret History of Domesticity: Public, Private, and the Division of Knowledge* (Baltimore, MD: Johns Hopkins University Press, 2005). For McKeon, the constitution of the private is never absolute, but rather always in an evolving relation to a notion of the public. Within the private spaces of economy, society, home, sexuality, and psychology are always elaborated a publicly relevant or observable domain.

42. As is the case throughout this chapter, my claims is about Hume's theory of actions. The argument would have to change somewhat were I discussing the theory of ideas in book 1 of the *Treatise*.

43. Here I would modify slightly Blakey Vermeule's argument that, in Hume, "we come to make inferences of this sort only by first crediting ourselves with an internal life and then by drawing an analogy to another person." Vermeule, *The Party of Humanity: Writing Moral Psychology in Eighteenth-Century Britain* (Baltimore, MD: Johns Hopkins University Press, 2000), 156. My argument here is that we come by a sense of motives for acting by crediting them first in other people.

44. Annette Baier, *A Progress of Sentiments: Reflections on Hume's Treatise* (Cambridge: Harvard University Press, 1991), 136.

45. I will discuss in Chapter 4 how the first edition of Locke's *Essay* makes the opposite point: reason is something one can know from the outside, whereas the passions (or desire at least) are not. With respect to Hume and the literary culture of the period, Adam Potkay is certainly right to say that Hume "unseats reason from its earlier Platonic and Christian throne, whence it presided as an organ of morality." See *The Passion for Happiness: Samuel Johnson and David Hume* (Ithaca, NY: Cornell University Press, 2000), 81. My point is that this is something that had been underway in different quarters of English language philosophy since Hobbes. As

Potkay further and persuasively observes, "Hume's devilish innovation is to assert that reason not only is but *ought to be* a slave" (86).

46. Reason is thus reduced, as Potkay puts it, to "a role of pure instrumentality, the calculation of logical propositions." *The Passion for Happiness*, 81.

47. A. O. Hirschman's classic study of the passions in the eighteenth century—*The Passions and the Interests: Political Arguments for Capitalism before Its Triumph* (Princeton: Princeton University Press, 1977)—pays short shrift to the doctrine of the "calm passions," which he argues are merely equivalent to the making of money. The theory of benevolence in writers like Shaftesbury, Hutcheson, and Hume is, for my purposes, more tied to ways of conceiving of society as a complicated aggregate. See G. J. Barker-Benfield, *The Culture of Sensibility: Sex and Society in Eighteenth-Century England* (Chicago: University of Chicago Press, 1992); and Lawrence Klein, *Shaftesbury and the Culture of Politeness* (Cambridge: Cambridge University Press, 1994).

48. Kripke (in *Wittgenstein*, 110) observes, however, that Hume's point turns on the way in which we conceive of the agent, not with his actual situation: "The falsity of the private model need not mean that a *physically isolated* individual cannot be said to follow rules; rather that an individual, *considered in isolation* (whether or not he is physically isolated), cannot be said to do so."

49. Hume, *An Enquiry Concerning Human Understanding*, 68. Further references are to this edition and in parentheses.

50. Davidson, "Introduction" to *Essays on Actions and Events*, xv.

Chapter 2

1. Readers interested in the larger Epicurean revival of which Lucretius translations were a part should consult Catherine Wilson's definitive new study, *Epicureanism at the Origins of Modernity* (Oxford: Oxford University Press, 2008); and Richard Kroll, *The Material Word: Literate Culture in the Restoration and Early Eighteenth Century* (Baltimore, MD: Johns Hopkins University Press, 1991). Wilson's study replaces Thomas Mayo, *Epicurus in England 1650–1725* (Dallas, TX: Southwest Press, 1934). Wilson and Kroll both extend well beyond Lucretius to the culture of Epicureanism. Kroll is especially interested in the works of Pierre Gas-

sendi, the Continent's atomist critic of Descartes, brought to England via Walter Charleton. Wilson presents a conspectus of atomist thinking from Leucippus to Leibniz. For a discussion of Lucretian ideas of matter with respect to sexuality as well as literary history, see Jonathan Goldberg, *The Seeds of Things: Theorizing Sexuality and Materiality in Renaissance Representations* (New York: Fordham University Press, 2009). Finally, while this chapter is about Creech's translation and some problems in the metaphysics of consciousness and mental causation, it is not about the wider circulation of Epicurean or Lucretian ideas in the period, beyond Rochester and Locke, nor about the Latin poem as such. I treat the translation as a seventeenth-century poem, which of course it is.

2. John Evelyn translated book 1 of the poem in 1656 along with a prefatory essay. Lucy Hutchinson's translation of the entire poem—circulated among an unknown number of associates—was completed at some point in the 1640s or 1650s but not published until 1996: see *Lucy Hutchinson's Translation of Lucretius*, De rerum natura, ed. Hugh De Quehen (Ann Arbor: University of Michigan Press, 1996). Rochester's translations of bits of the poem were done at some point in the 1670s, although the exact date, like that of all of his works, is unknown. Interestingly, his translation of the opening lines is one of the few poems to survive in his holograph. Creech's translation was a major success, and the third edition of 1683 was prefaced with thirteen commendatory poems, by Aphra Behn, Thomas Otway, John Evelyn, and others. On Hutchinson's translation, see Jonathan Goldberg, "Lucy Hutchinson's Writing Matter," *ELH* 73, no. 1 (Spring 2006): 275–301, and *Seeds of Things*. On Aphra Behn's interest in Lucretius and relation to Creech, see Alvin Snider, "Atoms and Seeds: Aphra Behn's *Lucretius*," *Clio* 33, no. 1 (Fall 2003): 1–24.

3. I will use the terms "atom," "seed," and "particle" interchangeably in this chapter. In the Latin original, Lucretius is similarly varied, changing the Greek *atom* into, among others, *materia, semina,* and *corpora*. Creech typically prefers "seed." In contemporary physics, atoms are not the same as particles. Rather, they are made from them (protons, quarks, electrons, and so forth). For Lucretius, atoms by definition cannot be divided. Likewise, Lucretius uses various terms for "mind" and "soul" (*mens, anima, animus*). Creech sometimes obeys the distinction; at other times he does not. I'll be interested in how atoms think and cause movement.

4. My use of the term "monism" here and "monist" elsewhere is to distinguish materialism from dualism. Not all monism is materialist, now or during the period, however. On the question of materialism and Christianity, see the discussion in Wilson, *Epicureanism at the Origins of Modernity* and Kroll, *The Material Word*, of Pierre Gassendi, and of Walter Charleton, whose *Epicurus's Morals* (1656)—a partial translation and apology—attempts to reconcile Christianity with atomism.

5. The distinction between persons and piles of atoms in the shape of persons is inspired by recent work in the ontology of material objects, especially work on mereology (the relation of parts and wholes) and composition (the adding of parts into wholes). See in particular Peter van Inwagen, *Material Beings* (Ithaca, NY: Cornell University Press, 1990); and Trenton Merricks, *Objects and Persons* (Oxford: Oxford University Press, 2003). I use expressions like "atoms in the shape of persons," whereas van Inwagen and Merricks would both say "atoms arranged personwise." The "wise" suffix means that the atoms may or may not actually compose a whole separate from its parts. Thus Merricks argues that there are no tables, no books, and no baseballs, just atoms arranged tablewise or bookwise or baseballwise. He does hold that there are people, owing to mental causation; on his view, minds cause events that masses of atoms could not. Van Inwagen argues that living beings form composites while other objects do not. Lucretius comes close to the opposite point on personal identity, as we shall see.

6. Thomas Creech, *T. LUCRETIUS CARUS, The Epicurean Philosopher, His Six Books, De Rerum Natura, Done into English Verse* (London, 1682), 1.6. Further references to Creech are to this edition and referenced to book and page (since Creech didn't include line numbers). I will also provide in brackets the book and line number Creech translates, all referring to the standard Latin edition, *De Rerum Natura*, ed. Cyril Bailey (Oxford: Clarendon Press, 1922), and identified by book and line number—in this case [1.158]. Creech's translation is loose, to the say the least. One thing he did was shorten the poem by cutting out most of the didactic comments to Memmius. I take the overall looseness as further reason to treat Creech's translation as a Restoration-era poem, which (again) it is. On the occasions when Creech's departure is significant for the present discussion, I will provide the original lines (from the Bailey edition) in the notes.

7. "nil igitur fieri de nilo posse fatendumst, / semine quando opus

est rebus quo quaeque creatae / aeris in teneras possint proferrier auras" (1.205–7). Creech makes the lines only about composition and leaves out the image of living beings brought into soft breezes of the air.

8. "rerum magnarum parva potest res / exemplare dare" (2.123–4). Once again, Creech turns the poem to his own interest. The original has "a small thing may give an analogy of great things," whereas Creech has "small things rise to great." He pushes on Lucretius' notion of material composition while not bringing up analogy.

9. As van Inwagen puts it, "Instead of asking about the conditions a pair of objects must satisfy if one is to be a part of the other, therefore, we shall ask about the conditions a plurality (or aggregate, array, group, collection or multiplicity) of objects must satisfy if they are to compose or add up to something." *Material Beings*, 22. On mereological relations, see Peter Simons, *Parts: A Study in Ontology* (Oxford: Oxford University Press, 1987); and Theodore Sider, "Parthood," *Philosophical Review* 116 (2007): 51–91.

10. The definition of a composite object as one with parts is basic mereology. See note above, as well as Kit Fine, "Compounds and Aggregates," *Noûs* 28 (1994): 137–58, and "Things and Their Parts," in Peter French and Howard K. Wettstein, eds., *Midwest Studies in Philosophy XXIII: New Directions in Philosophy* (Oxford: Basil Blackwell, 1999), 61–74.

11. Lucretius follows the Epicurean criticism of Democritus, who argued that atoms move in straight lines and that all wholes were merely illusions of our faulty perception. In the extreme, the argument entails that composite objects (like people) don't really exist. In the current philosophical scene, this position is known as mereological nihilism or elimitivism and can be found, for example, in the early work of Peter Unger. See his "I Do Not Exist," in G. F. MacDonald, ed., *Perception and Identity* (London: Macmillan, 1979), 235–51. A more moderate version may be found in Merricks, who argues for an elimitivism that will get rid of tables and chairs but not persons. See *Objects and Persons*, 1–55.

12. This all-important passage translates the following: "gigni posse ex non sensibu' sensus" (2.930). Although the line deals with sensation, the same concern about emergent properties applies to other mental terms found in the poem, such as *anima, animus,* or *mens,* words that Creech tends to run together. Lucretius might distinguish *anima* and *animus* as the rational and vital parts of the soul and *mens* as reason or cogitation and

sensus as feeling, but Creech loosely translates them as mind or sense or thought or soul, and defines each as a species of consciousness. The effect is a kind of compression: mind emerges from matter. See, for example, Creech's translation of 4.881–91 discussed in note 32, in which Creech makes both *mens* and *animus* "mind" in a single passage. In these cases, a singular mental-state term suffices to describe what matter in motion does. The question is not how various types of thought or emotions might arise from physical matter; it is only how atoms without sense might be able to produce entities that have sense, how a physical object might be the locus of experience.

13. See Chalmers, "Facing Up to the Problem of Consciousness," *Journal of Consciousness Studies* 2, no. 3 (1995): 200–19, and the book-length expansion, *The Conscious Mind*.

14. Chalmers, *The Conscious Mind*, 25.

15. Chalmers, "Facing Up to the Problem of Consciousness," 201. In addition to Chalmers, the recent work of Galen Strawson is also of interest to the present chapter. Stawson has argued against the kind of emergence one finds in Lucretius and in favor of a contrasting model of panpsychism. Whereas Lucretius argues that consciousness emerges from atoms that are not conscious, Strawson argues that this is impossible, and so therefore elementary particles must, in some sense, be conscious. See his *Consciousness and Its Place in Nature,* a book that contains responses from more than a dozen philosophers.

16. Qualia is the plural form of quale or qualis (in the masculine nominative singular) and refers to the subjective character of experience—what something is like. Qualia is thus, Dennett says, a most unfamiliar word for a very familiar thing. See his "Quining Qualia" (1988), reprinted in Chalmers, ed., *The Philosophy of Mind: Classical and Contemporary Readings* (Oxford: Oxford University Press, 2002), 226–46. For the neuroscience of qualia, see Christof Koch, *The Quest for Consciousness: A Neurobiological Approach* (Englewood, CO: Roberts and Co., 2004), 1–4 and passim. I'll stick close to Koch's definition: "The elemental feelings and sensations making up conscious experience (seeing a face, hearing a tone, and so on). Qualia are at the very heart of the mind-body problem" (343).

17. The expression "what it is like" was made famous by Nagel in his seminal essay, "What Is It Like to Be a Bat?," 435–50. The important sen-

tences for our current purposes appear near the beginning: "But no matter how the form may vary, the fact that an organism has conscious experience *at all* means, basically, that there is something it is like to *be* that organism. There may be further implications about the form of the experience; there may even (though I doubt it) be implications about the behavior of the organism. But fundamentally an organism has conscious mental states if and only if there is something that it is to *be* that organism—something it is like *for* the organism.

We may call this the subjective character of experience. It is not captured by any of the familiar, recently devised reductive analyses of the mental, for all of them are logically compatible with its absence" (436). For Nagel as for Chalmers, it is the plausible absence of consciousness from the physical domain that means that it is something that has to be explained.

18. Chalmers, "Facing Up to the Problem of Consciousness," 200. The expression "further fact" as far as I know comes from Derek Parfit's famous account of personal identity discussed below. In either case, further fact indicates a nonreductive position on the topic at hand. In our present-day philosophy, as in Creech's, attention to the hard problem of consciousness comes from knowing more not less about the parts of nature. Even as we discriminate the workings of a physical system, much remains unanswered; "Why does conscious experience exist? If it arises from physical systems, as seems likely, how does it arise?" Chalmers, *The Conscious Mind*, 5. In the words of Joseph Levine, there would seem to be an "explanatory gap" between sense and seeds void of sense. See "Materialism and Qualia: The Explanatory Gap," *Pacific Philosophical Quarterly* 64 (1983): 354–61. One important difference is that talk about the hard problem in our period distinguishes "consciousness" from other aspects of mind, such as propositional attitude psychology, for example, or concept possession. Consciousness is phenomenal, while other aspects of mind are functional. The situation in the seventeenth and eighteenth centuries was not so cleanly divided, though as I'll argue below, indications of the distinction are available as early as Locke.

19. See, for example, Richard Bentley's aptly titled *Matter and Motion Cannot Think: Or a Confutation of Atheism from the Faculty of the Soul* (London, 1692). For a historical account of this problem in the seventeenth and eighteenth centuries, see John Yolton, *Thinking Matter: Materialism in*

Eighteenth-Century Britain (Minneapolis: University of Minnesota Press, 1983).

20. Not every version of dualism held every single one of these points. Aquinas, for example, says that the soul is an immaterial substance yet perception, images, and memory hinge on the cooperation of the body. See *Summa Theologica* part 1, questions 88 and 89. For a contemporary defense of substance dualism, see Richard Swinburne, *The Evolution of the Soul* (Oxford: Clarendon Press, 1986).

21. Creech's notes are at the end of the poem, and are separately paginated. The quotation in this case appears on page 22, hereafter cited in parentheses.

22. Creech's dualism is relatively ad hoc and owes as much to Christian Platonism as to Descartes. Of course, not all Christian theology was dualist during the period; as Hobbes points out, ideas of the resurrection and heaven prominently feature notions of the body. Moreover, not all dualism was as absolute as that of Descartes: "Because on this side I have a clear and *distinct Idea* of my self, as I am only a *thinking Thing, not extended*; and on the other side because I have a *distinct Idea* of my *Body,* as it is onely an *extended* thing, *not thinking,* 'tis from hence *certain,* that I *am really distinct from my Body,* and that I can *exist without* it." *Six Metaphysical Meditations*, trans. William Molyneux (London, 1680), 93–4.

23. Margaret Cavendish, *Observations on Experimental Philosophy*, ed. Eileen O'Neil (Cambridge: Cambridge University Press, 2001). Cavendish differs from Lucretius in denying the ultimate level of solid, unbreakable atoms. For Cavendish, nature is one, without void and without minimal units. In recent work on literature and seventeenth-century philosophy, Cavendish has thus been understood to stand with Milton as part of a vitalist and Monist tradition of viewing all of creation as at once material and living. For Milton, this view links to a defense of free will and (for some) a defense of the individual over and against the state. See, for example, John Rogers, *The Matter of Revolution: Science, Poetry and Politics in the Age of Milton* (Ithaca, NY: Cornell University Press, 1995). Cavendish's panpsychism finds an echo in the recent work of Galen Strawson, who argues that the smallest units of nature—whatever these are—must be "experiencing involving" since the kind of emergence that would give us something from nothing is impossible. See Strawson, "Realistic Monism,"

in *Consciousness and Its Place in Nature*, 25. Whereas Lucretius argues that consciousness emerges from atoms that are not conscious, Strawson argues that this is impossible and so therefore elementary particles must, in some sense, be conscious.

24. Creech's translation compresses the argument somewhat, so that the option of sense in one part versus sense across the whole is left out (2.907–9). In some ways, this highlights the argument about micro- into macro-experience.

25. The classic statement of emergence is C. D. Broad's *The Mind and Its Place in Nature* (London: RKP, 1925). On emergentism especially in the nineteenth and twentieth centuries, see Brian P. McLaughlin, "The Rise and Fall of British Emergentism," in Ansgar Beckermann et al., eds., *Emergence or Reduction? Essays on the Possibility of Non-Reductive Physicalism* (New York: W. de Gruyter, 1992), 49–93.

26. It is the atoms that create sense and the wood that creates fire. For some, like Heraclitus, fire is one of the basic elements of the world.

27. Marshall Brown, *Preromanticism* (Stanford: Stanford University Press, 1991), 58–81. Deidre Lynch, *The Economy of Character: Novels, Market Culture and the Business of Inner Meaning* (Chicago: University of Chicago Press, 1998), 47–56. Ian Watt, *The Rise of the Novel* (Berkeley: University of California Press, 1957), 9–59. Lynch and Watt concentrate on empiricism, with its connection of consciousness to experience. Lynch locates a certain turn to inwardness at the midcentury. My own view is that the "flat" and "round" dichotomy, at least with respect to consciousness and actions, is not so abrupt. Brown views consciousness as something that is achieved by the Romantics when they disassociate the term from experience. See also his *The Gothic Text* (Stanford: Stanford University Press, 2005), in which this notion is developed at greater length with reference especially to Kant.

28. In the recent formulation of Jaegwon Kim, "The problem of mental causation is to answer this question: How can the mind exert its causal powers in a world that is fundamentally physical?" Kim, *Physicalism, Or Something Near Enough*, 7. The problem emerges from the heart of the physicalism to which the poem is so wed. "If you pick any physical event," Kim writes, "and trace out its causal ancestry or posterity, that will never take you outside the physical domain." *Mind in a Physical World:*

An Essay on the Mind-Body Problem and Mental Causation (Cambridge: MIT Press, 1998), 40. So if every event has such a physical cause, what work is there left for the mental cause of the same event? Those who want to say that matter gives rise to mind, yet want at the same time to say that mind has a causal role to play separate from its status *as* matter, "must give an account of how the mental cause and the physical cause of one and the same event are related to each other" (*Mind in a Physical World*, 37). Thus the problem of overdetermination, or, the problem of having two or more causes for the same effect (in which case, the lower-level physical explanation is typically given pride of place). This is Merricks's definition (*Objects and Persons*, 58): "An effect is overdetermined if the following are true: that effect is caused by an object; that object is causally irrelevant to whether some other—i.e. numerically distinct—object or objects cause that effect; and the other object or objects do indeed cause that effect."

29. On May 6, 1643, Elisabeth of Bohemia wrote to Descartes to ask "how the soul of a human being (it being only a thinking substance) can determine the bodily spirits, in order to bring about voluntary actions. For it seems that all determination of movement happens through the impulsion of the thing moved, by the manner in which it is pushed by that which moves it, or else by the particular qualities and shape of the surface of the latter. Physical contact is required for the first two conditions, extension for the third. You entirely exclude the one from the notion you have of the soul, and the other appears to me incompatible with an immaterial thing. This is why I ask you for a more precise definition of the soul than the one you give in your *Metaphysics*, that is to say, of its substance separate from its action, that is, from thought." *The Correspondence between Princess Elisabeth of Bohemia and Rene Descartes*, ed. and trans. Lisa Shapiro (Chicago: University of Chicago Press, 2007), 62. The most important of Epicurus' and Lucretius' seventeenth-century defenders, Pierre Gassendi, asked a similar question in his "Fifth Objection" to Descartes, published with the *Meditations* in 1642 and later continued in the *Disquisitio Metaphysica* (Amsterdam, 1644).

30. "Epiphenomenalism" is a nineteenth-century term, developed by writers like Thomas Huxley (see the discussion of Rochester's *Satyr against Reason and Mankind* in the next chapter). It has some but few defenders now, including Frank Jackson in his famous essay "Epiphenomenal Qua-

lia," *Philosophical Quarterly* 32 (1982): 127–36. I discuss Jackson's essay with reference to the Molyneux problem in Chapter 4. Perhaps of most interest, epiphenomenalism along with panpsychism are entertained, if not defended, by Chalmers in *The Conscious Mind*, 150–60 and 293–301.

31. Creech combines as one word—"mind"— Lucretius' distinction between the cognitive mind (*mens*) in 4.884 and soul (*animus, anima*) 4.881–2.

32. The Lucretian position on free will is opposed to both the compatibilism of Hobbes and Hume I discussed in the last chapter and the determinism of the Stoics and Spinoza. For the latter, there is no void and thus no free movement. For Lucretius, void is the precondition of free will. Collins makes this point against "Epicurians" in his first treatise.

33. A *Void is space intangible*: Thus prov'd.
　　For were there none no Body could be mov'd,
　　Because where e're the brisker motion goes,
　　It still must meet with stops, still meet with foes,
　　'Tis natural to Bodies to oppose.
　　So that to move would be in vain to try,
　　But all would fixt, stubborn, and moveless lie,
　　Because no yielding Body could be found
　　Which first should move, and give the other ground.
　　　　　　　　　　　　　　(i.12–3 [1.334–9])

34. Now *Seeds* in downward motion must *decline*,
　　Tho *very litle* from th' exactest line;
　　For did they still move *strait*, they needs must fall
　　Like drops of Rain dissolv'd and scatter'd all,
　　For ever tumbling thro the mighty space,
　　And never *joyn* to make one single mass. (i.41 [2.216–24])

35. David Skrbina, *Panpsychism in the West* (Cambridge: MIT Press, 2005), 53.

36. Ibid.

37. Sarah Ellenzweig, *The Fringes of Belief: English Literature, Ancient Heresy, and the Politics of Freethinking, 1660–1760* (Stanford: Stanford University Press, 2008), 42.

38. Rochester, *De Rerum Natura*, lines 1–6, in Harold Love, ed., *The*

Works of John Wilmot, Earl of Rochester (Oxford: Oxford University Press, 1999). All further citations are to this edition and noted in parentheses.

39. See *Troades*, lines 398–408, in *Seneca VIII: Tragedies*, trans. and ed. Frank Justus Miller (Cambridge: Harvard University Press, 1968).

40. Charles Blount, "To the Right Honourable The most Ingenious Strephon. Concerning the Immortality of the Soul," in *The Miscellaneous Works of Charles Blount* (London, 1695), 117–8.

41. Charles Gildon, "To Charles Blount, esq." in *The Miscellaneous Works of Charles Blount*, 189.

42. On the pragmatics of belief in Blount and Rochester, see Ellenzweig, *The Fringes of Belief*, 31–52.

43. The *OED* credits the *Essay* with coining its modern meaning as "impressions, thoughts, and feelings," rather than the older, transitive meaning of being aware of some object or state of affairs. The *OED* holds a separate definition for "The state or faculty of being conscious, as a condition and concomitant of all thought, feeling, and volition," and credits Locke with the second use. The first goes to Ralph Cudworth's 1678 *True Intellectual System of the Universe*. Importantly for my current purposes, Cudworth's use occurs in the process of addressing the "hard problem": "Neither can life and cogitation, sense and consciousness . . . ever result from magnitudes, figures, sites, and motions."

44. See Derek Parfit, *Reasons and Persons* (Oxford: Oxford University Press, 1984), 204–8 and passim, and Cameron, *Impersonality*.

45. For Taylor's chapter on Locke's "punctual" model of personal identity, see *Sources of the Self*, 159–76.

46. Lynch, *The Economy of Character*, 34.

47. Armstrong, *How Novels Think*, 11.

48. Ibid., 4.

49. These topics are again more ontological and metaphysical than Locke's typical epistemological concerns. They concern "what is" not how we know what is. As the discussion gets thorny, however, Locke does attempt to turn ontological discussion back to epistemology, back to how we know what's there, not what the world actually is.

50. This chapter was added to the second edition in 1694 and, along with remarks on thinking matter made in book 4, was a subject of his controversy with Bishop Stillingfleet. See note 59, below.

51. Locke, *An Essay Concerning Human Understanding*, 115, hereafter cited in parentheses. The point he is drawing at this exact instance has to do with the argument with Descartes over whether the soul always thinks. To have a soul is simply to be possessed of some variety of (most likely) immaterial substance, the precise nature of which is the concern of revealed religion and well outside the scope of what we can know. To think is to have ideas, every single one of which derives in some fashion from experience. Thus Locke further reasons that the soul does not always think, as when, for example, one is asleep and not dreaming. Were this constraint not in place, we would be able to acquire ideas without having experiences—sleeping ideas, say—which Locke is in the process of arguing is impossible.

52. "For this Organization being at any one instant in any one Collection of *Matter*, is in that particular concrete distinguished from all other, and is that individual Life, which existing constantly from that moment both forwards and backwards in the same continuity of insensibly succeeding parts united to the living Body of the Plant, it has that Identity, which makes the same Plant, and all the parts of it, parts of the same Plant, during all the time that they exist united in that continued Organization, which is fit to convey that Common Life to all the Parts so united" (331).

53. Were we to define the world as everything, it would also include the immaterial substance from which God and angels and (probably) souls are made. Of course, Locke makes it clear that he is not interested in explaining the nature of God or angels, so for the purposes of his philosophy, their nature is irrelevant.

54. Van Inwagen, *Material Beings*, 144.

55. Ibid., 145.

56. One difference would be that the planks always have the same dimensions and so the ship is the same size. "John Locke" loses parts and gains others as he grows older and changes shape. Yet the question of endurance over time remains otherwise the same. For the Ship of Theseus argument for physical continuity, see Parfit, *Reasons and Persons*, 203–4. For the four-dimensionalist use of the Ship of Theseus, see Sider, *Four-Dimensionalism*, 6–10. Sider's argument is that the ship has spatial parts (in this case planks) and temporal parts (moments in time), so the identity of the ship *perdures* as a "spacetime worm" (that is, extended in both

directions); the same could be said for the original planks, thought not *as* the ship itself.

57. Hence Parfit's updating (*Reasons and Persons*, 206) of Locke's psychological criterion for personal identity as "continuity" rather than "connectedness," not "the holding of particular direct psychological connections" but the "holding of overlapping chains of *strong* connectedness."

58. See Locke, *Essay Concerning Human Understanding*, 336–7.

59. The most important example would be Edward Stillingfleet, with whom Locke carried on a debate across the 1690s. See Stillingfleet's *The Bishop of Worcester's answer to Mr. Locke's letter, concerning some passages relating to his Essay of humane understanding* . . . (London, 1697), and *The Bishop of Worcester's answer to Mr. Locke's second letter* . . . (London, 1698).

60. The earlier date also might explain why the category of thinking crops up here more than consciousness. Since consciousness is the awareness of one's thinking—for Locke, that is, a flip side to the same thing—the question of can matter think is for him also a question of can matter be conscious: the hard problem as it is now called.

61. The discussion is about whether God could be a material thing. As Locke sets it up, however, the question applies to any thinking entity.

62. Strawson, *Consciousness and Its Place in Nature*, 8.

63. See, for example, book 2, chapter 23, on the complex ideas of substances. For a contemporary version of this point, see Colin McGinn's contribution to the Strawson volume, "Hard Questions," in *Consciousness and Its Place in Nature*, 90–9. Like Locke, McGinn wonders why the sentient particles of panpsychism don't amount to miniselves. Among philosophers considering the consciousness problem, McGinn's position—"mysterianism," as he puts it—is that emergence is insoluble and the hard problem beyond our grasp, a mystery. For the initial formulation of this position, see "Can We Solve the Mind-Body Problem?" *Mind* 98, no. 391 (July 1989): 349–66.

64. The full quotation might be called the consciousness sublime:

"Consciousness is all the rage just now. It boasts new journals of its very own, from which learned articles overflow. Neuropsychologists snap its picture (in colour) with fMRI machines, and probe with needles for its seat in the brain. At all seasons, and on many continents, interdisciplinary conferences about consciousness draw together bizarre motleys that include philosophers, psychologists, phenomenologists, brain scientists, MDs, computer scientists, the Dalai Lama, novelists, neurologists, graphic artists, priests, gurus and (always) people who used to do physics. Institutes of consciousness studies are bountifully subsidised. Meticulous distinctions are drawn between the merely conscious and the consciously available; and between each of these and the preconscious, the unconscious, the subconscious, the informationally encapsulated and the introspectable. There is no end of consciousness gossip on Tuesdays in the science section of the *New York Times*. Periodically, Nobel laureates pronounce on the connections between consciousness and evolution, quantum mechanics, information theory, complexity theory, chaos theory and the activity of neural nets. Everybody gives lectures about consciousness to everybody else. But for all that, nothing has been ascertained with respect to the problem that everybody worries about most: what philosophers have come to call 'the hard problem.' The hard problem is this: it is widely supposed that the world is made entirely of mere matter, but how could mere matter be conscious? How, in particular, could a couple of pounds of grey tissue have experiences?" *London Review of Books*, May 24, 2007.

Chapter 3

1. Carole Fabricant, "Rochester's World of Imperfect Enjoyment," *Journal of English and Germanic Philology* 73 (1974): 343.

2. For the epistemological argument, see Reba Wilcoxon, "Rochester's Philosophical Premises: A Case for Consistency," *Eighteenth-Century Studies* 8, no. 2 (1974–5): 183–201; and, more recently, Marianne Thormählen, *Rochester: The Poems in Context* (Cambridge: Cambridge University Press, 1993), 162–89. For Rochester's position within religious debate, see Ellenzweig, "The Faith of Unbelief: Rochester's 'Satyre,' Deism and Religious Freethinking in Seventeenth-Century England," *Journal of British Studies* 44 (January 2005): 27–45 and *The Fringes of Belief*, 31–5 and passim; and Gillian Manning, "Rochester's *Satyr against Reason and Mankind* and Contemporary Religious Debate," *Seventeenth Century* 8, no. 1 (Spring 1993): 99–121.

3. Love, ed., *The Works of John Wilmot, Earl of Rochester*, 66–7. Hereafter cited by line number in parentheses.

4. Wilcoxon ("Rochester's Philosophical Premises," 194) argues that "Hobbes's metaphysical materialism, however, receives no explicit statement in the 'Satyr Against Mankind.' (It is possible to adopt an epistemology of sense perception and still be a metaphysical idealist, as Bishop Berkeley demonstrates.)" Explicit statements are hard to come by in poetry, yet in this case I'm not sure how one can be more so than with "material sense."

5. On the ignis fatuus metaphor in the period, see Dustin Griffin, *Satires against Man: The Poems of Rochester* (Berkeley: University of California Press, 1973), 186–7; and Thormählen, *Rochester*, 194–5.

6. On Rochester in the epistemological vein, see Wilcoxon, "Rochester's Philosophical Premises"; Thormählen, *Rochester*; Griffin, *Satires against Man*. For the debts to Hobbes as well as Montaigne, see Thomas H. Fujimura, "Rochester's 'Satyr against Mankind': An Analysis," *Studies in Philology* 55 (1958): 576–90; K. E. Robinson, "Rochester and Hobbes and the Irony of *A Satyr against Reason and Mankind*," *Yearbook of English Studies* 3 (1973): 108–19. On the false light of the Cambridge Platonists as it made its way into normative Anglicanism, see Manning, "Rochester's *Satyr.*" Ellenzweig puts the argument around religion together with the ancient and modern skepticism.

7. Huxley's steam-whistle metaphor is perhaps the most widely quoted of all descriptions of epiphenomenal mental states. It appeared originally in *The Fortnightly Review* (1874) as "On the Hypothesis that Animals Are Automata, and Its History." See *Method and Results: Essays by Thomas H. Huxley* (New York: D. Appleton and Company, 1898), 240.

8. I find the category of right reason less baffling than do many critics, as I don't think Rochester was concerned wholly with epistemology and skepticism. See the interesting reflections of Charles A. Knight, "The Paradox of Reason: Argument in Rochester's 'Satyr against Mankind,'" *Modern Language Review* 65, no. 2 (1970): 254–60; and James E. Gill, "Mind against Itself: Theme and Structure in Rochester's *Satyr against Reason and Mankind*," *Texas Studies in Literature and Language* 23, no. 4 (1981): 555–76.

9. The impertinence of thought without action does of course suggest that a split is possible. The poem seems to toggle between describing the ways things are to describing the ways things ought to be. Glossing these

lines, Dustin Griffin (*Satires against Man*, 8) has written that "[m]orality, for Rochester, was the product of rational thought, not revelation." This strikes me as half correct. While it is surely right to say that the poem prefers the secular to the religious, it is nevertheless misleading to suggest that the solution dwells in the very category the poem insists upon questioning.

10. Howard Erskine-Hill, "Rochester and Falstaff," in Nicholas Fisher, ed., *That Second Bottle: Essays on the Earl of Rochester* (Manchester: Manchester University Press, 2000), 41.

11. See, for example, Gill, "The Fragmented Self in Three of Rochester's Poems," *MLQ* 10 (1988): 19–39. Gill's description of the poem is less succinct than Erskine-Hill's, though essentially the same: "Unframed by a physical or social setting, except the extreme unlikelihood that any traditional Phyllis [*sic*] would calmly acquiesce in the speaker's argument, 'Love and Life' conveys a sense of the radical contingency of a subject barely grounded in a fragmented, disappearing past, simultaneously generated and alienated from himself in the present . . . and uneasily projected into the uncertain, perhaps nonexistent future. What remains is the vital moment—true, wholehearted, utterly given, and miraculous in its brevity. But even as this gift is proffered, its evanescence is emphasized in the speaker's final comment, which can be read both as an extension of his basic insecurity and as a threat whose aim is to forestall his mistress from making unrealistic demands" (20–1). My reading will run contrary to Gill's in several respects. I don't think that the speaker has an argument by which he attempts to persuade the addressee. I don't think that the livelong minute is miraculous in its brevity (following the allusion to Augustine, I argue that it is quite the opposite). I don't think that the end is a threat. I address the first and last points in my attempt to unravel the poem's three- (as opposed to four-) dimensional ontology. I address the middle point first, as a question of the structure of time, presented in the poem through its reworking of Augustine and Hobbes.

12. Parfit, *Reasons and Persons*, 178.

13. I am quoting from the translation most commonly circulated during the seventeenth and eighteenth centuries, that of William Watts, *Saint Augustines Confessions* (London, 1631), 755. The Watts translation is still the basis for the Loeb classical edition.

14. This does not entail that a person's or a poem's qualities may be

explained by their atoms, though as we've seen, Lucretius does suggest something like that.

15. In *A Natural History of the Passions* (1674), Rochester's contemporary Walter Charleton gives a more discursive account of how the present is infused sense. "The Passions receiving their most notable diversity from certain *circumstances* of *Time*, may therefore be most intelligibly distinguished by having respect to the same Circumstances. For there are of *Conceptions* three sorts, whereof one is of that which is *present*, which is *sense*; another of that which is *past*, which is *Remembrance*; and the third, of that which is *to come*, which is called Expectation." Sense gives to the past and future a certain immediacy: "[We] are pleased, or displeased even at things past; because the *Memory* reviving and reviewing their images, sets them before the Soul as present, and she is affected with them no less than if the things themselves were present. So also of things *future*; forasmuch as the Soul by a certain providence preoccupying the images of things that she conceives to come, looks upon them as realy present, and is accordingly pleased or displeased by *Anticipation*: every conception being pleasure, or displeasure *present*." Charleton, *A Natural History of the Passions* (London, 1674), 86–7.

16. According to Hobbes's eclectic reading of Scripture, neither the soul nor its reward or punishment is eternal. See *Leviathan*, IV.38, 306–20, on the afterlife. For further reflections on the larger problem of time in *Leviathan*, see J. G. A. Pocock, "Time, History and Eschatology in the Work of Thomas Hobbes," in *Politics, Language, and Time* (New York: Atheneum, 1971), 148–201.

17. Gill, "The Fragmented Self," 24.

18. Gill refers to the speaker as a "split subject" (ibid., 24). In keeping with Rochester's commitment to the physical, I will refer to the identities in question as objects—in this case, persons—rather than "subjects," since the latter implies in this situation a dualist account of mental states.

19. Theodore Sider, "Four-Dimensionalism," *Philosophical Review* 106, no. 2 (April 1997): 197. Sider's thesis is extended in book-length form in *Four-Dimensionalism*, which, among other things, contains a response to the mereological elimitivism of van Inwagen (176–80). The definition from the original article is, in my view, more crisp than the longer elaboration; so I've stuck with that.

20. Sider, "Four-Dimensionalism," 204.

21. An instructive comparison might be *The Disabled Debauchee,* which *does* consider identity in four dimensions. The grammar of that poem establishes the speaker in relation to a future version of himself who then validates his own past. The future, present, and past versions of the speaker are all, in this respect, temporal parts in the way they are not in *Love and Life.*

22. For a contrary reading, that "thoughts" are represented as "a natural part of lovemaking," see Griffin, *Satires against Man,* 96.

23. Augustine was, needless to say, interested in erections he'd rather not be having, while Rochester's speaker—at least in the first half of the poem—is interested in the opposite. See *De nuptiis et concupiscentia* [*On Marriage and Concupiscence*], book 1, chapter 7.

24. For the classical and Continental sources of the libertine impotence poem (in Ovid, *Amores* III.7; and Petronius, *Satyricon,* 128–40), see Leo Braudy, "Remembering Masculinity: Premature Ejaculation Poetry of the Seventeenth Century," *Michigan Quarterly Review* 33 (1994): 177–201; James Grantham Turner, *Schooling Sex: Libertine Literature and Erotic Education in Italy, France, and England, 1534–1685* (Oxford: Oxford University Press, 2003), 273–7; and Richard Quaintance, "French Sources of the Restoration 'Imperfect Enjoyment' Poem," *Philological Quarterly* 42 (1963): 190–9.

25. This is to take a different approach from Reba Wilcoxon's claim that "Rochester is redefining the interplay of body and soul, and skillfully suspending the grounds of judgment between the two." See "Pornography, Obscenity, and Rochester's 'The Imperfect Enjoyment,'" *Studies in English Literature, 1500–1900* 15, no. 3 (1975): 380. Wilcoxon is able to maintain the "suspension" between body and soul by defining the former in terms of crude materialism that Rochester's aesthetic achievement overcomes.

26. Most readings of the poem treat the premature ejaculation simply in passing, as a matter of fact. Braudy attempts to give it a literary history of its own (see "Remembering Masculinity"). Turner (*Schooling Sex,* 274–5) is the most prominent of the minority tradition of reading these lines not as a premature ejaculation but rather as a transitory moment of idealized physical love at the precipice of intercourse.

27. The problem of redundancy in mental causation goes by the name of "overdetermination" (a term with no relation, incidentally, to the concept in psychoanalysis and Althusserian Marxism). "Overdetermination" in causal relations refers to the systematic reduplication of the physical to physical and the mental to physical. So, in mental causation, there's a physical cause and a mental cause, and the latter does the same work as the former. For a defense of overdetermination, see Theodore Sider, "What's So Bad about Overdetermination?" *Philosophy and Phenomenological Research* 67 (2003): 719–26; and Michael Tooley, *Causation: A Realist Approach* (Oxford: Oxford University Press, 1987). For a criticism, see E. J. Lowe, "Causal Closure Principles and Emergentism," *Philosophy* 75 (2000): 571–85.

28. For an early elaboration of the difference between emotions like shame and rage and propositional attitudes like intention (though the term was not, of course, used), see Hobbes, *Leviathan,* I.vi.

29. This is a principle of causal closure. For its current elaboration, see Kim, *Physicalism or Something Near Enough;* and Tim Crane, "The Mental Causation Debate," *Proceedings of the Aristotelian Society* 69 (1995): 1–23.

30. Melissa Sanchez, "Libertinism and Romance in Rochester's Poetry," *Eighteenth-Century Studies* 38, no. 3 (2005): 451.

31. But see Wilcoxon's interesting argument that Rochester places form before matter in the poem *Upon Nothing.* Reba Wilcoxon, "Rochester's Philosophical Premises," 188. I think Wilcoxon somewhat strains this point, since the lines (12–3) have matter spring assisted by form. A better strategy for claiming a certain immaterialism in Rochester would be the anti-Lucretian notion in *Upon Nothing* that something could come from nothing.

32. Sanchez, "Libertinism and Romance in Rochester's Poetry," 451.

33. On the circulation and meaning of Aretino's "postures" in sixteenth- and seventeenth-century Europe, see Turner, *Schooling Sex,* 31–71.

34. Ibid., 269. Turner further argues that "[t]ransgression becomes the norm and aestheticized pleasure the goal." Rochester's antipathy, on this account, is a "fear of *insufficient* artistic prowess" (269).

35. The model would be Juvenal's third satire, on Rome, especially par. 232.

36. The stance of the speaker with respect to social mingling is the same as elsewhere in Rochester's poetry. Casual sex between commoners and aristocrats is to be approved of, while sex between aristocrats and parvenus is not.

37. Thormählen, *Rochester*, 97.

38. The last mention of mental states is line eighty's "Joyful, and pleas'd, away she flew."

39. Stephen Clark, "'Something Gen'rous in Mere Lust': Rochester and Misogyny," in Edward Burns, ed., *Reading Rochester* (New York: St. Martin's Press, 1995), 27; and Sarah Wintle, "Libertinism and Sexual Politics," in Jeremy Treglown, ed., *Spirit of Wit: Reconsiderations of Rochester* (Oxford: Blackwell, 1982), 165.

40. James Grantham Turner, *Libertines and Radicals in Early Modern London: Sexuality, Politics, and Literary Culture, 1630–1685* (Cambridge: Cambridge University Press, 2002), 222 and 240.

41. Thormählen (*Rochester,* 98) argues that "[w]hat motivates her is one of the three defects which are always seen as inexcusable in Rochester's *oeuvre*: vanity, or pride . . . folly and hypocrisy (or stupidity and insincerity)." I think, rather, she has no motivation at all.

42. The poem was written in the immediate aftermath of the Treaty of Dover (1670), which secretly aligned England with France against Holland. Against this background, the poem consistently views international relations through the lens of sexual practice; so, for example, Charles is criticized for preferring the French Duchess of Portsmouth to the homegrown Nell Gwynn. For Rochester's place in this context, see Ronald Paulson, "Rochester: The Body Politic and the Body Private," in Lewis Martz and Aubrey Williams, eds., *The Author in His Work: A Problem in Criticism* (New Haven: Yale University Press, 1978), 103–21, Turner, *Libertines and Radicals in Early Modern London,* esp. 219–21; Michael McKeon, *Secret History of Domesticity,* 304–5 and passim; and Jeremy Webster, "Rochester's Easy King: Rereading (Sexual) Politics in the Scepter Lampoon," *English Language Notes* 42, no. 4 (2005): 1–19. Webster is particularly interesting on the coterie context for Rochester's complaint. For the context of Charles's sexuality, see Rachel Weil, "Sometimes a Scepter is Only a Scepter: Pornography and Politics in Restoration England," in Lynn Hunt, ed., *The Invention of Pornography: Obscenity and the Origins of Modernity, 1500–1800* (New York: Zone, 1993), 125–53.

43. Love, ed., *The Works of John Wilmot, Earl of Rochester*, "Group-E text," 89.

44. Love's statement (ibid., xviii) about the status of the original in Rochester holds true for this poem as well as most others: "[W]hat we possess is a body of contemporary manuscripts, some made by private readers and some by professional scribes, with a much smaller number of unauthorized, and generally inferior, printed texts taken from fortuitously encountered manuscripts." In an article on the scepter poem published in the lead-up to the edition, Love tracked its various manuscripts and versions in scribal miscellanies. See " 'Rochester's I' th' Isle of Britain': Decoding a Textual Tradition," *English Manuscript Studies* 6 (1997): 175–223.

45. Neither desires nor designs emanate from the poet, however, or at least not in any sense that would assign regularity or precision to them. See Love, " 'Rochester's I' th' Isle of Britain,' " 204–5.

46. As we shall see, Locke makes a different argument, and claims that desire must be felt as "uneasiness" in order for it to serve as a cause. The attention to "uneasiness" as the conscious end of the formal property of desire recognizes the difference between the two.

47. Love, *The Works of John Wilmot, Earl of Rochester*, 574–7.

48. See Love, "Dryden, Rochester and the Invention of the Town," in Claude Julien Rawson and Aaron Santesso, eds., *John Dryden (1631–1700)* (Newark, NJ: University of Delaware Press, 2004), 36–51. Love argues that the two writers refer across their works to a distinctive, post-Restoration sense of the town as a place and mentality, as distinct from both court and city. "Dryden shows up as pro-Town and Rochester as anti-Town." Located in the newly filled parishes of St. Martin, St. James, St. Anne, and St. Giles, the town was filled with "the lower aristocracy and wealthier country gentry now become urban dwellers" (37).

49. Ibid., 44.

50. *Artemisa to Cloe. A Letter from a Lady in the Town to a Lady in the Country, Concerning the Loves in Town, By a Person of Quality* (London, 1679), title page.

51. See, for example, Howard D. Weinbrot, "The Swelling Volume: The Apocalyptic Satire of Rochester's Letter from Artemisia in the Town to Chloe in the Country," *Studies in the Literary Imagination* 5, no. 2 (October 1972): 19–37. For a more recent, and sympathetic, treatment,

see Thormählen, *Rochester,* and her subsequent discussion, "Dissolver of Reason: Rochester and the Nature of Love," in Fisher, ed., *That Second Bottle,* 21–33.

52. For the long trajectory in which passions like fear, hope, envy, shame, and so forth turn from passive afflictions to motivations for actions, see Susan James, *Passion and Action: The Emotions in Seventeenth-Century Philosophy* (Oxford: Oxford University Press, 1997).

53. In what follows, I focus specifically on the use of one couplet, and do not attempt to trace the afterlife of Rochester more broadly, in for example Defoe, where he is cited frequently in *Moll Flanders,* or Richardson, where he is one model for Lovelace, who cites his play *Valentinian* just before the rape:

'Tis nobler like a lion to invade
When appetite directs, and seize my prey,
Than to wait tamely, like a begging dog,
Till dull consent throws out the Scraps of Love.

Samuel Richardson, *Clarissa, or, the History of a Young Lady,* 8 vols., ed. Florian Stuber (New York: AMS Press, 1990), 5:29. Lovelace also cites *Artemiza to Chloe* in his letter to Belford proposing a scheme for annual marriages. The polite world will consult the papers, he writes, to see "who and who's together" (5:273). For readings of *Clarissa* that see Rochester as an important precursor for Lovelace, see Jocelyn Harris, "Protean Lovelace," in *Eighteenth-Century Fiction* 2, no. 4 (July 1990): 327–46; and Turner, "Lovelace and the Paradoxes of Libertinism," in Margaret Anne Doody and Peter Sabor, eds., *Samuel Richardson: Tercentenary Essays* (Cambridge: Cambridge University Press, 1989), 70–88. For Defoe and Rochester, see John McVeagh, "Defoe and Rochester: A Study in Influence," *Studies in English Literature* 14, no. 3 (1974): 327–41.

54. *Poems on several occasions by the Right Honourable, the E___ of R___* (1680); and Jacob Tonson's *Poems, &c, on several occasions with the Valentian, a Tragedy. Written by the Right Honorable John, late the Earl of Rochester* (1691).

55. See Gilbert Burnet, *Some Passages in the Life and Death of the Right Honourable John, Earl of Rochester, who died the 26th of July, 1680* (1680).

56. On the question of audience for poems, see Rochester's *An Allusion*

to Horace, which says one ought to "Scorn all applause the Vile Rout can bestow / And be content to pleas those few who know" (102–3), a few then listed by name at the poem's close:

> I loath the Rabble, 'tis enough or me
> If Sydley, Shadwell, Shepheard, Wicherley,
> Godolphin, Butler, Buckhurst, Buckinghame
> And some few more whome I omitt to name
> Approve my sence, I count their Censure Fame. (120–4)

57. Thus, for example, in the first number of *The Tatler*, Steele apologizes that he has "troubled the public" with so much discussion of the death of Mr. Partridge. This sort of usage is, needless to say, completely ordinary for Steele in a way it wouldn't have been for Rochester.

58. Richard Steele, *The Tatler*, ed. Donald Bond, 3 vols. (vol. 1, no. 5) (Oxford: Oxford University Press, 1987), 45. Further references are to this edition and noted parenthetically.

59. Delarivier Manley, *New Atalantis*, ed. Ros Ballaster (London: Penguin, 1992), 5.

60. Here is part of Manley's long exposition (*New Atalantis*, 15) of how Fortunas's "ambition would not rest": "The lovely youth knew punctually how to improve those first and precious moments of good fortune, whilst yet the gloss of novelty remained, whilst desire was unsated, and love in the high spring-tide of full delight; having an early forecast, a chain of thought, unusual at his years, a length of view before him, not born a slave to love, so as to reckon the possession of the charmingst woman of the court as a zenith of his fortune, but rather the auspicious, ruddy streaks of an early morning, an earnest to the meridian of the brightest day." On Manley's use of this sort of portrait as a kind of propaganda, see Paula McDowell's discussion in *The Women of Grub Street: Press, Politics, and Gender in the London Literary Marketplace, 1678–1730* (Oxford: Oxford University Press, 1998). For the turn from political domestication to domesticity in Manley—the devolution of politics to "private" relations and the recapitulation in privacy of such politico-public terms as ambition —see McKeon, *Secret History*, 589–98.

61. Jane Barker, *Love Intrigues: Or, the History of the Amours of Bosvil and Galesia, As Related to Lucasia in St. Germains Garden. A Novel* (1713), in Paula Backsheider and John Richetti, eds., *Popular Fiction by*

Women, 1688–1750 (Oxford: Oxford University Press, 1998), 82. Further citation is to this edition and noted parenthetically in text.

62. Barker's skepticism about third-person access is in this respect unflagging. When Bosvil claims at the end that he loved her all along, she can only say to Lucasia, "How far all this was sincere or pretended, I know not" (110). And neither therefore do her readers.

Chapter 4

1. The chapter is typically discussed by Locke scholars as either a question of his ethics, which I will take up below, or his position on free will versus determinism. Most helpful in this regard have been Michael Ayers, *Locke: Epistemology and Ontology*, vol. 2 (New York: Routledge, 1991), 184–202; Vere Chappell, "Locke on Freedom of the Will," in G. A. J. Rogers, ed., *Locke's Philosophy: Content and Context* (Oxford: Oxford University Press, 1994), 101–21; Stephen Darwall, *The British Moralists and the Internal 'Ought'* (Cambridge: Cambridge University Press, 1995), 149–75; Philippa Foot, "Locke, Hume, and Modern Moral Theory: A Legacy of Seventeenth- and Eighteenth-Century Philosophies of Mind," in G. S. Rousseau, ed., *The Languages of Psyche and Mind in Enlightenment Thought* (Berkeley: University of California Press, 1990), 81–104; Raymond Polin, "John Locke's Conception of Freedom," in John Yolton, ed., *John Locke: Problems and Perspectives* (Cambridge: Cambridge University Press, 1969), 1–18; and Peter Schouls, *Reasoned Freedom: John Locke and Enlightenment* (Ithaca, NY: Cornell University Press, 1992), 117–72.

2. Locke, *An Essay Concerning Human Understanding*, 1st ed. (London, 1690), 117. Subsequent quotations to this edition, unless otherwise identified, will be cited parenthetically in the text.

3. The canonical statement on these matters was *A Practical Discourse Concerning a Future Judgment* (1692), written by William Sherlock, Dean of St. Paul's, and reprinted in seven editions over the next fifty years. Sherlock's "works versus grace" model presented knowledge of the everlasting as the guarantor of subjective volition: "[A] wise being will take care to govern the Creatures which he makes, and to govern them in such a way as is agreeable to the natures he has given them; and since Man, who is a free Agent, can be governed only by Hopes and Fears, God would never have made Man, had he not intended to judge him; that is, he would never have made such a Creature as can be governed only by the hope of rewards and

by the fear of punishments, had he not resolved to lay these restraints upon him, to reward and punish him according to his works" (11).

4. Chapter 20 on pleasure and pain contains the only sustained use of the word "uneasiness" in the first edition. Interestingly, the first use in that edition is very early on, in book 2, chapter 1, "Of Ideas in General," in the definition of "reflection," where it likewise describes a state of passivity: "By *REFLECTION* then, in the following part of this Discourse, I would be understood to mean, that notice which the Mind takes of its own Operations, and the manner of them, by reason whereof, there come to be *Ideas* of these Operations in the Understanding. These two, I say, *viz.* External, Material things, as the Objects of *SENSATION*; and the Operations of our own Minds within, as the Objects of *REFLECTION*, are, to me, the only Originals, from whence all our *Idea's* take their beginnings. The term *Operations* here, I use in a large sence, as comprehending not barely the Actions of the Mind about its *Ideas*, but some sort of Passions arising sometimes from them, such as is the satisfaction or uneasiness arising from any thought" (38).

5. Here is the full quotation from the chapter on the passions: "Pleasure and Pain, and that which causes them, Good and Evil, are the hinges on which our *Passions* turn: and if we reflect on our selves, how these under various Considerations operate in us, what Modifications or Tempers of Mind, what internal Sensations, (if I may so call them,) they produce in us, we may thence form to our selves the *Ideas* of our Passions" (113).

6. Molyneux first posed the problem in a letter written in 1688 in response to the redaction of the *Essay* that had appeared in France in the *Bibliotheque Universelle et Historique*. He asks Locke again when their correspondence takes off three years later. For a history of the Molyneux problem, see Marjolein Degenaar, *Molyneux's Problem: Three Centuries of Discussion on the Perception of Forms*, trans. Michael Collins (Dordrecht: Kluwer, 1996).

7. Maurice Cranston, *John Locke: A Biography* (London: Longmans, 1957), 360.

8. Quoted in ibid., 359.

9. *The Correspondence of John Locke*, vol. 4, ed. E. S. De Beer (Oxford: Clarendon, 1979), 480. All subsequent references are to this volume of this edition and will be cited parenthetically in the text.

10. This is to adopt the definition of qualia provided by Chalmers in *The Conscious Mind*, 4 and passim. See my discussion in Chapter 2.

11. The two had noted in their first letters that they were in Holland at the same time but had not met. See also Locke's next letter, which begins, "You have given me those marks of your kindness to me, that you will not think it strange that I count you amongst my friends, and, with those, desiring to live with the ease and freedom of a perfect confidence, I never accuse them to my self of neglect or coldness," only to note with some sadness the expanse of geography that blocks their friendship (663). "That request of yours you press earnestly upon me," he responds to an appeal for manuscripts, "makes me bemoan the distance you are from me, which deprives me of the assistance I might have from your opinion and judgment, before I ventur'd any thing into the publick" (664). A fuller account of the Molyneux correspondence may be found in my "Locke's Desire," *Yale Journal of Criticism* 12, no. 2 (Fall 1999): 189–208.

12. The second edition includes it in book 2, chapter 9, on perception: "I shall here insert a Problem of that very Ingenious and Studious promoter of real Knowledge the Learned and Worthy Mr. *Molineux*, which he was pleased to send me in a Letter some months since; and it is this, *Suppose a Man born blind, and now adult, and taught by his touch to distinguish between a Cube, and a Sphere of the same metal, and nighly of the same bigness, so as to tell, when he felt one and t'other, which is the Cube, which the Sphere. Suppose then the Cube and Sphere placed on a Table, and the Blind Man to be made to see: Quære, Whether by his sight, before he touch'd them, he could now distinguish and tell, which is the Globe, which the Cube.* To which the acute and judicious Proposer answers, *Not, For though he has obtain'd the experience of, how a Globe, how a Cube affects his touch; yet he has not yet attained the experience, that what affects his touch so or so, must affect his sight so or so; Or that a protuberant angle in the Cube, that pressed his hand unequally, shall appear to his eye, as it does in the Cube:* I agree with this thinking Gent. whom though I have never had the happiness to see, I am proud to call my Friend, in his answer to his problem; and am of opinion that the Blind Man, at first sight, would not be able with certainty to say which was the Globe, which the Cube, whilst he only saw them; though he could unerringly name them by his touch, and certainly distinguish them by the difference of their Figures

felt. This I have set down, and leave with my Reader, as an occasion for him to consider how much he may be beholding to experience, improvement and acquired notions, where he thinks, he had not the least use of, or help from them: And the rather, because this observing Gent. farther adds, that *having, upon the occasion of my Book, proposed this to divers very ingenious Men, he hardly ever met with one that at first gave the answer to it which he thinks true, till by hearing his reasons they were convinced*" (2nd edition, 67–8).

13. For Leibniz, see *Nouveaux essais sur l'entendement d'humain* (1704/1764), II, ix, 8. For Berkeley, see *An Essay Towards a New Theory of Vision* (Dublin, 1709), 154 and passim. For Voltaire, see *Elémens De La Philosophie De Neuton* (1738), chapter 7. For Diderot, see *Lettre sur les aveugles* (1749).

14. Frank Jackson, "Epiphenomenal Qualia," 130.

15. Ibid. Like Nagel and Chalmers, Jackson is concerned to argue that consciousness cannot be reduced to physical states. Mary had "*all* the physical information," yet her knowledge of color was incomplete (130). Qualia provide additional information or further facts over the physical. A complete theory of consciousness therefore needs to account for qualia without reducing them to the facts of physics.

16. Qualia are, on Jackson's view, epiphenomenal because they are "causally impotent" (133). They are closely associated with certain behaviors but both may be joint effects of underlying brain processes.

17. That the very form of the thought experiment is antiempirical, and relies upon intuitive forms of ratiocination, is not noticed or remarked upon.

18. He also asks him on several occasions to write a separate book of morals. His solution instead is that Locke should compose a separate "Treatise of Morals" that might make good on the claim that morality can be described according to a mathematical method (508). He asks Locke to write such a book in his first letter and repeats his appeal frequently. (For example, October 15, 1692: "I am wonderfully pleased that you give Me Hopes of seeing a Moral Essay from Your Hand, Which I assure you Sir with all sincerity is highly respected by . . ." [533]. This unrequited plea is repeated in virtually every letter; here is March 2, 1693: "On this Consideration of Usefulnes to Mankind, I wil presume again to remind you of your

Discourse of Morality; And I shall think my self very Happy, if by putting you on the Thought, I should be the least Occasion of so Great Good to the World" [649].) The letter that worries about the finely spun thread of the theory of actions closes with a dramatic appeal along these lines. "There Remains only that I again put you in mind of the Second Member of your Division of Sciences, the Ars Practica or Ethicks; you cannot Imagine what an earnest desire and Expectation I have raised in those that are acquainted with your Writings by the Hopes I have given them from your Promise of Indeavouring something on that subject. Good Sir Let me renew my request to you herein, for believe me Sir twill be one of the Most useful and Glorious undertakings that can Imploy you . . . . Be as large as tis possible on this subject, and by all means let it be in English" (602). The reminder draws two related points. In making reference to the desires, expectations, and hopes of Locke's audience, Molyneux places mental states, including emotions, in the vicinity of actions. By insisting that the treatise will only be useful if it is written in English, he asks Locke to fill in the abstract model so it might serve as a guide in making choices. The first point would require considerable revision of the theory; the second would ask for some clarification of how a formal account might include actual agents. For whatever reason, Locke never wrote such a book.

19. See the enumeration of the subsections of the chapter in the letter dated July 15, 1693 (700–1), and the synopsis of the argument in the letter dated August 23, 1693 (722–3).

20. On the distinction between the phenomenal and the functional, see Chalmers, *The Conscious Mind*, 3–31.

21. In the first edition, as we have seen, the word "uneasiness" appears in chapter 20 on the passions as a phenomenal description of desire.

22. Locke, *An Essay Concerning Human Understanding*, 2d ed. (London, 1694),125, emphasis added. All subsequent references to this edition are cited parenthetically in the text.

23. This move requires him to separate the will from desire, something Hobbes and others had not done. "I find the Will often confounded with several of the Affections, especially *Desire;* and one put for the other, and that by men, who would not willingly be thought, not to have had very distinct notions of things, and not to have writ very clearly about them" (2nd ed., 133). In language besotted with compound negatives, Locke affirms

clearly that "[t]he *Will* is perfectly distinguished from *Desire*" (2nd ed., 133). Two points will turn out to be important about this distinction. Having gone to great pains to avoid desire in the first edition of the *Essay*, Locke now transforms that faculty from a passive condition of suffering to the motor principle of action. At the same time, distinguishing the will from desire provides a structure for the consequential act of forbearance, for the not doing of something one seemingly wants to do.

24. Locke repeats his having come to second thoughts several more times across the new version of the chapter. The sense is of a kind of conversion. Where once he agreed with the "establish'd and settled a maxim . . . that good, the greater good, determines the will," now he has "ventur'd to recede from so received an Opinion" (2nd ed., 135). When he "first publish'd" his thoughts on the subject, he "took it for granted" that we act in response to the good, but now "upon a stricter enquiry" he is "forced to conclude, that *good*, the *greater good*, though apprehended and acknowledged to be so, does not determine the *will*, until our desire, raised proportionately to it, makes us uneasy in the want of it" (2nd ed., 135).

25. He does not confront the overdetermination problem we saw in chapter 2 because he does not address how matter could have experiences like uneasiness. This being so, he doesn't have to answer how atoms and qualia could both cause the same effect. His overall position on how mind actually causes matter to move is that it's a mystery though a matter of fact, as I discussed in the introduction.

26. The skeptical perspective has a special bearing on Locke's revisions. His shift from assuming that objects solicit longings to postulating that we are uneasy about objects we may never have encountered adjusts the chapter to the *Essay*'s disinclination to discuss the actual material nature of objects. The outcome is an object thrown into an unexpected instability. Now that "the power of preferring" is no longer "determined by the good," Locke is free to multiply and expand the variety of items that fall into the orbit of wanting: "We are seldom at ease, and free enough from the sollicitation of our natural or adopted desires, but a constant succession of uneasinesses, out of that stock, which natural wants, or acquired habits have heaped up, take the *will* in their turns, and no sooner is one action dispatch'd, which by such a determination of the *will* we are set upon, but another uneasiness is ready to set us on work" (140). For an

incisive discussion of Locke's nominalism along these lines, see Nicholas Hudson, "John Locke and the Tradition of Nominalism," in Hugo Keiper, Christoph Bode, and Richard J. Utz, eds., *Nominalism and Literary Discourse, New Perspectives* (Amsterdam: Rodopi, 1997), 283–300.

27. See my discussion of Locke in Chapter 2.

28. Locke, *An Essay Concerning Human Understanding*, 5th ed. (London, 1706), 171–2.

29. Perhaps the most strident version of this is to be found in Charles Taylor's *Sources of the Self*, in which Locke augurs "a radical disengagement and reification of human psychology" (173). But see also Jonathan Lamb's *Preserving the Self in the South Seas* (Chicago: University of Chicago Press, 2001), 28 and passim.

30. "*That which has the power, or not the power to operate, is that alone, which is, or is not free*; and not the Power it self" (1st ed., 121; 2nd ed., 129).

31. See, for example, letters 58 and 60, both written over the summer of 1659, in *The Correspondence of John Locke*, v. 1, 82, 85–8.

32. See, for example, letter 121, dated April 1661, in ibid., 174–5. Cranston details Locke's taste for the romance in *John Locke*, 67–74.

33. Gaultier de Coste, seigneur de La Calprenède, *Cassandra the Fam'd Romance: The Whole Work in Five Parts* (1652), III.136.

34. In the eighteenth-century reprinting of the translation, the passage is changed to: "[In] all his Actions he shewed an Uneasiness which could not proceed merely from his Zeal, and Fidelity to a King. When he was near her, his Eyes perpetually fix'd upon her face, but 'twas with Troubles and Distractions of Mind, which took away part of his Understanding." *Cassandra, a romance. In five parts. Written originally in French and faithfully translated into English by Sir Charles Cotterell*, III (1715), 100–1.

35. *The Works of Aphra Behn*, ed. Janet Todd, vol. 3 (Columbus: Ohio State University Press, 1992), 221.

36. Locke wrote to Trotter after the publication of her *Defence* and included a gift of books along with thanks for the "generosity above the strain of this groveling age." See *The Correspondence of John Locke*, v. 7, ed. E. S. De Beer, 730–1.

37. [Catharine Trotter], *The Adventures of a Young Lady, Written by her self, in several letters to a Gentleman in the Country*, in *Letters of Love*

and Gallantry and Several Other Subjects, All Written by Ladies V. 1 (London, 1693), 1. Hereafter cited in parentheses.

38. Trotter, *A Defence of the Essay of Human Understanding, written by Mr. Lock* (London, 1702), 4. Hereafter cited in parentheses.

39. She reviews quickly the idea of person, man, and soul in Locke against his detractors, lighting on the connection of consciousness to person and soul to man (the latter in a relatively strained reading of the *Essay*). See ibid., 28–30.

Chapter 5

1. The full titles are *Love in Excess or the Fatal Enquiry* and *Fantomina: or Love in a Maze. Being a Secret History of an Amour between Two Persons of Condition.* On the Haywood revival, see Margaret Case Croskery, "Who's Afraid of Eliza Haywood?" *Literature Compass* 4, no. 4 (May 2007): 967–80.

2. I return to citation from Locke, *An Essay Concerning Human Understanding*, ed. Peter Nidditch (Oxford: Oxford University Press, 1975), 67, hereafter cited in parentheses.

3. In this respect, consent is, in Anscombe's terms, "under a description." One is Xing with consent. One is not consenting in private, absent relations with others. The Lockean idea of tacit consent will strain against Anscombe's notion that some actions are intentional or not depending on how they're described. In Locke's world, one is almost always consenting (at least to be governed) from almost all descriptions. I take up the notion of "under description" at some length in the next chapter in the discussion of Clarissa's intentions. See Anscombe, *Intention*, 11–12.

4. "Though the earth, and all inferior creatures, be common to all men, yet every man has a *property* in his own *person*: this no body has any right to but himself. The *labour* of his body, and the *work* of his hands, we may say, are properly his. Whatsoever then he removes out of the state that nature hath provided, and left it in, he hath mixed his *labour* with, and joined to it something that is his own, and thereby makes it his *property*. It being by him removed from the common state nature hath placed it in, it hath by this *labour* something annexed to it, that excludes the common right of other men." Locke, *Second Treatise of Government*, ed. C. B. Macpherson (Indianapolis: Hackett, 1980), 19. Hereafter cited in parentheses.

5. John Dunn, "Consent in the Political Theory of John Locke," in Gordon Schochet, ed., *Life, Liberty, and Property: Essays on Locke's Political Ideas* (Belmont, WA: Wadsworth, 1971), 138. See also Dunn's *The Political Thought of John Locke: An Historical Account of the Argument of the 'Two Treatises of Government'* (Cambridge: Cambridge University Press, 1969), esp. 129–35; Iain Hampsher-Monk, "Tacit Concept of Consent in Locke's Two Treatises of Government," *Journal of the History of Ideas* 40 (1979): 135–9; and Don Herzog, *Happy Slaves: A Critique of Consent Theory* (Chicago: University of Chicago Press, 1989).

6. The notion that one could have consented without consciously knowing so would seem to violate Locke's position in the *Essay* that all thinking must be accompanied by consciousness. His response might be that consent is a kind of power rather than a kind of idea. Locke's emphasis on consciousness, however, usually predicates that powers are also experienced when in use.

7. On the "unsexed" nature of the mind with relation to action, see Helen Thompson's *Ingenuous Subjection: Compliance and Power in the Eighteenth-Century Domestic Novel* (Philadelphia: University of Pennsylvania Press, 2005). Thompson argues that Locke's neuter model of the mind leads to a willingness to submit to authority, one then often undercut within the novel.

8. See Mary Astell, *Some Reflections on Marriage* (1700), in *Political Writings*, ed. Patricia Springborg (Cambridge: Cambridge University Press, 1996), 1–79; and Carole Pateman, *The Sexual Contract* (Stanford: Stanford University Press, 1988).

9. See, for example, the very different accounts of Haywood in Ros Ballaster's *Seductive Forms: Women's Amatory Fiction 1640–1740* (Oxford: Oxford University Press, 1992); and William Warner's *Licensing Entertainment: The Elevation of Novel Reading in England, 1684–1750* (Berkeley: University of California Press, 1998).

10. Citing Lacan, for example, Warner (*Licensing Entertainment*, 121) says of *Love in Excess* that "the two characters and the reader flow into one scene of polymorphous sexual arousal, where the drive exceeds the subject position through which it operates." I might extrapolate from this statement a more generalized account of Haywoodian erotics, but I would observe that this is less an anticipation of mid-twentieth-century French psychoanalysis than an engagement with eighteenth-century empiricism.

11. Eliza Haywood, *Love in Excess: or the Fatal Inquiry*, ed. David Oakleaf (Ontario: Broadview Press, 1994), 60, hereafter cited in parentheses.

12. As John Richetti puts it, "[T]he balanced phrases and clauses just about contain the rushing participles which do the actual describing." See *Popular Fiction before Richardson: Narrative Patterns, 1700–1739* (Oxford: Oxford University Press, 1969), 188. See also his "Voice and Gender in Eighteenth-Century Fiction: Haywood to Burney," *Studies in the Novel* 19 (1987): 263–72.

13. See the discussion of Nagel's "What Is it Like to Be a Bat?"; and Chalmers, *The Conscious Mind*, chapters 2 and 4.

14. Warner, *Licensing Entertainment*, 113.

15. On the fictional representation of public opinion, see Frances Ferguson's brief but suggestive remarks in her discussion of free indirect discourse in "Jane Austen, Emma, and the Impact of Form," *MLQ* 61, no. 1 (2000): 157–80.

16. Hence Anna Howe's quip to Clarissa: "If every-body would speak out, as I do (that is to say, give praise where only praise is due; dispraise where due likewise), *Shame*, if not *Principle*, would mend the world—Nay, Shame would *introduce* Principle in a generation or two" (3:208).

17. René Descartes, *The Passions of the Soule in three Books* (London, 1650), 167.

18. Bernard Mandeville, *The Fable of the Bees, or Private Vices, Public Benefits*, ed. F. B. Kaye (Indianapolis, IN: Liberty Press, 1988), 68.

19. Ludwig Wittgenstein, *Philosophical Investigations*, trans. G. E. M. Anscombe (Oxford: Blackwell, 2001), 136.

20. Ibid.

21. *Fantomina* was one among many novels that Haywood published during the 1720s; it was included only in an omnibus collection, never published alone. It is presently in every major teaching anthology (the Norton, Longman, Broadview, and Blackwell) and a subject of ongoing scholarly discussion. Surely the *Fantomina* craze must be credited in part to Ballaster's *Seductive Forms: Women's Amatory Fiction 1640–1740*, which drew attention to *Fantomina* as a rewriting of the conventional seduction plot of the amatory romance (see 181–92). I will disagree with certain details of Ballaster's reading below. Nevertheless, the field is in her debt for drawing attention to this remarkable novel. For Margaret Case Cros-

kery, *Fantomina* creates an ethics of eroticized constancy, within which female desire is no longer equated with moral culpability; see "Masquing Desire: The Politics of Passion in Eliza Haywood's *Fantomina*," in Kirsten Saxton and Rebecca P. Bocchicchio, eds., *The Passionate Fictions of Eliza Haywood* (Lexington: University of Kentucky Press, 2000), 69–94. For Tiffany Potter, Fantomina is an example of Haywood's attempt to create a "powerful and distinct idiom for the expression of that which is culturally defined to be feminine and therefore private"; see "The Language of Feminised Sexuality: Gendered Voice in Eliza Haywood's *Love in Excess* and *Fantomina*," *Women's Writing* 10, no. 1 (2003): 169. Potter's perspective is shared by Catherine Craft, "Reworking Male Models: Aphra Behn's *Fair Vow Breaker*, Eliza Haywood's *Fantomina*, and Charlotte Lennox's *Female Quixote*," *Modern Language Review* 84 (October 1991): 821–38. Closest to the perspective of the present chapter, Helen Thompson reads *Fantomina* within a tradition of viewing persons as material entities; see "Plotting Materialism: W. Charleton's *Ephesian Matron* and E. Haywood's *Fantomina*," *Eighteenth-Century Studies* 35, no. 2 (Winter 2002): 195–214. My argument also concurs with Emily Anderson's conclusion that "Haywood casts the impulse to probe beneath a woman's 'mask' in search of her true sentiments as misleading." Anderson's particular point has to do with Haywood's indebtedness to the theater. See Emily Hodgson Anderson, "Performing the Passions in Eliza Haywood's *Fantomina* and *Miss Betsy Thoughtless*," *The Eighteenth Century: Theory and Interpretation* 46, no. 1 (2005): 3.

22. Haywood, *Fantomina, or Love in a Maze* (1725), in Alexander Pettit, Margaret Case Croskery, and Anna C. Patchias, eds., *Fantomina and Other Works* (Peterborough: Broadview Press, 2004), 41. Further citation is to this edition and noted in parentheses.

23. Croskery, "Masquing Desire," 73.

24. Glossing this scene, Ballaster (*Seductive Forms*, 188) writes, "Fantomina engages to meet Beauplaisir the following night at the theatre and takes lodging near the playhouse. Here she entertains him but finds her play-acting has gone further than she imagined. Despite her revelation that she is a virgin, Beauplaisir rapes her. Haywood employs her characteristic rhetoric of victim and victor to describe the scene, and it appears that Fantomina will go the way of her sisters, seduced, abandoned, and fall-

ing into hysteria: 'He was bold;—he was resolute: She fearful,—confus'd, altogether unprepar'd to resist in such Encounters.'" This reading seems suspect to me in several respects. When Ballaster cuts off the final clause in the sentence, which has the young lady rendered more unprepared to resist "by the extreme Liking she had to him," she seems to want to clarify what Haywood represents as ineluctably obscure, namely, the lines between consent and compliance, agency and supplication, individual desire and social expectation. The same could be said for Ballaster's claim that up to this point the young lady had been "play-acting," a term Haywood does not use, and that sexual intimacy lies beyond what she might have "imagined." Everything up to this point has suggested that the desire itself is consequential and imagining a kind of acting. Even though Croskery ("Masquing Desire," 72–3) stresses the "compatibility of female agency and female passion in all of Haywood's works," she also reads the ambiguity out of the scene and, even more than Ballaster, cuts and pastes the text to fit her reading: the episode is reduced to "Shock'd . . . at the Apprehension of really losing her Honour, she struggled all she could. . . . In fine, she was undone; and [Beauplaisir] gain'd a Victory, so highly rapturous, that had he known over whom, scarce could he have triumphed more."

25. When Beauplaisir tires of her soon after, he is said to have grown "tir'd of her Conversation" (51). *Fantomina* regularly describes sex as conversation and conversation as sex.

26. Thompson, "Plotting Materialism," 202.

27. Ibid., 204.

28. Ibid.

29. Thompson (ibid., 205) does something like this in arguing that Judith Butler's account of performance "glosses the impossible consistency of Haywood's heroine."

Chapter 6

1. So whereas William Warner's deconstructive account of the novel argues that Clarissa models a "self" that is the basis of moral authority, I am arguing that this sort of modeling focuses on the one question of intentions. Selfhood is quite a broad term and can't really support the sort of work that Clarissa wants intentions to do in the sorting of actions. See *Reading Clarissa: The Struggles of Interpretation* (New Haven: Yale University Press, 1979), 16–20.

2. An action is reasonable only if it is both good and rational. So Clarissa would, in other words, disagree with Hume's claim that it is "not contrary to reason to prefer the destruction of the world to the scratching of my finger."

3. Richardson, *Clarissa, or, The History of a Young Lady*, 3:256; further references are to this edition and cited in parentheses. The AMS edition is based on the third edition and preserves the spelling and punctuation. For the sake of convenience, I have also placed in brackets the equivalent pages from *Clarissa; or, The History of a Young Lady*, ed. Angus Ross (London: Penguin, 1985), based on the first; in this case, 508. Clarissa's theory of intentions remains relatively consistent: "I am, in my own opinion, a poor lost creature: And yet cannot charge myself with one criminal or faulty inclination." She then says in the same letter, of Lovelace, that she might "acquit his *intention*, if not his *action!*" (4:37, 38 [565–6]). Much later, as she's dying, she returns to the faultlessness of her intentions in leaving home, in a letter to her mother, composed in the third person: "[S]he met the Seducer, with a determination not to go off with him: That the rash step was owing more to compulsion than infatuation: And that her heart was so little in it, that she repented and grieved from the moment she found herself in his power; and for every moment after, for several weeks *before* she had any cause from him to apprehend the usage she met with" (7:77 [1108]).

4. Anscombe, *Intention*, 24. My point is not to do an "Anscombian" reading of the novel, whatever that might be. It is rather to say that Anscombe's slim volume abstracts and crystallizes questions about actions that preoccupied philosophers during the period of this study.

5. Ibid., 29.

6. This is to adapt Anscombe's famous example of the man pumping poisoned water into a meeting of Nazis. His muscles contract in a certain way while he moves his arm; the pump makes a certain clanking noise, but it would be hard to describe the action in such a way that clanking out a rhythm or contracting certain muscles are the intentions "with which" the action is performed (ibid., 37–41).

7. Terry Castle, *Clarissa's Ciphers: Meaning and Disruption in Richardson's "Clarissa"* (Ithaca, NY: Cornell University Press, 1982), 49.

8. Criticism has a long tradition of treating the novel as a series of epistemological riddles, many of which come down to knowing what's on Cla-

rissa's mind, dating back to Ian Watt's somewhat notorious claim (*The Rise of the Novel*, 229) that "we are fully entitled to suspect Clarissa herself of not knowing her own feelings." For a recent and provocative attempt to use the methods of cognitive science—especially "theory of mind"—to talk about the attribution of mental states in *Clarissa*, both the reader's wondering about those of the characters and the characters wondering about each other's, see Lisa Zunshine, *Why We Read Fiction: Theory of Mind and the Novel* (Columbus: Ohio State University Press, 2006), 82–99.

9. See Letter 35, 1:235–8 (164).

10. Anscombe, *Intention*, 46. Thus again, the man pumping a supply of poisoned water: He is moving arms, operating the pump, replenishing the water supply, poisoning the Nazis. These are four ways of describing the one action, with four separate intentions or one large intention that "swallows" them all depending on how the event is described.

11. Ibid.

12. Davidson, "Intending," in *Essays on Actions and Events*, 88.

13. Like Wittgenstein, Anscombe tends to avoid talk about private mental states, separate from actions: thus her notion that "motive" is ineluctably obscure. In this light, Davidson's interest in "pure intending" is part of a larger return to the mental (in Chomsky, Putnam, and Fodor) that we now recognize as the first cognitive revolution.

14. See for example Harris, "Protean Lovelace," 327–42.

15. This notion of the fixity of Lovelace's intentions despite the changing nature of his actions slightly revises Frances Ferguson's argument that "Lovelace's account of himself is that he will discover what it was that he intended when he sees how things turn out, so that his account of his intentions is that they are infinitely variable precisely because they are defined as arbitrary, operating as a fictional code in which he assumes different parts at the will of the imaginary text that he is elaborating." See "Rape and the Rise of the Novel," *Representations* 20 (Fall 1987): 101. My point is that the discovery of intentions when he sees how things are worked out leaves them *invariable* precisely because, for Lovelace as for Anscombe, intentions are logically and grammatically dependent on actions. Both Lovelace and Anscombe would deny the privacy and causal role of mental states. In this Anscombe is certainly following Wittgenstein and perhaps Ryle. See, for example, *Intention*, 17–20 and passim. "But it appears to me that the

mental causes are seldom more than a very trivial item among the things that it would be reasonable to consider" (19). Davidson responds by insisting on the causal role of intentions and reasons, yet not their essential privacy. See not only "Intending" but also the foundational essay "Actions, Reasons, Causes" in *Essays on Actions and Events*, 3–21.

16. Watt, *The Rise of the Novel*, 195.

17. Ibid., 192.

18. Tom Keymer, *Richardson's Clarissa and the Eighteenth-Century Reader* (Cambridge: Cambridge University Press, 1992), 11. I am not sure that Watt thought these things either—Keymer surely imputes to him a naïveté he did not have—but the difference falls on where each critic would put the accent. So Keymer's revision of Watt places emphasis on rhetorical distortions, and Watt places emphasis on effects of authenticity.

19. Ibid., xvi.

20. Watt, *The Rise of the Novel*, 228–9.

21. See note 27 in the introduction on the concept of "direction of fit." One important example in Anscombe concerns "a man going round a town with a shopping list in his hand" and "a list . . . made by a detective following him about" and recording his purchases. The conclusion she wants to draw is that the former is an "expression of intention" and therefore endeavors to influence the world (items in the shopping cart) in a certain way, while the latter endeavors to record the world accurately without changing it. The former has a world-to-mind direction of fit (fits the world to the mind) and the latter a mind-to-world direction of fit (fits the mind to the world). "What then is the identical relation to what happens, in the order and the intention, which is not shared by the record? It is precisely this: if the list and the things that the man actually buys do not agree, and if this, and this alone constitutes a *mistake*, then the mistake is not in the list but in the man's performance . . . whereas if the detective's record and what the man actually buys do not agree then the mistake is in the record." Anscombe, *Intention*, 56.

22. Scott Paul Gordon has argued that "[t]he Harlowes' position paradoxically construes Clarissa's refusal to act as aggression, an attempt by a daughter to victimize the powerful patriarchal family." Yet this is a paradox only from the perspective that understands refusal as separate from the world, as an entirely internal action or no action at all. Scott Paul

Gordon, *The Power of the Passive Self in English Literature 1640–1770*
(Cambridge: Cambridge University Press, 2002), 188.

23. Peggy Thompson, "Abuse and Atonement: The Passion of Clarissa
Harlowe," in David Blewett, ed., *Passion and Virtue: Essays on the Novels
of Samuel Richardson* (Toronto: University of Toronto Press, 2001), 153.
Or as Mary Poovey writes: "It is a paradox of the faith that the action
which Clarissa's perfected heart dictates is complete passivity, patient
acquiescence to the mysterious workings of the hand of God." See "Journeys from This World to the Next: The Providential Promise in *Clarissa*
and *Tom Jones*," *ELH* 43 (1976): 305. An interesting account of Clarissa's
passivity may be found in Gordon's *The Power of the Passive Self*, which
situates the novel in the context of eighteenth-century theories of disinterest. From this perspective, Richardson strives to show that Clarissa's suffering is void of cunning and in line with Christian and neo-Shaftesburian
ideals of sincerity and virtue (those that prefer the social good to individual
desire). For the reading of Clarissa's selflessness as an *Imitatio Christi*, see
John Dussinger's influential essay, "Conscience and the Pattern of Christian Perfection in Clarissa," *PMLA* 81 (1966): 236–45; Dussinger concentrates more on the rejection of worldliness than on passivity as such.

24. I am thus not entirely sure what to make of Gordon's contention
(*The Power of the Passive Self*, 194) that "[t]he novel both struggles to
preserve Clarissa's will and denies her use of it; this 'will' that has remained
'inviolate' has remained equally unassertive." This is true if the assertion of
the will means acting in her interest, but not if it means refusing to accept
what is offered.

25. In addition to the exchange with Anthony, below, see her letter to
John of March 11, where the demand of her father "will deprive me of my
free-will" and make her "contend perhaps, in breach of a vowed duty, for
every innocent instance of free-will" (1:206, 207 [148, 149]).

26. The chapter on power contains in all its versions a criticism of "that
long agitated and, I think, unreasonable, because unintelligible, Question
viz. Whether Man's Will be free or no" (1st ed., 119). The will is only a
means to get from a reason to an action and can no more be free than a
line that joins one point to another. "'Tis plain then, That the *Will* is nothing but one Power or Ability, and *Freedom* another Power or Ability: So
that to ask, whether the Will has Freedom, is to ask, whether one Power

has another Power, one Ability another Ability; a Question at first sight too grosly absurd to make a Dispute, or need an Answer. For who is it that sees not, that *Powers* belong only to Agents, and *are Attributes only of Substances, and not of Powers* themselves?" (ibid., 120). It is therefore "as insignificant to ask, whether Man's Will be free, as to ask, whether his Sleep be Swift, or his Vertue square" (ibid., 119). Barring evidence to the contrary, one may infer from an action an agent's willingness to commit it. Unless an action is compelled, like being pushed off a cliff or kidnapped from home, its mere performance implies the freedom of its agent, as "*That which has the power or not the power to operate, is that alone, which is, or is not free*; and not the Power itself" (ibid., 121).

27. Recent advocates of this position would include Henry Frankfurt and David Velleman. See Frankfurt, *The Importance of What We Care About* (Cambridge: Cambridge University Press, 1988); and Velleman, *The Possibility of Practical Reason*, 123–43.

28. Either "obstinacy and perverseness" or "prepossessions in another's favour."

29. Hume, *A Treatise of Human Nature*, 477.

30. The novel's exploration of how one agent attributes motive to another has made it a rich resource for critics interested in cognitive science, especially "theory of mind" (the subfield devoted to mental state attribution). See, for example, Zunshine, *Why We Read Fiction*; Vermeule, *The Fictional among Us: Why We Care about Literary Characters* (Baltimore, MD: Johns Hopkins University Press, 2010); and Jonathan Kramnick, "Empiricism, Cognitive Science and the Novel," *The Eighteenth Century: Theory and Interpretation* 48, no. 3 (Fall 2007): 263–85.

31. On the religious meaning of Clarissa's retreat, see Dussinger, "Conscience and the Pattern of Christian Perfection in Clarissa" (1966), which reads Clarissa's "complete renunciation of the world" in terms of the "perfectionist doctrine" of William Law, contemporary theologian and associate of Richardson, that "the mark of a true Christian is the utter denial of sublunary pleasures and the striving towards perfect devotion to God" (242).

32. Once the Harlowes realize that her consent is not to be gained, they accordingly abandon their attempt to reach her consent and simply demand that she "acquiesce" or "comply" (2:265, 266 [180]). "But let

me repeat, that it is your *duty* to acquiesce, if you *can* acquiesce: Your father has given your Brother's schemes *his* sanction; and they are now *his*. Mr. Lovelace, I doubt, is not a man that will justify *your* choice so much as he will *their* dislike. It is easy to see that your brother has a *view* in discrediting you with all your friends, with your Uncles in particular: But for that very reason, you should comply, if possible, in order to disconcert his ungenerous measures" (2:265–6 [180]). Clarissa's duty arises from the sanction her father has given to James's plan. This more than her consent is ultimately what is at stake for the family, though it remains unclear precisely how the marriage will be put in effect should Clarissa persist in her refusal. The claim near the end of the novel that the Harlowes had planned to withdraw the scheme at the eleventh hour seems little more than an attempt to stave off their guilt. For more on Richardson's representation of the authority of the family, see Ruth Perry, *Novel Relations: The Transformation of Kinship in English Literature and Culture, 1748–1818* (Cambridge: Cambridge University Press, 2004) 65–77 and passim.

33. Ferguson, "Rape and the Rise of the Novel," 101.

34. Ibid.

35. Ferguson tends to run meaning together with intention (semantics with actions) so that attention is paid more to "intending to mean" than "intending to act." This is, it seems to me, a natural result of the disciplines. From Wimsatt and Beardsley onward, we literary critics tend to be concerned with questions of intention as they impact upon questions of meaning. What did Pope intend to mean by the symbol of the lock, anyway? For the more technically minded philosophical disciplines, intention and meaning might be related but are distinct dimensions to the mind. Indeed, intentionality has a whole other significance as, following Brentano, "aboutness" or the "mark of the mental." This is a source of much confusion for those trying to approach literary questions with help from contemporary philosophy.

36. The term "stipulate" has a special importance in Ferguson's essay (ibid., 91) as the objective characterization of a mental state as opposed to its subjective experience.

37. Ibid., 102. According to Margaret Doody, pregnancy would also stipulate consent: "If Clarissa brought forth a young Lovelace, the conception would signify consent, and Lovelace would indeed have proved at last

that the 'Yielding in resistance' he had hoped for was there—below all the resistance, beneath even the drugged insensibility." Doody, "Disguise and Personality in Richardson's *Clarissa*," *Eighteenth-Century Life* 12 (1988): 34.

38. Long-standing though perhaps now in permanent decline; see two recent and compelling readings of the novel, Sandra Macpherson's argument for a kind of consequentialist ethics that leaves intentions beside the point: "*Clarissa* progressively detaches responsibility from character, redescribing criminality, liability—and ultimately exemplarity itself—in terms of the consequences of rather than the motives behind action"; see "Lovelace Ltd.," *ELH* 65 (1998): 115. (Macpherson's revision of this argument in the very recent *Harm's Way: Tragic Responsibility and the Novel Form* (Baltimore, MD: Johns Hopkins University Press, 2010) appeared as this book was going to press); and Katherine Binhammer's argument that the novel concerns not sexual desire but love and thus that one should "resist reading the novel simply as an originary text of modern subjectivity, not least because the epistemological model that paints Clarissa's heart as betraying a truth that the owner does not consent to positions the critic as Lovelace, since both claim to know what she does not—her hidden desire for the rake"; see "Knowing Love: The Epistemology of *Clarissa*," *ELH* 74 (2007): 861.

39. Ferguson, "Rape and the Rise of the Novel," 109.

40. Turner, "Lovelace and the Paradoxes of Libertinism," 71.

41. See Doody, *Natural Passion* (Oxford: Clarendon, 1974), 145 and passim. Doody's larger argument is that Lovelace's attempts at seduction make use of a romantic idiom that turns out to fail him, as Clarissa is not at heart a rake but rather a paragon. To Doody's list of the parallels between Lovelace's discourse and Haywood's, I would add the striking similarity between Fantomina's and Lovelace's account of why strangers make better lovers than spouses. Recall the young lady's account:

> Had he been faithful to me, (*said she, to herself,*) either as *Fantomina*, or *Celia*, or the Widow *Bloomer*, the most violent Passion, if it does not change its Object, in Time will wither: Possession naturally abates the Vigour of Desire, and I should have had, at best, but a cold, insipid, husband-like Lover in my Arms; but by these Arts of passing on him as a new Mistress whenever the Ardour, which alone makes Love a Bless-

ing, begins to diminish, for the former one, I have him always raving, wild, impatient, longing, dying.—O that all neglected Wives, and fond abandon'd Nymphs would take this Method!—Men would be caught in their own Snare, and have no Cause to scorn our easy, weeping, wailing Sex! (65)

Here is Lovelace:

Whence, for a by-reflection, the ardent, the complaisant Gallant is so often preferred to the cold, the unadoring Husband. And yet the Sex do not consider, that Variety and Novelty give the Ardor and the Obsequiousness; and that, were the Rake as much used to them as the Husband is, he would be [and is to *his own Wife*, if married] *as* indifferent to their favours, as their Husbands are; and the Husband, in his turn, would, to another woman, be the Rake. Let the women, upon the whole, take this Lesson from a Lovelace—"Always to endeavour to make themselves as New to a Husband, and to appear as elegant and as obliging to him, as they are desirous to appear to a *Lover*, and actually were to *him* as *such*; and then the *Rake*, which all women love, will last longer in the *Husband* than it generally does." (4:126 [609–10])

42. Lovelace here layers his reading of Haywood with one of his "worthy friend Mandeville," who argues in the *Fable of the Bees* that "the Modesty of Women is the Result of Custom and Education," hence women blush only when they are in company, a sentiment echoed by Lovelace to Belford as his own: "I wonder whether [the modestest women] ever blush at those things by themselves, at which they have so charming a knack of blushing in company" (5:222, 4:305 [847]). See Mandeville *The Fable of the Bees*, 65. On Richardson's relation to Mandeville, see Gordon, *The Power of the Passive Self*, 186; and Heather Zias, "Who Can Believe? Sentiment vs. Cynicism in Richardson's *Clarissa*," *Eighteenth-Century Life* 27, no. 3 (2003): 99–123.

43. The decision to go to Sinclair's performs in miniature Lovelace's larger theory of actions. He orchestrates the options so that she will decide to go to Sinclair's on her own, and so "chuse what was before chosen for her" (3:183 [472]).

44. Jocelyn Harris ("Protean Lovelace," 332) has argued that "Lovelace inhabits a state of nature," and so imagines he "enjoys absolute power,

even over the body of Clarissa." I would argue in contrast that Lovelace wants the postnatural state of contract. Carol Kay argues similarly to Harris, though with an intriguingly qualified observation: "It takes only one restless Hobbesian man to destabilize a balance of power. His encroaching imagination takes him far beyond the commandments of Clarissa's family, partly because he lacks any formal basis for authority. He is attracted to the jealous tyranny traditionally associated with usurpers. Even his images of monarchical power are extreme." See *Political Constructions: Defoe, Richardson, and Sterne in Relation to Hobbes, Hume, and Burke* (Ithaca, NY: Cornell University Press, 1988), 174. Kay then further observes, however, that Lovelace "shows the manipulative scope of the moral amphibian . . . complete with 'stratagems,' abject apologies, petty resentments, and fits of generosity" (176). Kay contrasts this to the more traditional assertion of patriarchal sovereignty evinced by the Harlowes, who are not so much usurpers as absolutists (hence father and son are named James). Kay nicely points to the slipperiness of Lovelace's version of power, but she nowhere engages the question of consent, save for very briefly at the end of her chapter on *Clarissa,* where she remarks that Clarissa prefers "the noncoercive relationships of sympathy and generosity . . . to contractual relationships" yet offers little to substantiate the claim (192).

45. See also 5:203–4 [837–8] and 5:283 [879].

46. I would therefore qualify Castle's argument (*Clarissa's Ciphers,* 108) that a "kind of demented fatality leads Lovelace from hermeneutic violence against her to actual sexual violence: his very literal infiltration of Clarissa's body is intimately related to that infiltration of sign systems he has already effected in order to control her. Rape is the culminating interruption in a long pattern of interference and intrusion, a climax in the drama of 'penetration' to which he subjected her." The intimate relation between Lovelace's earlier attempts at control and his later act of sexual violence is uneven: the deceptions to which she was subjected ought to have elicited consent but did not. The rape in this respect demonstrates the failure of Lovelace's theory of tacit consent.

47. The point is close to Ferguson's observation that "[w]hile there may be two bodies—Lovelace's and Clarissa's—involved in the rape, only one person is present" (104). This is certainly true from the perspective of Clarissa's dualism; whether Lovelace would agree is more difficult to say.

48. See Doody, *A Natural Passion*, 151–88; Watt, *The Rise of the Novel*, 216–9; and Jolene Zigaravich, "Courting Death: Necrophilia in Samuel Richardson's *Clarissa*," *Studies in the Novel* 23 (2000): 111–27; Thompson, "Abuse and Atonement"; and Allan Wendt, "Clarissa's Coffin," *Philological Quarterly* 34, no. 4 (1960): 481–95.

49. In response, they have offered a range of answers to the question of why Clarissa dies, from a "disengagement with patriarchal and class society" to disorders of the nerves to, as we shall see, self-starvation. Class and patriarchy is from Terry Eagleton, *The Rape of Clarissa: Writing, Sexuality, and Class Struggle in Samuel Richardson* (Minneapolis: University of Minnesota Press, 1982), 73. Nervous disorder is from Raymond Stephanson, "Richardson's Nerves: The Physiology of Sensibility in *Clarissa*," *Journal of the History of Ideas* 49 (1988): 267–85. For self-starvation, see the discussion below. For the case against natural causes, see Adam Budd, "Why Clarissa Must Die: Richardson's Tragedy and Editorial Heroism," *Eighteenth-Century Life* 31, no. 3 (Fall 2007): 1–28. Budd observes that illness and death are everywhere else in the novel provided a natural cause yet in Clarissa's case deliberately obscured.

50. From the religious perspective, Clarissa's death is seen as the consummate retreat from the world—what Doody calls "holy dying," after Jeremy Taylor, the seventeenth-century theologian of whom Clarissa is fond. Taylor's *Holy Living* (1650) and *Holy Dying* (1651) were reprinted as one volume throughout the eighteenth century. Lovelace picks up and thumbs through the volume when he catches up with Clarissa in Hamstead (6:156 [1001]). On this account, the "long process of true repentance" denies everything sublunary and wills a state of grace akin to the suffering of Christ. Doody, *A Natural Passion*, 169. In John Dussinger's words ("Conscience and the Pattern of Christian Perfection in *Clarissa*," 242, 244): "[A] penitent after the catastrophe, she belongs in her 'shining time' to the higher order of the faithful," for whom "redemption from the world, the flesh, and the devil" involves a "perfect denial" of material living. Dussinger emphasizes (again) the importance of William Law, the eighteenth-century nonjuror and associate of Richardson who was the author of, among other works, *A Practical Treatise upon Christian Perfection* (1726). Law was a friend of the physician and mystic George Cheyne, who administered to and corresponded with Richardson. On a similar set

of terms, Poovey ("Journeys from This World to the Next," 302, 314) writes: "[T]he particulars of the compromised world emphasize the disparity between Clarissa's physical surroundings and her spiritual purity," hence "the necessity of Clarissa's death. Tom Jones can realize his reward in this world, but Clarissa must leave her father's house in order to reach its divine counterpart . . . . [T]he absolute nature of Clarissa's consolation cannot be represented in the details of compromise." On this view Clarissa not only exemplifies a larger trend within her culture of depicting perfect modes of exiting the world but also, in her singularity, serves to criticize aspects of her culture that have contributed to her demise: her grasping family, her libertine vanquisher.

51. Clarissa expresses a hope for death at many points after the rape (and indicates that she would rather die than marry Solmes beforehand). Most expressive, perhaps, is the tenth "mad paper," in the form of a poem, the fifth stanza of which begins "When Honour's lost, 'tis a relief to die" (5:308 [893]), or her subsequent complaint that her healthy constitution will delay her demise (6:188 [1018]). For a discussion of Clarissa's "death wish," see Zigaravich, "Courting Death." Zigaravich is certainly right to argue that *Clarissa* is haunted by the death of its heroine, but I would disagree with the conclusion that both Clarissa and Lovelace "actually fetishize, are aroused by and obsess upon, the exquisite corpse," that both "in their own manner, are necrophiliacs" (114).

52. The Augustine prohibition from the City of God is discussed below; for the historical background of the prohibition in the Christian church, see Georges Minois, *History of Suicide: Voluntary Death in Western Culture*, trans. Lydia G. Cochrane (Baltimore, MD: Johns Hopkins University Press, 1999), 27–40 and passim. For the eighteenth-century debates, see Lester Crocker, "The Discussion of Suicide in the Eighteenth Century," *Journal of the History of Ideas* 13 (1952): 47–72; Michael MacDonald, "The Secularization of Suicide in England, 1660–1800," *Past & Present* 111 (1986): 50–100, and "Suicide and the Rise of the Popular Press in England," *Representations* 22 (1988): 36–59; Minois, *History of Suicide*, 179–277. Samuel Sprott, *The English Debate on Suicide: From Donne to Hume* (Lasalle, IN: Open Court, 1961).

53. Capitalizing on the controversy, the second edition printed above the title the following: "On Account of the Bold Truths contain'd in this

PAMPHLET, the Author (who wrote it in *Italian*) was oblig'd to fly the Kingdom; the translator was sent to *Newgate*, and the Publisher confin'd in the *Fleet*." On Radicati, see Jonathan Israel, *Radical Enlightenment: Philosophy and the Making of Modernity, 1650–1750* (Oxford: Oxford University Press, 2002), 68–72; and Margaret Jacob, *The Radical Enlightenment: Pantheists, Freemasons and Republicans* (London: Allen and Unwin, 1981), 171–4.

54. [Alberto Radicati], *A Philosophical Dissertation upon Death. Composed for the Consolation of the Unhappy. By a Friend to Truth* (London, 1732), 5. Hereafter cited in parentheses.

55. According to Merricks, a material object cannot be at once identical with and reduced to its parts, since this would assume that one can be identical with many, and that the many would stay the same. Since objects lose microscopic parts all the time, identity cannot reduce to composition. His conclusion is therefore that, with the exception of people, macroscopic objects do not exist. See *Objects and Persons*, 20–2 and passim.

56. The collection the essay finally appeared in is interesting; it includes a response by the editor as well as the also unpublished "On the Immortality of the Soul" and selections on suicide from Rousseau. The full title is: *ESSAYS ON SUICIDE, AND THE IMMORTALITY OF THE SOUL, ASCRIBED TO THE LATE DAVID HUME, ESQ. Never before published. With REMARKS, intended as an Antidote to the Poison contained in these Performances, BY THE EDITOR. TO WHICH IS ADDED, TWO LETTERS ON SUICIDE, FROM ROSSEAU'S ELOISA* (1783).

57. Ibid., 5. Hereafter cited in parentheses.

58. Budd has made this argument recently, with respect to Belford particularly. See "Why Clarissa Must Die," 12.

59. As with wishing for death, promising not to kill herself is also something she does on several occasions, in addition to those cited here; see 7:205 [1249] and Dr. H's assertion on 7:361 [1332]. Thus while I agree with Carol Houlyhan Flynn that Clarissa "refuses to accommodate herself to the world," I do not reach the same conclusion: "Clarissa's refusal to accommodate ends in her death, which on at least one level must be seen as suicide." See *Samuel Richardson: A Man of Letters* (Princeton: Princeton University Press, 1982), 37.

60. Richardson revises the framing of this statement slightly in the third

edition, allowing the wish plausibly to refer to the retraction of her father's curse. Compare 1106 in the Penguin to 6:358 in the AMS.

61. As Budd ("Why Clarissa Must Die," 13) observes, Richardson "protects Clarissa from the charge of killing herself" by having the possibility raised by Sally Martin and by her asking her doctor if remaining at her final lodgings would ensure her life not be unnaturally curtailed.

62. See Lovelace's remarks on 5:323, 7:14, and 8:146 [900, 1108, and 1439]. Richardson alludes to the Lucretia story early in *Pamela* as well, during an early attempt by Mr. B: "He by Force kissed my Neck and Lips; and said, Who ever blamed *Lucretia*, but the Ravisher only? And I am content to take all the Blame upon me; as I have already borne too great a Share for what I have deserv'd. May I, said I, *Lucretia* like, justify myself with my Death, if I am used barbarously? O my good Girl! said he, tauntingly, you are well read, I see; and we shall make out between us, before we have done, a pretty Story in Romance, I warrant ye!" Samuel Richardson, *Pamela: Or, Virtue Rewarded*, ed. T. C. Duncan Eaves and Ben D. Kimpel (Boston: Houghton Mifflin, 1971), 42. Belford worries that Clarissa might behave like "another Lucretia" and kill herself (4:342 [710]); Clarissa says of Lovelace, "A less complicated villainy cost a Tarquin" (5:311 [895]).

63. See Augustine, *The City of God against the Pagans,* ed. and trans. R. W. Dyson (Cambridge: Cambridge University Press, 1998), book 1, chapter 20 and passim.

64. Ibid., 29.

65. Ibid., 30.

66. The classical literature on the topic is rich and extensive, beginning with Plato's account of Socrates' death in the *Phaedo,* but more appositely, in the case of *Clarissa,* the writings of Stoics like Marcus Aurelius, who defend suicide in the face of suffering as part of what "does the work of man" as opposed to the Gods (see tenth meditation, section eight), or Seneca who views suicide as part of what it means to live well: "Life has carried some men with the greatest rapidity to the harbour, the harbour they were bound to reach even if they tarried on the way, while others it has fretted and harassed. To such a life, as you are aware, one should not always cling. For mere living is not a good, but living well. Accordingly, the wise man will live as long as he ought, not as long as he can. He will mark in what place, with whom, and how he is to conduct his existence,

and what he is about to do. He always reflects concerning the quality, and not the quantity, of his life. As soon as there are many events in his life that give him trouble and disturb his peace of mind, he sets himself free. And this privilege is his, not only when the crisis is upon him, but as soon as Fortune seems to be playing him false; then he looks about carefully and sees whether he ought, or ought not, to end his life on that account. He holds that it makes no difference to him whether his taking-off be natural or self-inflicted, whether it comes later or earlier. He does not regard it with fear, as if it were a great loss; for no man can lose very much when but a driblet remains. It is not a question of dying earlier or later, but of dying well or ill. And dying well means escape from the danger of living ill." Seneca, *Epistulae Morales*, 3 vol., trans. R. M. Gummere (Cambridge: Harvard University Press, 1917), 57–9. Augustine's prohibition is later codified in Aquinas, *Summa Theologica* 2. 2. Q64. A5. For a Christian defense of suicide, see John Donne's *Biathanatos* (1607). Charles Gildon defends Blount's suicide in the introduction to Blount's collected works (which I discuss with respect to Rochester on death in Chapter 2). Locke (*Second Treatise of Government*, 19, 9) remains within the orthodox view in the *Second Treatise* where he writes: "[E]very man has a *property* in his own *person*" only a few pages after he argues that every man is the property of a wise and omnipotent maker and so "bound to preserve himself and not leave his station willfully." In keeping with the idea that the wrongness of suicide shows the limits of self-ownership, Kant views the act as an act of agency that destroys the agent and so is not only contradictory but also a destruction of human dignity and therefore of moral law. Suicide is in this way a consummate example of what it means to act from inclination as opposed to acting from duty. See Kant, *Groundwork of the Metaphysics of Morals*, ed. and trans. Mary Gregor (Cambridge: Cambridge University Press, 1998), 31–8.

67. For a recent statement of the no causes argument, see Budd; for nervous disorders, see note above; for "galloping consumption," see Doody. The self-starvation thesis is worthy of its own note. Rita Goldberg writes that Clarissa "cannot actually choose to die," yet "the *physical* cause of her death is starvation." See *Sex and Enlightenment: Women in Richardson and Diderot* (Cambridge: Cambridge University Press, 1984) 123, 124. Since Goldberg, two separate monographs have argued that Clarissa is a

"holy anorexic" who achieves autonomy and self-mastery through deny-
ing her physical desire to eat. The term "holy anorexic" is from Rudolph
Bell's *Holy Anorexia* (Chicago: University of Chicago Press, 1985). See
Maud Ellmann's *The Hunger Artists: Starving, Writing, and Imprisonment*
(Cambridge: Harvard University Press, 1993), half on *Clarissa* and half on
twentieth-century Irish political prisoners; and Donallee Frega, *Speaking
in Hunger: Gender, Discourse, and Consumption in* Clarissa (Columbia:
University of South Carolina Press, 1998). See also Raymond E. Hilliard,
"*Clarissa* and Ritual Cannibalism," *PMLA* 105 (1990): 1083–97, which
situates Clarissa's alleged anorexia in an anthropological context. The
anorexia reading understandably makes much of the fact that Clarissa, for
a time after the rape, eats only bread and tea or, at the extreme, nothing
at all. See, for example, Belford's description of finding Clarissa at break-
fast with Hickman: "The Doctor [said he] has ordered nothing for you,
but weak jellies, and innocent cordials, lest you should starve yourself,"
to which Clarissa responds, "What sir . . . can I do? I have no appetite.
Nothing you call nourishing will stay on my stomach. I do what I can:
And have such kind directors in Dr H. and you, that I should be inexcusable if I did not" (6:400–1 [1129]). The anorexic reading would thus have
Clarissa deceiving others and perhaps herself when she says that she is not
willing herself to avoid food. It would also credit the interpretation of Sally
Martin (6:253 [1054]). Clarissa's long promise to Anna culminates thus:
"When appetite serves, I will eat and drink what is sufficient to support
nature," and, as with all her promises, this is one she keeps, even if her
appetite sometimes falters (6:378 [1117]). Indeed when Belford visits her a
month after this statement is made he reports, as if to allay any suspicions,
that her day was punctuated by meals: "[S]he was rowed to Chelsea, where
she breakfasted; and after rowing about, put in at the Swan at Brentford-
Aight, where she dined" (7:200 [1249]). Ellmann (*The Hunger Artists*, 75)
therefore exaggerates some when she writes that Clarissa "systematically
refuses food." At the same time, Ellmann does not exaggerate quite so
much when she writes that Clarissa "starves in order to refuse all traffic
with a world that threatens to invade her every orifice" (81). Ellmann simply conflates spiritual disengagement with the world with actual starvation
of the body. What recent interest in Clarissa's putative anorexia reveals, I
think, is the extent to which the novel dwells upon causation in its closing

pages. Clarissa does not starve herself to death, but the novel plausibly solicits this misreading. We are led to suspect Clarissa dies from starvation even when she doesn't because she is so strongly pitched against appetite in the broad sense of the term. Because we read about Clarissa refusing to take a causal role in events, we think she starves when she doesn't and miss her eating when she does. We therefore suspect her of acting in her death when she only desires that end.

68. See Sandra Macpherson, *Harm's Way*.

Index